teach yourself…

Excel 97

for Windows

teach yourself...

Excel 97
for Windows

**John Weingarten
& Garrett Riddle**

A Subsidiary of
Henry Holt and Co., Inc.

A Subsidiary of
Henry Holt and Co., Inc.

MIS:Press
A Subsidiary of Henry Holt and Company, Inc.
115 West 18th Street
New York, New York 10011
http://www.mispress.com

This book is based on Betas 2 and 3 of Microsoft Office 97, not final code. Although the product we declared is stable, and the majority of the features enabled and finalized, there may be some differences between these builds and final product. For the latest information on Microsoft Office 97 differences, please visit http://www.microsoft.com.

teach yourself… and the ty logo are registered.

First Edition—1997

MIS:Press and M&T Books are available at special discounts for bulk purchases for sales promotions, premiums, and fundraising. Special editions or book excerpts can also be created to specification.

For details contact: Special Sales Director
MIS:Press and M&T Books
Subsidiaries of Henry Holt and Company, Inc.
115 West 18th Street
New York, New York 10011

10 9 8 7 6 5 4 3 2 1

Associate Publisher: *Paul Farrell*

Executive Editor: *Cary Sullivan*

Technical Editor: Chris Kelley

Copy Edit Manager: *Shari Chappell*

Editor: *Rebekah Young*

Production Editor: *Maya Riddick*

Copy Editor: *Gwynne Jackson*

ACKNOWLEDGMENTS

This book was a team effort, and we want to thank everyone who helped make it possible. If we left anyone off the following list, please know that you are appreciated.

Matt Wagner, of Waterside Productions, is more than just a great agent. We can't thank him enough for his help and guidance.

Rebekah Young, our terrific editor at MIS:Press, has been a driving force in the completion of this book. Her organization and poise during these busy times proved invaluable.

Maya Riddick, our production editor at MIS:Press, did an outstanding job getting the manuscript into the terrific-looking book you are holding.

Chris Kelley, tech editor extraordinaire, helped ensure the accuracy of this book. His attention to detail and wonderful suggestions were greatly appreciated.

Special thanks to Arturo Torres, June Stewart, Cecelia McMullen, and the rest of the gang at Gonzaga University School of Law Library. They make it a joy to come to work every morning at the finest Law School in the beautiful Pacific Northwest.

In addition, we'd like to individually thank:

My wife Julie for her love and support. Nothing I write can adequately express just how much that means to me. Thanks also to my father Gerald, mother Susan, and sister Tara for all their help and encouragement.

Garrett Riddle

CONTENTS-IN-BRIEF

CONTENTS

Introduction

This book is for people who want to learn the essentials of Excel 97 quickly. You won't find details of arcane and seldom-used features here. What will you find are step-by-step procedures for putting Excel to work for you.

The examples in the book are based on real world situations and should provide you with enough practical insight to tailor the procedures to your own requirements. Tasks and concepts are presented in a logical order, progressing from simple navigation and data entry to more complex tasks, such as charting, database manipulation, and linking multiple worksheets. Don't be intimidated if some of these terms seem foreign to you. They are all clearly defined and explained in the appropriate part of the book.

We hope you find the writing style clear, concise, and friendly, with even a bit of humor thrown in. You shouldn't have to be bored to tears to learn the basics of Excel. It should be fun!

Who Should Read This Book

No previous knowledge of spreadsheets or computers is required. Even if you have never seen a spreadsheet before, you will easily be able to follow the procedures. You'll be amazed at how quickly you will become comfortable working with Excel.

If you have worked with a previous version of Excel, or another spreadsheet without mastering the ins and outs, this book helps you learn Excel 97 while providing a refresher on general spreadsheet basics.

The Highlights of Excel 97

This version offers many powerful new features, as well as refinements, to make working with the program easier and more intuitive. The following are some of the more interesting features covered in this book.

Improved Help Facilities

The help Excel provides is more extensive than in previous versions. The new animated Office Assistant will answer your questions and offer tips to help make your work with Excel more efficient.

World Wide Web Tools and Functions

Whether you want to convert your Excel worksheet into an HTML document or scan the Web, Excel is up to the task. The Internet Assistant Wizard converts your Excel charts and data into HTML documents, and the Web toolbar will help direct your travels through cyberspace.

More Chart Options

The Chart Wizard makes creating data presentations as simple as a few clicks of your mouse. You can choose from over a hundred different chart formats, so finding the right look for your data is easier than ever.

Conventions Used in This Book

Keyboard combinations are separated by commas and/or hyphens (-). A combination separated by commas means press and release the first key and then press and release the second key. A combination separated by a hyphen means press and hold down the first key, then press the second key, and finally release both keys. For example, if you instructed to press **Ctrl-X**, press and hold down the **Ctrl** key and then, while still pressing the **Ctrl** key, tap the **X** key. **Ctrl-X**, **Y** means press and hold the **Ctrl** key while pressing the **X** key, then release them and tap the **Y** key.

The first time an important term is used in the book, it appears in italics. The term is defined and explained in the chapter and in the glossary at the end of the book.

A FINAL THOUGHT

If you take the time to work through all the chapters in this book, you are rewarded with a new skill that allows you to perform many of your business and personal tasks in much less time than you currently spend. You have more time for the things you really enjoy. And don't let this be the last of your Excel explorations. Excel is a rich program with vast capabilities. You'll have plenty to explore when you finish. Enjoy the journey.

John Weingarten and Garrett Riddle
Spokane, Washington

CHAPTER 1

Excel: The Big Picture

SPREADSHEETS: HOW THE COMPUTER REVOLUTION STARTED

The spreadsheet is a formidable computer tool that lets you record the past, analyze the present, and predict the future. Spreadsheets allow for easy preparation of accounting records and financial statements, as well as budgets and forecasts.

Because of their ability to use mathematical formulas and functions to calculate results when numbers are changed, spreadsheets are marvelous facilities for playing "what if." In a business, you might want to know the answer to, "What if the costs of our supplies increase by ten percent next year?" or "What if we raised our selling price by three percent?" Spreadsheets can provide the answers to those questions, and more.

Before the development of the first spreadsheet program about 15 years ago, few people thought of computers as personal. Large corporations used huge mainframe computers that often cost millions of dollars for very specific accounting applications such as accounts receivable and inventory control. The only contact most corporate workers had with these computers was by way of printed reports—or perhaps entering data through dumb terminals.

When the first spreadsheet program (Visicalc) appeared on the scene shortly after the introduction of the first Apple personal computers, small and medium-sized businesses quickly realized that they could exercise greater control over their business. They could do budgeting and forecasting on their own desktop computers.

Computers and software have come a long way since those early Visicalc days. Other categories of software, such as word processing, databases, and desktop publishing programs, now share spots on the software best-seller lists along with spreadsheets. But spreadsheets remain one of the primary reasons for the tremendous proliferation of personal computers.

WHAT SPREADSHEETS ARE (AND AREN'T) GOOD FOR

Almost any task that requires numeric calculations is a good candidate for spreadsheet consideration. Budgeting and forecasting are the tasks that first come to mind when thinking about what spreadsheets are good for, but virtually anything requiring the storage and manipulation of data can be done with a spreadsheet. This includes such tasks as database management, drawing and graphics, charting, word processing, and more. However, a spreadsheet is not necessarily the best tool for any of these tasks.

It has become increasingly difficult in recent years to choose the most appropriate software category for a particular task. Many word processing programs offer spreadsheet-like features, and database programs include the ability to work with data in rows and columns, which makes them look like spreadsheets. Take Excel 97, for example. You can use Excel for several primary functions:

❖　Financial analysis
❖　Database management

❖   Charting and graphing

❖   Drawing and graphics

❖   Forms processing

❖   Word processing and text layout

There is no program better than a spreadsheet for financial analysis and numeric graphing. These are the primary functions of a spreadsheet. If the work you need to perform is heavily text-oriented, where reporting on certain aspects of the document's contents isn't required, a word processing program is likely your best bet. If your task requires heavy manipulation of graphics and the ability to draw detailed images, then a dedicated graphics program is what you need. A database program would make more sense if:

1.   You want to be able to restrict the types of data being entered, as in an inventory control system.

2.   Your database contains more than 10,000 records.

3.   You need to combine two or more databases into one front-end software system.

As we explore Excel, you'll see that you can accomplish most basic word processing and database tasks with this powerful spreadsheet program, but the fact that you *can* do it doesn't mean you *should* do it. The examples in this book will give you a good idea about the types of applications where Excel excels. Here are a few examples:

❖   Budgets and personal financial statements

❖   Expense reports and summaries

❖   Financial projections with charts and graphics

❖   Inventory control

❖   Job estimates and cost sheets

❖   Printing and storing business forms

❖   Customer and client lists

❖   Creating and updating tables of data for documents

❖   Database statistical analysis

WHAT SETS EXCEL APART FROM THE COMPETITION

Excel 97 includes every feature and refinement you could imagine in a spreadsheet. You'll find a wide variety of powerful financial and scientific functions, suitable for almost any type of business. Charting and database facilities, as well as proofing tools such as spell checking and spreadsheet analysis, round out Excel's impressive capabilities.

However, none of these features truly sets Excel apart from the competition. There are several other products that include the same basic features. So what does set Excel apart? Ease of use and integration.

Excel 97 includes a number of features that make the program easier to use and to troubleshoot when you run into problems. These ease-of-use features—such as the Office Assistant, tabbed dialog boxes, ToolTips, and tracing—are covered in detail later in the book.

For those seeking ease of use, there is the ability to switch easily between different types of computers without having to spend a great deal of time learning a new program. Excel's PC and Macintosh versions are practically identical. If your business uses both types of machines, you'll be able to use Excel on either without giving a thought to which computer you're using.

Excel works smoothly with other Windows 95 applications, especially other Microsoft applications. Microsoft has gone to great lengths to make its programs compatible with one another. An example of this is the large number of menu commands shared by all of the Office 97 programs.

CHARTING AND DATA MANAGEMENT

When you think of spreadsheets, you generally think of rows and columns of text and numbers. Back in the early days of spreadsheet programs, that was about all these programs could produce.

Most modern spreadsheet programs include at least basic facilities for turning numbers into charts and graphs and for performing database functions and manipulation. Many programs include charting and database facilities that rival the most powerful stand-alone programs in these categories.

No spreadsheet program has gone further in these areas than Excel 97. Excel's competitors cannot create a wider variety of charts and graphs or customize them in such seemingly endless ways. The data management capabilities (including easy creation of lists and nearly automatic sorting) let you do more with your normal worksheet data and may prove powerful enough to save you from having to invest time and money in a stand-alone database program.

WHAT YOU SEE IS WHAT YOU GET

Thanks to advances in both computer hardware and software, it's much easier to create great-looking documents than it once was. In the old days, if you wanted to print your documents with special fonts, characters, and graphic embellishments, you had to enter arcane printer codes into the spreadsheet program. As if that wasn't bad enough, you often didn't see the results of these codes until you actually printed your document. The result was a sense of flying blind, requiring repeated experimentation and wasted time and paper, until you attained the desired results.

With the introduction of computers that displayed reasonably accurate representations of what would be on the printed page, you no longer had to guess what would be coming out of your printer. It was right there in front of you on your screen.

The acronym *WYSIWYG* (What You See Is What You Get) has become as meaningless as the ubiquitous term *user-friendly*. Many programs claiming to be WYSIWYG don't provide a very accurate view of printed output. In this area, as in many others, Excel has raised the standard by providing a greater measure of accuracy and detail than was available before.

EXCEL 97 OVERVIEW

Excel 97 is the latest in a long line of groundbreaking versions of the Excel application. Here's a summary of the program's new features for those familiar with previous versions of Excel:

❖ Excel is now capable of understanding natural language formulas. You can refer to labels, rather than cell references, within formulas (e.g., `=Jan Sales - Cost` can replace `=B2 - B3`).

❖ Menus and toolbars have a flat appearance and some new controls.

❖ Help is now available through an animated Office Assistant. You can ask the Assistant questions or wait for it to offer tips based on the actions you perform.

❖ There is a new drawing package, shared between all the Office 97 applications, that offers more shapes and formatting options.

❖ Excel is compatible with the World Wide Web. You can put spreadsheets on-line, create hyperlinks between documents, and complete many other Web-related tasks—all without any HyperText Markup Language (HTML) programming.

A FINAL THOUGHT

This chapter set the stage for a better understanding of Excel's place in the computing world. While you can certainly use Excel productively without this information, this background should help shed some light on the big picture.

CHAPTER 2

Getting Started:
Excel and Windows Basics

WHAT WINDOWS 95 CAN DO FOR YOU

As mentioned in the previous chapter, Windows 95 lets you accurately see what your printed documents look like before you print them. But what exactly is Windows 95?

Glad you asked. Windows 95 is a software program that creates an environment that is friendly, intuitive, and graphical. Like previous versions of Windows, you can choose commands from menus and dialog boxes by simply pointing and clicking with a mouse. However, unlike its predecessors, Windows 95 is a true operating system—not just a Graphical User

11

Interface, or GUI (pronounced "gooey") which runs on top of a separate operating system. Because Windows 95 *is* the operating system, it's more stable, and less prone to some of the bugaboos that often plagued Windows 3.1 users.

Windows 95 displays everything on your screen as a graphic image, and you can use visual images and cues to lead you through the application you're working with. It also makes your computer life easier by providing a consistent user interface. User interface is just a fancy term for the way you and your computer interact.

In addition to making it easier to enter commands, the user interface also makes it easier to learn new programs. Most Windows 95 programs adhere, more or less, to the same structure of menus and other tools for communicating with Windows 95. Once you learn how to use one Windows 95 program, you've already gone a long way toward learning the next. For example, the procedures for opening, closing, and saving documents are virtually identical from one Windows 95 program to another.

Windows 95 can increase your productivity by allowing you to run more than one program at a time and share information between them. This may seem trivial, but imagine you are working in your word processing program on a report that requires a portion of a worksheet from Excel. The ability to move between the two programs without having to exit one before starting the other saves time and effort.

N O T E If you're used to older versions of Windows or other user interfaces, it may feel like Windows 95 is getting in your way and slowing you down. Let us assure you that as you become familiar with all the shortcuts available to you, you'll be flying through commands as quickly as you did in previous versions.

The next few sections provide a brief explanation about navigating through Windows 95. We know you want to dive right in and begin using Excel, but please work through the tutorial if you're not familiar with Windows 95. You'll find that using Excel and other Windows 95 programs is much easier if you have at least a basic understanding of the Windows 95 environment. Keep in mind that the following sections just scratch the surface of what Windows 95 has to offer. If you want to learn more of the ins and outs of Windows 95, take a look at *teach yourself...Windows 95* from MIS:Press, or use the tutorial included with Windows 95.

WELCOME TO WINDOWS 95

When you turn your computer on, Windows 95 automatically starts running. Your machine will go through a series of tests before eventually coming to rest on a screen similar to the one shown in Figure 2.1.

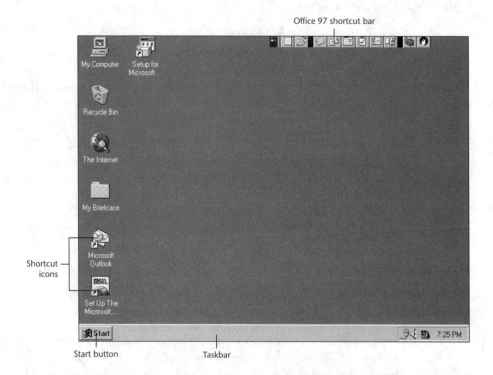

Figure 2.1 The Windows 95 opening screen.

Depending on how your computer is set up, the opening screen may look a little bit different from what you see in Figure 2.1. As you learn to work in the Windows 95 environment, you'll discover ways to rearrange the layout according to your needs. For now, don't worry if your screen doesn't look exactly like our example.

Finding Your Way Around the Desktop

The opening screen in Windows 95 is called the *desktop*. As the name suggests, the desktop is home to all your computer's resources. From this screen you can launch applications, manage files, and optimize the system to meet your needs.

The long rectangular bar at the bottom of Figure 2.1 is the *taskbar*. By clicking on the taskbar's **Start** button you can initiate a program, open a document, change system settings, and more. We'll be exploring some of these features later on in this chapter.

Telling Windows 95 What to Do

One of the benefits of using Windows 95 is that there are several different ways to accomplish the exact same task. You can communicate with applications by using either the keyboard, the mouse, or both. In this book, the mouse method is emphasized, but that doesn't mean it is always the most efficient way to carry out an operation. Where there is a keyboard method that is clearly a shortcut, we'll point it out. However, most people who are new to Windows 95 find the mouse action more intuitive and easier to remember.

The mouse pointer on the screen moves as you move the mouse on the surface of your desk. In addition to moving the mouse to reposition the pointer, there are several basic mouse operations you need to master:

❖ **Dragging**—moving the mouse while holding down the left mouse button.

❖ **Clicking**—pressing and releasing the left mouse button.

❖ **Right-clicking**—pressing and releasing the right mouse button.

❖ **Double-clicking**—clicking the left mouse button twice in rapid succession.

As the mouse is moved over various portions of the screen, its shape changes to indicate the type of action that can be performed. As the pointer is positioned over the border on the side of a window, it changes to a double-headed arrow. This indicates that you can change the height or width of the window by dragging the mouse in one of the directions the arrow is pointing. Placing the pointer over one of the corners of a window transforms it into a diagonal double-headed arrow, indicating that you can change both the height and width at the same time.

Running Programs

One of the first things you'll want to do in Windows 95 is run your programs. There are many ways to run programs and we'll discuss a few of them here.

The simplest way to run a program is to locate the application's name in the *Program Launcher* on the taskbar.

1. Click once on the **Start** button.

2. Move your mouse pointer up to **Programs**. A highlight bar will follow your pointer through the options, and when the bar rests on Programs another menu will appear to the right. The screen should look like Figure 2.2.

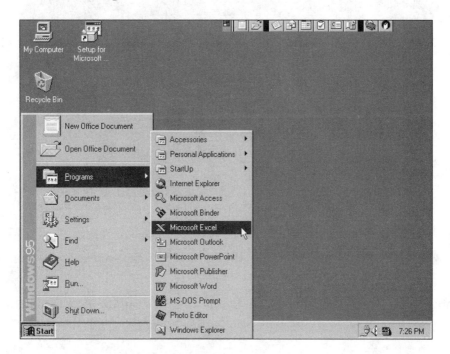

Figure 2.2 *Launching Microsoft Excel.*

3. Move the pointer to **Microsoft Excel** and click once. This launches the Microsoft Excel program. Depending on the options you selected while installing Office 97, and whether you've run Excel before, you may receive a dialog box like the one shown in Figure 2.3.

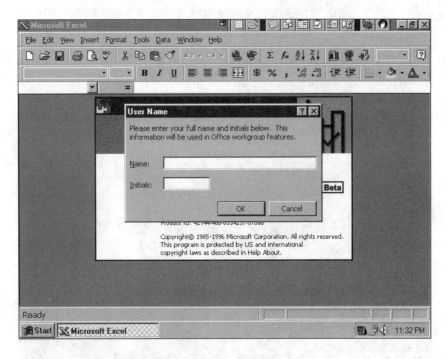

Figure 2.3 *The opening Excel screen.*

4. Type in your full name and press the **Tab** key.
5. Type in your initials and press **Enter**.

You can also open a program by double-clicking on its appropriate icon in the C: disk drive or desktop. We'll discuss these options later on in this chapter.

Putting Programs Away and Quitting

Now that Excel is up on the screen, there are several ways you can get back to the desktop. First you need to click on **Start using Microsoft Excel** in the cartoon bubble in the lower right-hand corner. Now you can either close Excel entirely, or *minimize* the program so you can return to your work at a later time. Let's try minimizing the program first.

1. Locate the **Minimize** button in the top right-hand corner of your screen.

NOTE You'll notice that there are two sets of buttons in the top right-hand corner of your screen. The outer set controls the application you are working with—this area is called the *application window*. The inner set of buttons control the document you are working with—this space is the *document window*. Figure 2.4 illustrates the difference between the application and document windows.

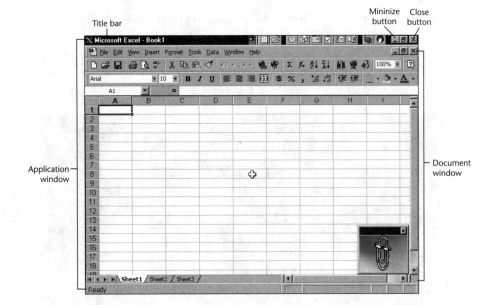

Figure 2.4 *Types of windows.*

2. Click on the **Minimize** button at the top of the application window.

The Excel program window is now temporarily hidden, and at the bottom of the desktop screen an Excel button has been added to the taskbar.

3. To get back to Excel, just click on the taskbar's **Microsoft Excel** button and the program will reappear.

NOTE Programs which appear in the taskbar are still running. Clicking on a window's •**Minimize** button merely puts the window out of view. If you want to completely quit the program and close the window, you'll need to click on the **Close** button.

4. Let's click on the **Close** button to completely exit the program. We'll do some more work with Excel later on in this chapter.

Opening and Arranging Windows

As you've already seen, Windows 95 displays just about everything in (what else?) windows. One of the many advantages of working with windows is that you can keep several of them open at the same time. What's more, you can arrange or resize these windows to meet your immediate needs.

For starters, lets take a closer look at how to arrange windows.

1. Double-click on the desktop's **My Computer** icon as shown in Figure 2.5. This will open the My Computer window, which is an area you can visit to look at your computer's contents, manage your files, etc.

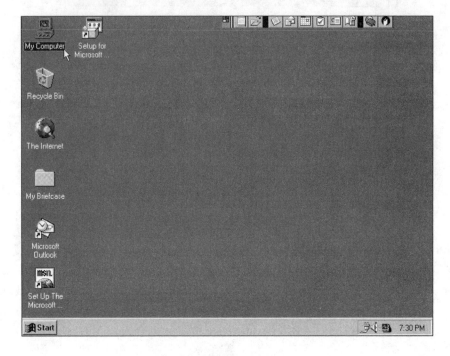

Figure 2.5 *The My Computer icon.*

N O T E If your [C:] icon is preceded by a name, such as Main, or Big Kahuna, that's just a label which was added to the drive. If your drive doesn't have a label and you want to add one, right-click on the icon above [C:], choose **Properties** from the shortcut menu, type the desired name in the **Label** text box, and click **OK**.

2. Double-click on the **Main [C:]** icon. This opens a window displaying the contents of your C: drive.

3. Double-click on the **Program Files** folder icon. This opens another window containing several different program groups.

4. Double-click on **Microsoft Office**. This displays the files inside the Microsoft Office folder, as shown in Figure 2.6.

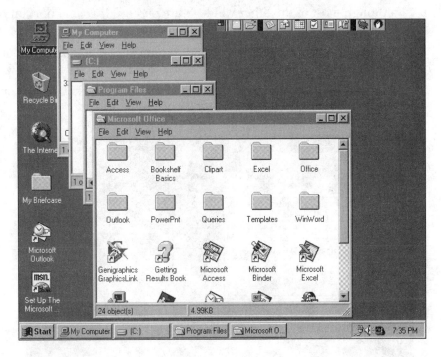

Figure 2.6 *Displaying the contents of the Microsoft Office folder.*

Depending on how you have Windows 95 set up, you may not be viewing a separate window for each folder you open. To change this, you'll need to go into **My Computer** and select **View, Options**. Click on the **Folder** tab, and

N O T E   choose **Browse folders by using a separate window for each folder**.

With several windows open at once, the screen becomes a little cluttered. Using the program buttons on the taskbar is one way to navigate among windows. Another option is to manually move the windows to separate areas of the screen.

Notice that the Microsoft Office window overlaps the other windows and its title bar is dark, indicating that it is the *active window*. This means it's the window you can work with now. Also notice that although most of the other windows are obscured, a small portion of each is still visible behind the Microsoft Office window.

5. Click on the **Program Files** window. Program Files is now on top of the other windows, and its title bar indicates that it is the active window.

6. Move your pointer to the title bar of the active window and drag it out of the way, as displayed in Figure 2.7.

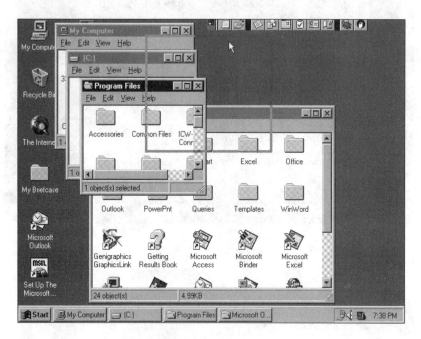

Figure 2.7 *Dragging a window.*

7.   Release the mouse button to complete the repositioning of the window as shown in Figure 2.8.

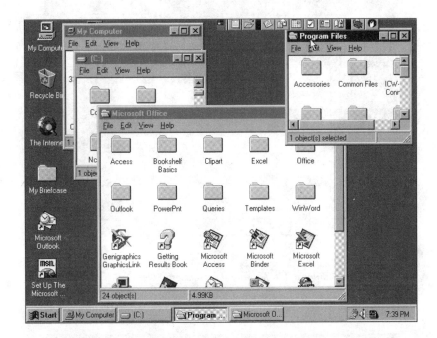

Figure 2.8 *The repositioned Program Files window.*

N O T E

You probably noticed the Excel program icon inside the Microsoft Office window. You now know the location of this program—inside the Program Files folder, which is inside the C: disk drive. If you double-clicked on the Excel program icon, you would run the program, just as you did earlier this chapter with the **Start** button. This is a second way to run programs, though it is a little bit more cumbersome because you constantly have to open the windows where the icons are located.

Resizing a Window

Let's try changing the size of the Microsoft Office window.

1.   Position your mouse pointer over the right border of the window, as displayed in Figure 2.9.

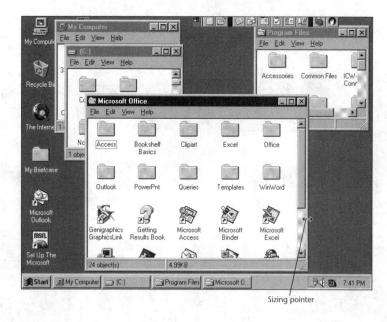

Sizing pointer

Figure 2.9 *Moving the mouse into position.*

2.   Drag the mouse to the left, as shown in Figure 2.10.

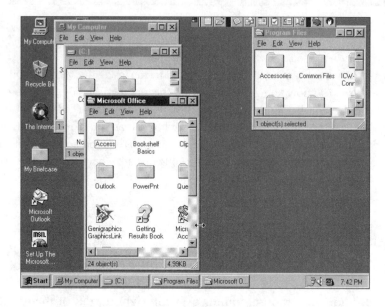

Figure 2.10 *The new right border's position.*

3. Release the mouse button to complete the resizing process.

Because the window isn't big enough to display all the group icons in their current positions, Windows 95 adds *scroll bars* to allow you to move through portions of the window that aren't currently visible.

Depending on its original size, your Office 97 window may already have had scroll bars, or you may need to reduce it further to make the scroll bars appear. If you don't have scroll bars, follow the steps above to reduce the window's size until you do.

Using Scroll Bars

Navigating through a window that contains scroll bars is easy. You can move up or down within a window by clicking on the *scroll bar buttons*, the scroll bar itself, or dragging the scroll box.

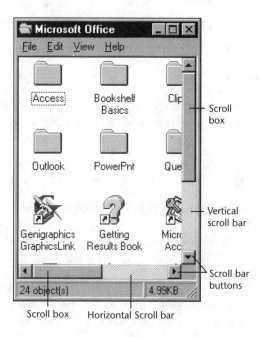

Figure 2.11 *The scroll bar buttons and boxes.*

The scroll boxes show you the current position of your window's contents. For example, if the scroll box in the horizontal scroll bar is at the far left, there are no more icons or other objects further left.

1. Drag the horizontal scroll box until it is in the middle of the scroll bar and release the mouse button, as shown in Figure 2.12.

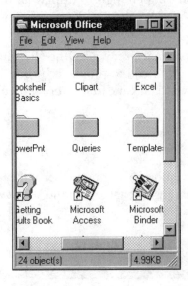

Figure 2.12 The scroll box in the middle of the scroll bar.

The scroll box in the middle of the scroll bar tells you that you have scrolled approximately halfway over in the window. Now, use the scroll bar button to scroll all the way to the right.

2. Point to the right scroll bar button and click several times until the scroll box is on the right side of the scroll bar.

The contents of the window have shifted to the left, so you are viewing what's on the right. Clicking in the scroll bar, or on either side of the scroll box, also moves the scroll box.

You'll find the scroll bar an invaluable tool for navigating large worksheets in Excel and large documents in other applications. If you feel like you could use some more work with scroll bars, don't worry, you'll get lots of practice when we start working with Excel.

Closing Windows

When you no longer need to work with a window, you may wish to close it to reclaim some screen real estate for the windows you are working with.

To close an active window, you've already seen that you can click on the close button in the upper-right corner of the application window. You can also close an application by clicking on the *Control menu box* in the upper-left corner of the window.

1. Click on the **Control** menu box of the Microsoft Office window (see Figure 2.13).

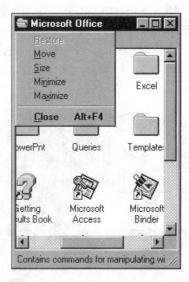

Figure 2.13 *The Control menu box.*

2. Choose **Close**.
3. Close the other group windows you have opened.

Your screen should now look the way it did when you first started Windows 95.

For the remainder of the book, when a step tells you to use a menu command, you'll be instructed to *choose* the command. For example, if you were being told to open a document, the instruction would look like this: "Choose **File**, **Open**." The choice of keyboard or mouse access is left up to you.

Creating a Shortcut Icon

If there are programs you use frequently, you might find it convenient to create shortcut icons for these programs on your desktop. A shortcut icon is simply a duplicate of another icon that is located in a more convenient place. Shortcut icons can be used for either general applications or specific documents. Let's try putting a shortcut icon for the Excel application on the desktop.

1. Click on the **My Computer** icon and re-open the Microsoft Office folder.
2. Press the **Ctrl** key and hold it down (this will copy, rather than move the icon, so the original stays where it was).

    By holding the **Ctrl** key down, you'll copy the original icon instead of just moving it.
3. Click and drag on the **Excel** icon located in the Microsoft Office folder.
4. Drag the Excel icon to a clear spot on the desktop, as shown in Figure 2.14.

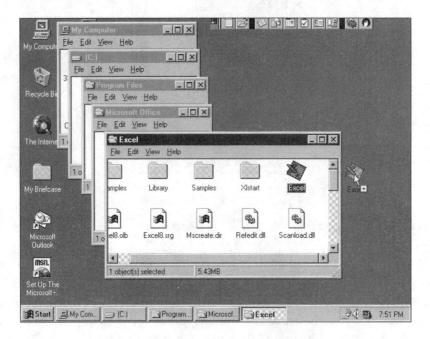

Figure 2.14 *Creating a shortcut icon.*

5.   Release the mouse button.

You can now position the icon at an appropriate spot on your desktop. You might want to close some windows to make more room.

STARTING EXCEL

Well, the big moment has arrived. It's time to start Excel and get this show on the road. Since we just created a shortcut icon on the desktop, let's try it out.

1.   Locate the Excel shortcut icon you created in the previous section.

2.   Double-click on the icon.

After a few seconds, the main Excel screen, as shown in Figure 2.15, will appear on your monitor.

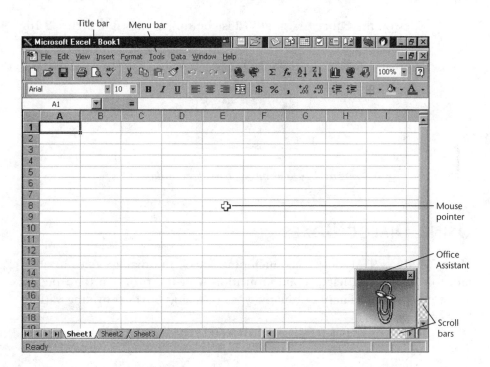

Figure 2.15 Starting Excel.

QUICK TOUR OF THE EXCEL SCREEN

Many parts of the opening Excel screen should seem a little familiar to you. The title bar, menu bar, control menu box, and scroll bars all work the same way as those in other windows. Of course, there are also quite a few new screen elements that will be discussed shortly.

When Excel is first started, you see a worksheet named Sheet 1 in a document window. The worksheet consists of lettered columns and numbered rows. The intersection of a column and a row is called a *cell* and its name is the column letter followed by the row number. The active cell is surrounded by a border, and its name is displayed in the cell reference area. The hollow cross on the worksheet is the mouse pointer, and it changes shapes as it moves to different parts of the worksheet. The animated character in the lower right-hand corner of the screen is the *Office Assistant*, which will be discussed in greater detail later in this chapter.

❖   Click on the Office Assistant's **Close** button, as shown in Figure 2.16.

Figure 2.16   Turning off the Office Assistant.

USING DIALOG BOXES

Many Windows 95 applications, including Excel, use dialog boxes to allow more detailed or efficient communication with the program than menus alone can provide. There are many types of dialog boxes providing various kinds of input.

Some dialog boxes appear automatically if you make some sort of mistake or ask Excel to do something that requires confirmation. They appear as a result of choosing a menu command that requires additional input. You can tell which menu commands produce dialog boxes because they are followed by an ellipsis (...). Let's examine one of the more complex dialog boxes to see how it works.

1.   Choose **Tools** to display the Tools drop-down menu (see Figure 2.17).

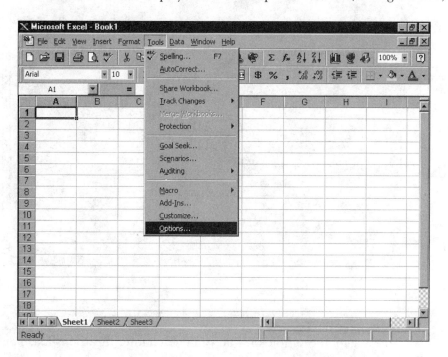

Figure 2.17 *The Tools drop-down menu.*

Notice that several of the menu commands have triangles next to them. These commands have submenus with additional commands. Submenus are used later. Other menu commands are followed by an ellipsis, indicating that choosing that command will produce a dialog box.

2. Choose **Options** to produce the Options dialog box, shown in Figure 2.18.

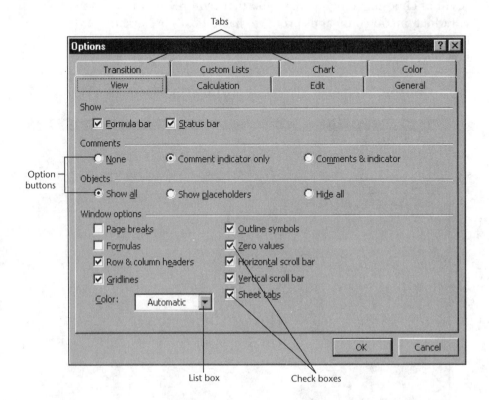

Figure 2.18 *The Options dialog box.*

This is a good example of what you'll encounter in various Excel dialog boxes. *Option buttons* allow you to choose only one of the options in a category. *Check box* categories can have multiple boxes checked. *List boxes* let you select a choice from a list.

Clicking on one of the tabs at the top of the dialog box will allow you to switch between various sets of options. Let's take a look at another set of options in the same dialog box.

3. Click on the **General** tab (see Figure 2.19).

This set of options includes yet another input method—a text box you can type information into.

4. Click on the **Cancel** button on the right side of the dialog box or press the **Esc** key to clear the dialog box. Don't worry if you changed some of these options while exploring the dialog box; choosing **Cancel** instead of **OK** means that none of your changes will be made.

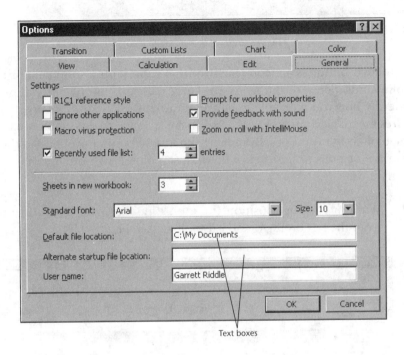

Text boxes

Figure 2.19 *The Options dialog box with the General tab highlighted.*

USING THE TOOLBARS

You've learned that there are often keyboard shortcuts for accomplishing certain tasks. Excel's toolbars are like shortcut keys that can be opened with a click of a mouse button. One of the advantages of toolbars is that the shortcuts are visible, so they're often easier to remember than keyboard shortcuts.

Excel supplies predefined toolbars for a variety of situations. Two default toolbars are set to automatically appear when you start Excel. The top toolbar is the *Standard toolbar*, and the one below it is the *Formatting toolbar*. See Figure 2.20.

Figure 2.20 *The default toolbars.*

Each toolbar button is an icon (picture) that represents a command or series of commands. Some of the icons are fairly self-explanatory, but you may be wondering how you'll be able to figure out what the rest of those cryptic little pictures mean. Never fear. Excel provides an easy way to determine what each of the toolbar buttons does. By moving the mouse pointer over one of the buttons, a *tool tip* pops up just below the mouse pointer with the button's name. Let's try it out.

1.   Without clicking, position the mouse pointer over the third button from the left on the Standard toolbar (see Figure 2.21).

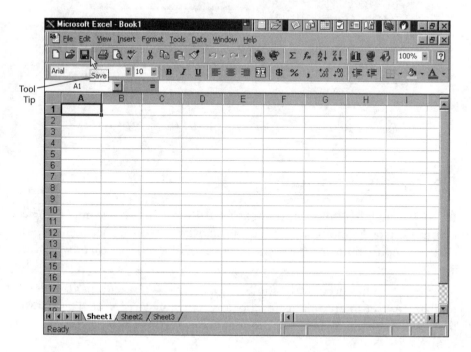

Figure 2.21 *The mouse pointer on the **Save** toolbar button.*

The tool tip says *Save*, and if you were to click on this button you would go to the Save window.

2. Move the pointer over some of the other toolbar buttons. Look at the tool tip to get an idea of what some of the other buttons can accomplish.

Depending on the options you selected while installing Office 97, you also may have an *Office 97 shortcut bar* on the right-hand side of the Microsoft Excel title bar. Let's turn this feature off for now.

1. Position your mouse pointer over the Office 97 logo in the toolbar's left-hand corner.

2. Right-click once and choose **Exit** from the drop-down menu (see Figure 2.22).

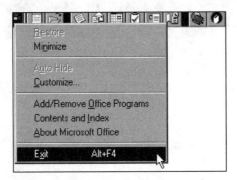

Figure 2.22 *Turning off the Office 97 shortcut bar.*

3. You will be asked if you want the Office Shortcut Bar to continue starting automatically.

4. Choose **No**.

If you ever want to turn on the Shortcut bar again, you can open the application from the Microsoft Office folder on your C: drive.

Throughout the book, we'll be working with various toolbars and toolbar buttons. Later on you'll learn how to select which toolbars you want to appear on the screen, how to change their position, and even how to create special toolbars to meet your personal needs.

NAVIGATING THE WORKSHEET

As you start entering and editing data in worksheets, you need to know how to move around. There are quite a few ways to navigate through the worksheet using either the keyboard or the mouse. The simplest method is clicking the mouse pointer on the cell you want to move to, or using the **Arrow** keys to move to the cell you want to be active.

1. Use the **Arrow** keys to move to several different cells. The *cell reference area* tells you what the active cell is (see Figure 2.23).

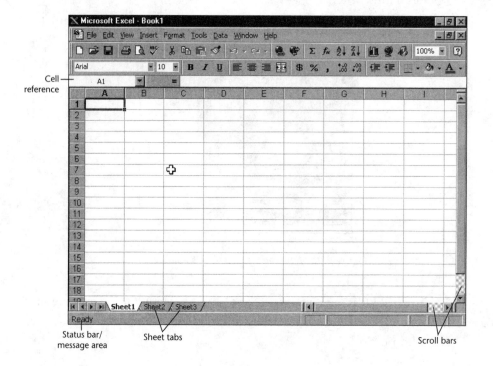

Figure 2.23 The cell reference area.

2. Use the mouse to click on several different cells.

While this method works well for moving short distances, it's very inefficient for moving long distances. Some of the more useful long-distance navigation techniques involve keyboard combinations (see Table 2.1).

Table 2.1 *Navigation Keyboard Combinations*

KEYS	RESULT
PageUp	Moves up one screen.
PageDown	Moves down one screen.
Alt-PageDown	Moves right one screen.
Alt-PageUp	Moves left one screen.
Ctrl-Home	Moves to A1.
Ctrl-End	Moves to the last used cell.

You can also move long distances by using the scroll bars. Use the same techniques you learned earlier to scroll to different parts of the worksheet:

❖ Click on the scroll bar buttons to move one row at a time.

❖ Drag the scroll box to move to a distant location.

❖ Click in the scroll bar to move up or down one screen.

Using the scroll bars doesn't change the active cell; it only changes what part of the worksheet you're looking at. Once you've moved to the right spot, click in the cell you want to become active.

One of the most useful ways to move around is to use the Go To dialog box. With the Go To dialog box, you can enter the cell address you want to move to, and zap! You're there. Let's try it.

1. Choose **Edit, Go To** (or press **F5**). The dialog box appears, as shown in Figure 2.24.

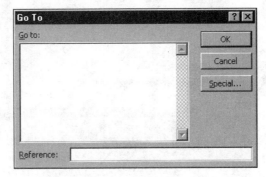

Figure 2.24 *The Go To dialog box.*

As we work through the book, we'll cover a number of ways to use the Go To dialog box. For now, let's just move to a new cell. Notice the vertical line in the Reference text box. This is called the *insertion point* and indicates that this is where you can start typing. If the insertion point isn't in the Reference text box, just click in the Reference text box and the insertion point will move there.

2.   Type **Z45** and click **OK** to make Z45 the active cell.

USING EXCEL'S HELP FACILITIES

One of the most important skills you can learn is how to get yourself unstuck when you run into trouble. Fortunately, Excel provides some very useful tools for getting help. Let's explore Help's contents to see what's available.

1.   Choose **Help** and then click **Contents and Index** to produce the Help screen shown in Figure 2.25.

Figure 2.25 The Excel Help Contents and Index window.

The Help window is an application window. Help runs concurrently with Excel, which means you can leave it open while you try things out on your worksheet. The Help window can't be resized, but it can be moved out of the way by dragging the title bar.

Help is divided into logical groups. Double-clicking on the **Creating**, **Opening** and **Saving Files** group, for example, will open a series of sections that deal with particular aspects of working with documents. Other sections lead to more information about related topics.

You can move to any of these sections by double-clicking on them. Let's try moving to one of the help sections now.

2. Position the mouse pointer over the **Creating, Opening, and Saving Files** heading and double-click to display additional topics within the heading, as shown in Figure 2.26.

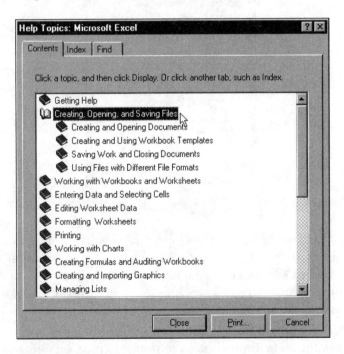

Figure 2.26　*The Creating, Opening, and Saving Files Help window.*

Now you can choose from further headings.

3. Double-click on **Creating and Opening documents**.

    Note that the choices under this heading each have a question mark beside them. This indicates that double-clicking on these topics will provide an actual help screen—not more topics. In other words, it's the end of the line.

4. Double-click on **Open workbooks when Microsoft Excel starts** to display a help screen as shown in Figure 2.27. Notice that the word shortcut is green and underlined with dashes. This means you can click on that item to display a definition.

Figure 2.27 A Help window.

    You can use the buttons just below the title bar to move to other portions of Help. For example, you can use the **Back** button to retrace your steps, one screen at a time, or the **Help Topics** button to return to the contents page. The **Options** button provides a list of options that you can perform with the Help information on the screen, such as printing out a topic.

5. Click the **Help Topics** button to return to the Contents page.

    You can search for specific information when you don't know what topic you need. This is like using the index of a book to find a specific word. Do this by accessing the Index page of the Help window.

6. Click on the **Index** page tab to view the index window, as shown in Figure 2.28.

Figure 2.28 *The Help Index.*

You can either scroll to a category item in the list or just start typing the name of the feature you need help with in the text box above the list. As you type, the category items starting with those letters will appear in the list. When the category item you want is visible, you can click on the **Display** button, or just double-click on the item.

Suppose you want more information about using Help.

7. Type **h** in the text box and notice that the list jumps to the first features that start with the letter h.

8. Type **help** and the Help categories come into view. Now you can double-click on any of the topics offered to view the corresponding help information. After you have found the help screen you are looking for and read the information, you can close the Help window by double-clicking on the control-menu box. You can close a Help topic by clicking on the **Close** button.

9.   Choose **File**, **Exit** from the main Help widow to exit Help.

Using the Office Assistant

Not only does Excel make it easy to find and use Help for the topics you are struggling with; the Office Assistant can even suggest better ways to perform the same tasks. Excel is a smart program.

   To turn the assistant on, click the **Office Assistant** button on the Standard toolbar, as shown in Figure 2.29.

Figure 2.29   *The Office Assistant button.*

The Office Assistant appears in the top right-hand corner of your screen. It will watch you and try to offer help based on the actions you perform. When the Assistant has a suggestion for you, a yellow light bulb will appear in the right corner of the Assistant's window.

   To display the Assistant's suggestion, just click on the light bulb. To clear the suggestion, all you have to do is click on the **Close** button. Let's see if the Assistant can show us a better way to move between cells than the Go To box we used in the last section.

1.   Press **F5**.
2.   Type **Z45** and click **OK**.

     A light bulb should now be showing in the Office Assistant window.

3.   Click on the **light bulb** to display the Assistant's suggestion.

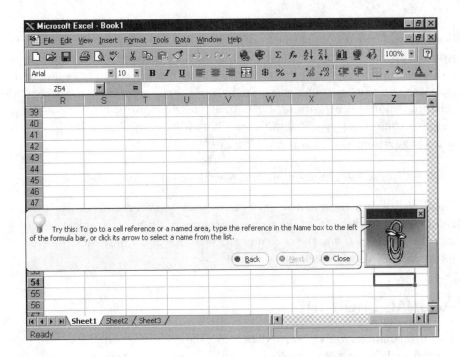

Figure 2.30 *The Office Assistant offers a suggestion.*

4.   Click on the **Close** option to resume working in Excel.

Because the Office Assistant uses a great deal of intelligence for providing tips, you may have gotten a different one than the example in the book. Don't worry, Excel is just trying to give you the best suggestion for your particular situation.

N O T E

You can also ask the Office Assistant questions. Just click on the **Assistant** and type your question in the text box. When you're finished, press **Enter** and the Assistant will provide you with a list of Help topics.

You can leave the Office Assistant open to automatically display suggestions, or you can keep it closed except when you want to see a suggestion. We won't keep the Assistant displayed for the figures in the rest of the book since it does take up some valuable screen real estate. However, don't hesitate to display it as you work through the book to see if there are better ways of accomplishing what you are doing. Of course, just because the Office Assistant suggests something, that doesn't mean it's the best approach. It's just giving you a suggestion. Use your own judgment.

❖ Choose **File**, **Exit**, or click on the **Close** button.

Excel closes and returns to the icon you started from. If you have made changes to a worksheet, Excel is considerate enough to ask you if you want to save the changes. If you see such a message at this point, just click the **No** button to finish exiting Excel.

A FINAL THOUGHT

The information you've learned in this chapter gives you the tools to get around in Windows 95 and Excel. In the next chapter, you'll finally get a chance to put Excel to work creating worksheets and entering data.

Creating a Worksheet

PLANNING A WORKSHEET

The worksheet is where you enter information you want to store and manipulate. Like almost anything you build, a worksheet is more useful, efficient, and understandable if you take the time to plan before diving in and entering data willy-nilly.

The first step is to decide on the purpose of your worksheet. For example, if the worksheet is going to contain a monthly budget for the next year, then the purpose is to forecast and gain greater control over inflows and outflows for your business.

Give some thought to the level of detail you want to include in the worksheet. Too little detail may render the worksheet useless by omitting critical information required to make decisions based on the analysis of data. Too much detail can make the worksheet unwieldy and mask the results, not letting you see the big picture.

You may also find it useful to use paper and pencil to sketch out the overall design of your worksheet. This lets you see how the worksheet looks to the user (whether that user is you or someone else) before you take the time to enter data.

One more planning tip to keep in mind: remember that the ultimate result of most worksheets is a printed report of some sort. Many things that seem obvious to you as you create or edit a worksheet can easily be obscured or invisible in the printout. For example, formulas you create to perform calculations can be revealed in the worksheet, but are generally not part of the printed output. The printed report is only a small portion of the entire worksheet, so the context that might make the worksheet understandable on-screen may not be a part of the printout.

Building a Text Framework

The most common and often the most practical way to start putting together a worksheet is to enter titles, column and row headings, and any other text elements that provide a structure for your worksheet as you enter the data. There are no hard-and-fast rules for the text framework but, traditionally, columns contain time periods such as months, days and hours, and row headings contain categories such as rent, insurance or cost of goods.

We are going to create a budget worksheet for a small locksmith business that also sells bagels. The Spokane Locks and Bagel Corporation decided to use Excel to create a budget worksheet to compare budgeted amounts with actual figures. Figure 3.1 depicts the initial text framework for this budget worksheet.

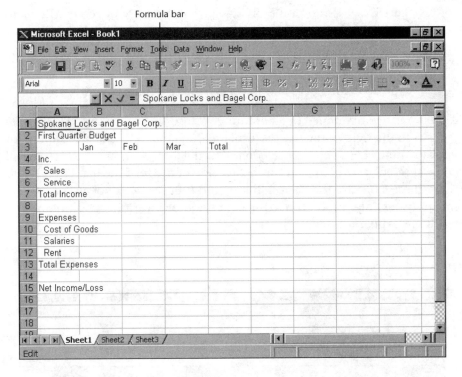

Formula bar

Figure 3.1 The text framework for the Spokane Locks and Bagel Corp. worksheet.

ENTERING TEXT

To enter text into an Excel worksheet, simply move to the cell where you want to enter the text and start typing. As you type, the text appears in both the cell and the formula bar. Let's start entering the text as displayed in Figure 3.1.

1. Start Excel if you don't already have it up on your screen. Refer to Chapter 2 if you don't remember the steps for starting Excel.

2. Be sure A1 is the active cell. Look at the cell reference area to double-check that you're in the right place.

3. Type **Spokane Locks and Bagel Corp.** Press **Enter**.

As you start typing, notice that a flashing vertical line called an *insertion point* appears to the right of the text, as displayed in Figure 3.2. The insertion point lets you know where text is to be entered or deleted. As soon as you start a cell entry, three new icons appear on the left side of the formula bar. From left to right, these icons are the **Cancel**, **Enter**, and **Edit Formula** boxes. Also notice that pressing **Enter** moves you to the next row of the worksheet, where you can type the next part of the heading.

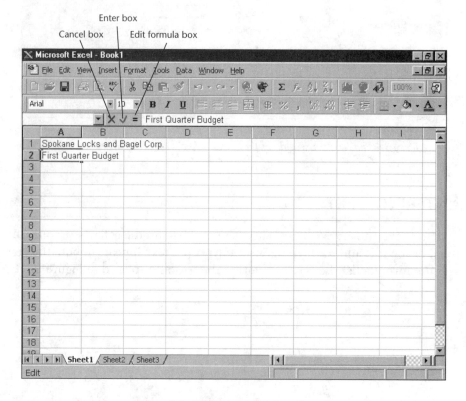

Figure 3.2 *The beginnings of a cell entry.*

If you make a mistake while typing, just press the **Backspace** key to erase the character(s) to the left of the insertion point. If you've really messed up and want to start over again, click on the **Cancel** box or press **Esc**.

While you are entering text in a cell, you cannot press the **Left Arrow** or **Right Arrow** keys to reposition the insertion point for editing. Pressing an arrow key causes Excel to complete the cell entry with what you've typed so far and move in the arrow's direction to the next cell on the worksheet.

N O T E

The text you typed in cell A1 has apparently spilled over into the adjacent columns B, C, D, and E. But do those other cells really contain part of the information? No. The entire worksheet title is in A1. The cell reference area says you are in A1 and the formula bar displays the whole title. If you were to move to B1, you'd see from the formula bar that B1 contains no data. In fact, it is because B1, C1, D1, and E1 are empty that the contents of A1 are allowed to spill over. If these cells contained data, even a space, the entry in A1 would be truncated.

To see how this works, let's enter something in B1. There are several ways to complete a cell entry, including clicking on the **Enter** box, pressing the **Enter** key, or moving to another cell. The last method is usually the fastest since you often need to make entries in other cells.

1. Press the **Up Arrow** and **Right Arrow** keys to move to cell B1. Notice that cell B1 is empty.

2. Press the **Spacebar** once and then click on the **Enter** box. The text in A1 is limited to what fits in the current column width. Now let's get rid of the space in B1 to restore the title.

3. While B1 is still the active cell, press the **Delete** key to erase all the contents and allow the title to flow across the columns.

Column widths can be changed to accommodate the amount of text entered. Changing column widths, which is covered in the next two chapters, is usually the preferred method for accommodating long text entries.

N O T E

4. Click on cell **A2** to make it the active cell.

5.   Type **First Quarter Budget**. Press **Enter**.

6.   Click on cell **B3** and type **Jan.**

T I P

Next you could move to cell C3 and type **Feb** and then go to D3 and type **Mar**, but there's an easier way. In the lower-right corner of the box surrounding the active cell is a small black rectangle called the *fill handle*. The fill handle allows you to perform several different copying actions. For now we'll use the fill handle to take advantage of Excel's intelligence. By dragging the fill handle to the right so the outline extends through cell D3, Excel automatically enters **Feb** and **Mar** for you.

7.   Position the mouse over the fill handle until the mouse pointer transforms into thin cross-hairs. Drag it to the right until the cell outline extends to cell D3, as displayed in Figure 3.3.

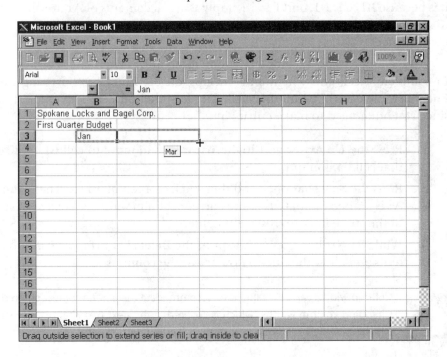

Figure 3.3 Dragging the fill handle.

8.   Release the mouse button to complete the fill (see Figure 3.4).

N O T E

Use of the fill handle isn't limited to months of the year. If a cell contains *Mon*, dragging the fill handle increments the days of the week as *Tue*, *Wed*, *Thu*, and so on. A cell containing text and a number, such as *1st Period*, fills as *2nd Period*, *3rd Period*, and so on.

You can also use the fill handle to increment a series by dragging to the right or down. If you want to use the fill handle to decrement a series, drag to the left or up. For example, if a cell contained *Jan*, dragging left or up would fill as *Dec*, *Nov*, *Oct*, and so on.

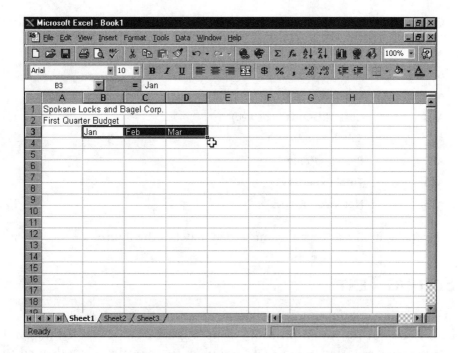

Figure 3.4 The results of the fill after releasing the mouse button.

9. Click in cell **E3** and type **Total**.

10. Move to cell A4 and type **Income**.

    If you're entering several contiguous cells in a column, pressing the **Enter** key is the most efficient way to complete a cell entry since it causes the next cell in the column to become the active cell.

11. Press the **Enter** key to complete the entry and move to the next cell in the column.

In Figure 3.1, the entries in cells A5–A6 and A10–A12 are slightly indented. This was accomplished by preceding the entries with two spaces.

N O T E

12. Press the **Spacebar** twice and type **Sales**. Then press **Enter**.

13. Enter the following text:

Table 3.1 *Text framework for Spokane Locks and Bagels worksheet*

CELL	TEXT TO BE ENTERED
A6	**Service** (*Indented*)
A7	**Total Income**
A9	**Expenses**
A10	**Cost of Goods** (*Indented*)
A11	**Salaries** (*Indented*)
A12	**Rent** (*Indented*)
A13	**Total Expenses**
A15	**Net Income/Loss**

Refer to Figure 3.1 to be sure your screen matches the figure.

EDITING TEXT

Making your worksheet look the best it can with accurate data is very important. Consequently, you'll probably spend a great deal of time editing and revising your worksheets. Let's take a look at some of the methods used to make editing easy.

Editing by Retyping

One of the easiest ways to edit cells that contain very little data is simply to click on the cell and begin typing. The new information you type will replace the data that was originally there. Let's try it by abbreviating the word *Income* in cell A4.

1. Double-click on cell **A4**.
2. Type **Inc.**
3. Press **Enter**.

That was pretty easy. *Inc.* has now replaced *Income.* But now you decide that it looked better spelled out after all. Let's change it back.

1. Double-click on cell **A4**.
2. Type **Income** and press the **Enter** key.

Editing Entries in the Cell

You may want to make revisions to a cell containing more than one or two words or data. Your cells may contain sentence-long and paragraph-long data, and you might need to revise only one word or number. This can be done with a few simple keystrokes. For example, suppose you decide to spell out the word *Corp.* in your worksheet title.

1. Double-click on cell **A1**.
2. Use your **Right Arrow** key to position your cursor between the letter *p* and the period (.) in *Corp*.
3. Press the **Delete** key once to get rid of the period and type **oration**.
4. Press **Enter**.

Try out some of the editing commands in Table 3.2 when you need to make a revision in a cell or formula bar that contains a lot of data. You'll need to double-click on the cell you want to change in order to enter edit mode.

Table 3.2 *Editing Commands*

ACTION	RESULT
Arrow	Moves cursor in the direction of the arrow
Home	Moves cursor to the beginning of the current line
End	Moves cursor to the end of the current line
Ctrl-Arrows	Moves cursor to the beginning of a word or segment in the direction of the arrow
Ctrl-Delete	Deletes all data to the right of the cursor
Shift-End	Highlights data to the right of the cursor
Shift-Arrows	Highlights data in the direction of the arrow
Delete	Deletes a single character to the right of the cursor
Backspace	Deletes a single character to the left of the cursor

Editing Entries in the Formula Bar

You can also edit information in the formula bar rather than in the cell itself. The formula bar is the area at the top of your screen that displays the information in the active cell. Suppose you've changed your mind again and decide that you really want the word *Corporation* abbreviated after all. These are the steps you would use to edit the title using the formula bar.

1. Click on cell **A1**. In the formula bar, click between the letters p and o in the word *Corporation*.
2. Hold down the mouse button and drag to the right so that *oration* is highlighted. See Figure 3.5.
3. Type a period (.) to replace the selected text.
4. Press **Enter**.

See Chapter 5, "Modifying a Worksheet," for more editing functions such as copying and moving.

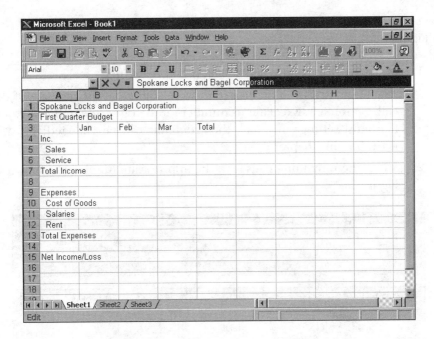

Figure 3.5 Editing an entry inside the formula bar.

ENTERING NUMBERS

Entering numbers is done in the same way as entering text. What you see on-screen depends on what type of number you enter. For example, if you enter **100**, the screen displays 100. If you enter **100.43**, the screen displays 100.43. But if you enter **100.00**, the screen displays 100 without the decimal point or trailing zeros. Now suppose you enter **1000000000000**. It is displayed as 1E+12. Hey, what the heck is going on here?

Let us reassure you that Excel isn't actually changing the number you enter, just the way it is displayed. The actual number you enter in the cell is used in any calculations Excel performs. Now, here's what's happening. Excel formats numbers using what it calls *General Formatting*. General Formatting doesn't display trailing zeros after a decimal point and converts very large numbers to scientific notation, which uses exponents.

The way numbers (or text, for that matter) are formatted can be changed to suit your taste and requirements. The techniques for changing cell formatting are covered in Chapter 6.

N O T E

Let's start entering the numbers for the budget worksheet that are displayed in Figure 3.6.

1. Move to cell B5 and type **228000**, then press **Enter**.

    The text entries you made earlier were aligned at the left side of the cell. Conversely, Excel aligns numbers at the right side of the cell. Just like most settings in Excel, these defaults can be changed; you will learn how in Chapter 6.

2. Fill in the remaining cells with the appropriate numbers as shown in Figure 3.6.

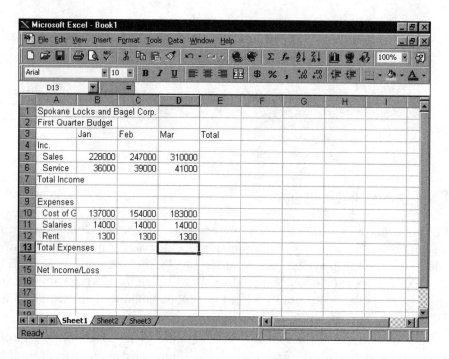

Figure 3.6 *The budget worksheet with its initial numbers entered.*

Since we're on the subject of entering numbers, there are several other features you will need to know about. Click on the **Sheet 2** tab at the bottom of the screen, and you can experiment with a few of the basics.

Characters Used When Entering Numbers

When entering numbers you may use any numeric characters from 0 to 9. You may also use the following special characters:

```
+ - ( ) , / $ % . E e
```

For example, you can type a minus sign prior to a number to create a negative number. A percent sign after a number makes it a percentage value. These characters will be discussed in more detail later in this chapter when we talk about formulas, and in Chapter 4, when we talk about formatting numbers.

Entering Numbers as Text

At times, you may want to enter numbers as text. For example, let's say you need to enter the zip code 05468 in a cell. Excel will drop the leading zero and display the zip code as 5468. So what do you do now? The easiest thing to do is to precede the numbers with an apostrophe ('). The computer will then treat this cell like all other text entries, and the numbers will be aligned on the left side of the cell. As shown in Figure 3.7, the apostrophe is visible in the formula bar but doesn't appear in the cell itself.

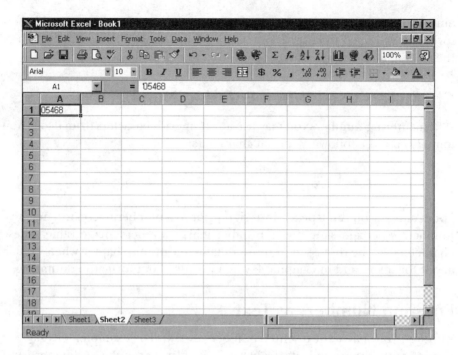

Figure 3.7 *Entering numbers as text.*

Entering Fractions

Fractions must be entered as mixed numbers—that is, as integer values that contain fractions. For example, if you want to enter the fraction one-third, you would need to type 0 1/3. If you enter 1/3, Excel will think you are entering the date of January 3. If you were to enter 5/95 for five-ninety-fifths, Excel will think that you are entering a date of May 1995. Always enter fractions as mixed numbers to prevent unwanted results.

You can also enter fractions as decimal values. For example, the fraction 2/5 equals .4 in decimal value. If you enter the fraction 0 2/5 in a cell, the formula bar will display the value *.4* because Excel converts the fraction automatically for its own purposes.

Entering Dates and Times

As you just saw, Excel 97 recognizes certain entries as dates. Date entries can be used in a wide variety of mathematical calculations. For example, you can determine the number of days between two dates or calculate 30 days from one date to another.

Excel uses a serial-numbering system for calculating dates. The dating system begins with January 1, 1900; its serial number equals 1. The serial number of January 2, 1900, equals 2, and so on.

Because mathematical calculations can be performed with dates, it's important to look at the formatting used by Excel. Try entering dates in a variety of ways to see how Excel handles them. Table 3.3 shows some examples.

Table 3.3 *Excel Dates*

You Type This	Excel Displays This
June 15, 1997	15-Jun-97
6/15/97	6/15/97
15 June 97	15-Jun-97
15-June-97	15-Jun-97
June 1997	Jun-97
June-97	Jun-97

 When you experiment with these dates, make sure you use a fresh cell for each one. Once you've chosen a format, the cell will remember it, and any other value you enter in the cell will adhere to that format unless you change it manually using the **Cell** command in the Format menu.

N O T E

Excel handles time the same way it handles dates. Both are stored as serial numbers. With time, the serial number is a decimal fraction of a 24-hour period beginning at midnight (12:00 a.m.). Therefore, noon (12:00 p.m.) is half of the day, and its serial number would be .5. Sound confusing? Well it's not as bad as it sounds. Come on, let's try it out. Enter the following times in separate blank cells and then look at the formula bar:

Table 3.4 *Excel times*

YOU TYPE THIS	FORMULA BAR SHOWS THIS
17:32	5:32:00 PM
5:32	5:32:00 AM
5:32:25	5:32:25 AM
5:32 PM	5:32:00 PM
5:32 AM	5:32:00 AM
12 am	12:00:00 AM

N O T E

The default format for time in Excel 97 is 24-hour format. Therefore, 9:30 p.m. should be entered as either **21:30** or **9:30 PM**.

Now that you've gotten a little experience with dates and times, it's time to put those skills to work. Click on the **Sheet 1** tab to return to the worksheet for Spokane Locks and Bagels. On this sample worksheet, the column headings Jan, Feb, and Mar are not technically date values; they are text labels. You know this because they align themselves with the left side of the cell, as all text entries do. Date values entered in one of the date formats shown in Table 3.4 align themselves with the right side of the cell, as do numbers. Try replacing the text entries with date values in the sample worksheet as follows:

1. Move to cell B3 and type the date value **Jan-97**.
2. Without pressing Enter, click on the fill handle and drag it to cell D3. (If you've already pressed Enter, move back to cell B3).

The cells now contain date entries and are aligned with the right sides of the cells.

See Chapter 4 to learn more about how to use date and time functions.

CREATING FORMULAS

Formulas are a spreadsheet's *raison d'etre*. If all we needed to do was put text and numbers in rows and columns, just about any word processing program would fill the bill. Formulas allow us to perform calculations using values from any cells and to have the result appear in the formula cell.

You build formulas using the four mathematical operators:

* ❖ The plus sign (+).
* ❖ The minus sign (-).
* ❖ The asterisk (*) for multiplication.
* ❖ The slash (/) for division.

You always start a formula by moving to an empty cell where you want the results of the formula to appear, and typing the equal sign (=), which tells Excel to get ready for a formula. For example, you could type the formula =2*2 in a cell and, after completing the cell entry, the cell would display the result of the formula as 4, but the formula bar displays the formula.

At this point, you know how to use your fancy spreadsheet program like a pocket calculator. Big deal, you say. Well, the real power of formulas comes into play when you use *cell referencing*. Instead of entering a formula using values, you can enter a formula using cell references, such as **=C12*D14**. If 2 is the value in both C12 or D14, the result is still 4. However, if the values in C12 and D14 change, the result automatically changes as well.

Let's create the formula for January's Total Income in our budget worksheet. The formula adds the values in cells B5 and B6.

1. Move to cell B7 and type **=B5+B6**, then click the **Enter** box to complete the cell entry while keeping B7 as the active cell.

    If you originally entered the values in B5 and B6 as specified (and we know you did), cell B7 now displays the value 264000, while the formula bar displays the formula, =B5+B6, as shown in Figure 3.8.

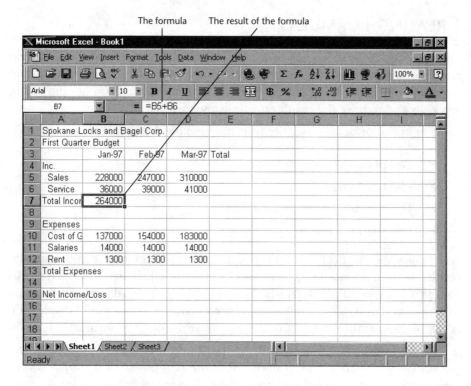

Figure 3.8 A formula and its result.

Now, let's try a different method of specifying the cells to be included in a formula. We'll use the pointing method to click on the cells we want to include, thus eliminating any possibility of entering an incorrect cell reference. To create the formula for January's Total Expenses:

2. Move to cell B13 and start the formula by typing =.

3. Click on cell **B10** to let Excel know that B10 is the first cell you want to include in the formula.

The beginning of the formula (=B10) followed by the insertion point appears in the formula cell, and a dashed border appears around B10, as displayed in Figure 3.9.

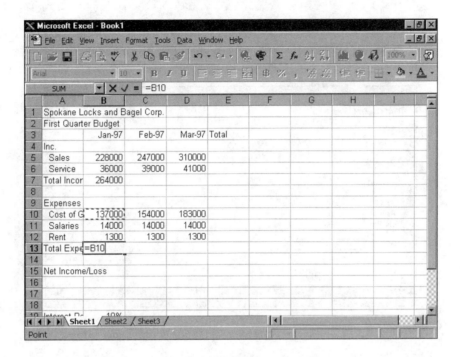

Figure 3.9 *The beginning of a formula using the pointed method.*

4. Type + then click on cell **B11**. Type + again and click on cell **B12**.

5. Click on the **Enter** box or press the **Enter** key to accept the formula.

   In this example, pointing may not appear more advantageous that just typing in the cell references, but when dealing with more distant cell references or specifying ranges of cells, pointing can make a substantial difference. We think you'll start to see the advantage of pointing as we create the formula for January's Net Income/Loss.

6. Move to cell B15 and type =.

7. Click on cell **B7** (January's Total Income), then type - (the minus sign). Now click on cell **B13** (January's Total Expenses) and press **Enter**.

With the three formulas entered, your screen should now look like Figure 3.10.

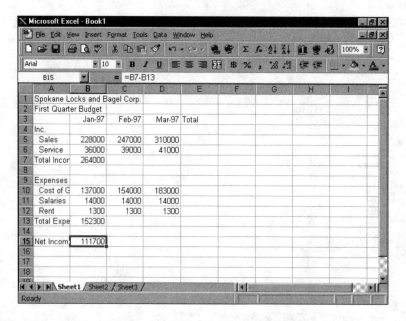

Figure 3.10 The budget worksheet with the first three formulas entered.

Understanding the Order of Operation

When creating formulas that involve more than a single mathematical operator, it's important to remember that your computer will follow a set of guidelines called *the order of operation*. This means instead of reading a formula from left to right, the computer will perform its calculations according to the mathematical syntax used. The order of operation is shown in Table 3.5.

Table 3.5 Excel's Order of Operation

OPERATOR	DESCRIPTION
-	Negative (as in –34)
%	Percent
^	Exponentiation
* and /	Multiplication and division
+ and -	Addition and subtraction
&	Text joining/concatenation
=<> <=> =<>	Comparison or relations

If you typed in the formula **=6*3+4/2**, Excel would find the value to be 20. That's because the computer will perform all multiplication and division before doing any addition or subtraction.

You can control the order of operation by using parentheses and creating an *expression*. All expressions inside parentheses are processed first. For example, you could change your formula to read **=(6*3+4)/2**, and Excel would find the value to be 11. If you're ever unsure about what order Excel will follow to process a sequence of operators, use parentheses, even if they aren't really necessary.

UNDERSTANDING AND USING FUNCTIONS

Think of *functions* as predefined formulas. Using just the four mathematical operators, you could duplicate just about any of the supplied Excel functions. It might take a long time to recreate a function with the math operators, particularly for some of the more complicated functions. Just as importantly, you'd have to go through the same process every time you wanted to use the formula.

Perhaps the most common function is the SUM function, which adds the values in a range of cells. Most functions require *arguments*, contained within parentheses, which are just pieces of information the function needs to complete the calculation. Only one argument is required for the SUM function—the range of cells to be added.

One advantage of using the SUM function (versus specifying plus signs between each cell reference) is that it's just plain easier. Using plus signs between each cell reference can become very unwieldy for a large range of cells. For example:

```
=C2+C3+C4+C5+C6+C7+C8+C9+C10+C11+C12
```

is much more cumbersome and error-prone than

```
=SUM(C2:C12)
```

don't you think?

The colon between the two cell references in the argument is the *separator*. It means *through*, as in C2 through C12.

Also, using the range argument makes it easier to insert or delete cells in the range without having to modify the function's argument. Let's say you needed to add a row for a new category within the range of C2 through C12. If you had used the SUM function, the new row would automatically be included in the range.

Let's use the SUM function to calculate February's Total Income.

1. Move to cell C7 and type **=SUM(**

   You are now ready to enter the range of cells to be totaled. We'll use the pointing method to enter the range, and we can do it in one fell swoop.

2. Point to cell **C5**, drag down to **C6** and release the mouse button.

   A dashed border surrounds the range of cells, C5 through C6, and the cell references have been entered after the left parenthesis, as shown in Figure 3.11.

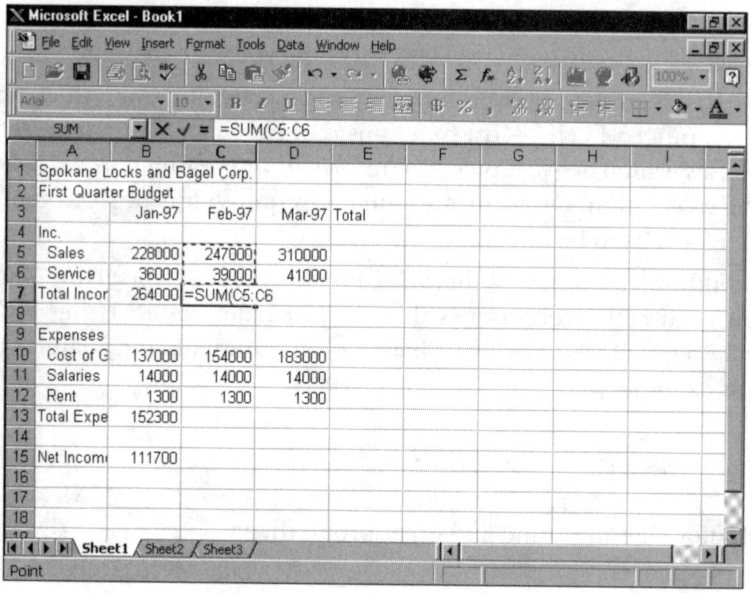

Figure 3.11 *The beginning of the SUM function with its argument.*

You probably think the next step is to enter the right parenthesis, but not so fast. Excel is so smart, it usually knows when a closing parenthesis is required and enters it for you when you complete the cell entry. Let's try it.

3. Press **Enter** to complete the cell entry.

The result of the function's calculation appears in cell C7 (286000), and the function with its argument and both parentheses appears in the formula bar.

Now get ready for some Excel magic. Most of the time when you want to SUM a range of numbers, you don't even need to enter the function or specify the range. You can put Excel's brains to work and usually figure out the proper range to sum. Let's try to SUM the March Total Income.

1.   Click in cell **D7**.

2.   Click on the **AutoSum** button on the toolbar, as shown in Figure 3.12.

Figure 3.12   The AutoSum button.

The SUM function is automatically entered and the closest contiguous range (D5 through D6) is specified as the argument, as shown in Figure 3.13.

	A	B	C	D	E	F	G	H	I
1	Spokane Locks and Bagel Corp.								
2	First Quarter Budget								
3		Jan-97	Feb-97	Mar-97	Total				
4	Inc.								
5	Sales	228000	247000	310000					
6	Service	36000	39000	41000					
7	Total Incor	264000	286000	=SUM(D5:D6)					
8									
9	Expenses								
10	Cost of G	137000	154000	183000					
11	Salaries	14000	14000	14000					
12	Rent	1300	1300	1300					
13	Total Expe	152300							
14									
15	Net Incom	111700							
16									
17									
18									

Figure 3.13 Using the AutoSum button.

3. Press the **Enter** key to complete the entry.

SHORTCUT If you are sure that Excel will select the correct range for the argument, you can double-click on the **AutoSum** button and the entry is completed for you. This isn't too dangerous, even if the wrong range is selected. You can always delete and start over.

Okay, that was pretty darned easy, but what about all those other functions that are hidden away somewhere in Excel? Don't worry, they aren't so hidden. In the following steps, we'll show you how easy it is to find just the function you need.

Let's use one of the more complex functions—one that requires several arguments to see what the monthly payments would be for a new piece of equipment the Spokane Locks and Bagel Corporation is thinking about purchasing. It's one of those fancy new combination key-duplicator-and-cream-cheese-spreading machines.

The function we'll use is the PMT function, which calculates the payments if we simply supply a few arguments. The information we need to supply is the interest rate per payment period, the number of payment periods, and the present value (the amount of the loan). We'll enter those three pieces of information onto the budget worksheet now.

1. Press the **PageDown** key to move to a new screenful of rows, click in cell **A19** and type **Interest Rate**.

2. In cell A20 type **Term**.

3. In cell A21 type **Loan Amount**.

4. In cell A22 type **Payment**.

5. In cell B19 type **10%** and press **Enter**.

6. In cell B20, type **5** to represent a five-year loan period.

7. Type **28500** in cell B21, which is the amount the company wants to finance over the five-year period.

   We could move to the cell that is to contain the function (B22) and enter the function name and the appropriate arguments, but with three arguments required, it can be difficult to remember what goes where. Never fear! Excel Paste Function to the rescue. Excel includes several *wizards*—specialized help systems that take you by the hand

and step you through some of the more mysterious procedures. Additional Wizards are covered later in the book, but we'll go over the Paste Function now because it's so useful.

You can invoke the Paste Function in a variety of ways. Choosing **Insert, Function** will do it, or you can click on the **Paste Function** toolbar button, which is what we'll do now.

8.   Click in cell **B22** and then click on the **Paste Function** button on the toolbar, shown in Figure 3.14.

Figure 3.14 *The Paste Function button.*

If the dialog box obscures the values in column B, point to its title bar, drag to the right about an inch, and release the mouse button.

If the function you want is visible in the Function Name list on the right side of the dialog box, you can click on it. Otherwise, click on the category of functions you think your function might be in and then use the scroll bar to find it. See Figure 3.15.

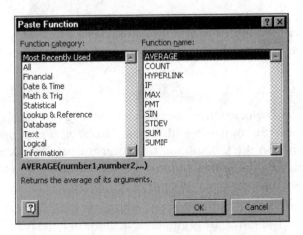

Figure 3.15 *The Paste Function dialog box.*

We'll go through the steps to find the PMT as if it weren't visible and we didn't know what category to choose.

9. Click on **All** in the Function Category list to display all the available functions in every category.

10. Click on any of the functions in the Function Name list.

11. Use the scrollbar to scroll down the list until **PMT** is visible and double-click on it, as shown in Figure 3.16.

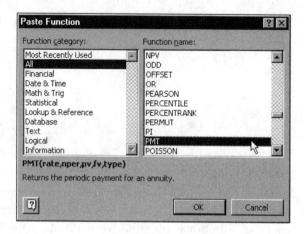

Figure 3.16 *The Paste Function dialog box with the PMT function selected.*

You can type the first letter of the function name, and the highlighter jumps to it. Then you only have to search through the functions that start with that letter.

SHORTCUT

With **PMT** selected, the Paste Function dialog box displays the proper syntax for the function and, below that, a brief explanation of what the function does. If you want to enter the arguments manually, you can click on the **Cancel** button, but it's much easier to let the Wizard step you through the argument entry process.

12. Click on the **OK** button to proceed to the Paste Function dialog box that lets you enter the arguments, as show in Figure 3.17.

The insertion point is in the rate text box. Just below a series of text boxes, a dialog box lets you know that you are ready to enter the interest rate per period.

You could type the cell reference for the rate, but it's easier to point and click.

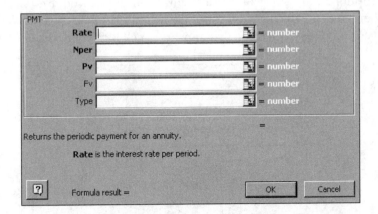

Figure 3.17 The Paste Function dialog box for entering arguments.

13. Click on cell **B19** (the interest rate).

B19 is entered in the rate text box and 0.1 is entered to the right of the text box. We need to make an adjustment here. Remember that the rate the function needs is the rate *per period*. Since we want to determine the monthly payment and 10% is the annual rate, we need to divide it by 12.

14. Type /**12**.

Notice that the rate to the right now displays the monthly interest rate, 0.0083333333.

15. Press the **Tab** key to move to the *Nper* (number of payment periods) text box and click on cell **B20**.

Again we need to modify the entry. Cell B20 contains the number of years for the loan and we want the number of months, so we need to multiply by 12.

16. Type *****12**.

The value to the right of the text box now displays the value 60, which is the correct number of months.

17. Press the **Tab** key to move to the *Pv* (present value) text box and click on cell **B21**.

This entry doesn't need to be altered, and the dialog box should now look like Figure 3.18. The *fv* (future value) and type arguments are optional, and we won't use them. With all the required arguments entered, the dialog box displays the formula result in the lower left-hand corner. This is the value that appears in cell B22 when we are finished.

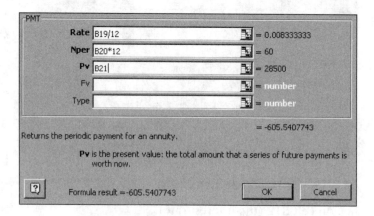

Figure 3.18 *The filled-in dialog box.*

18.   Click on the **Finish** button to complete the Paste Function.

The value in cell B22 is in parentheses and in red (if you have a color monitor) to let you know that this is a negative value. The monthly payment is negative because it results in an outflow from the business. If this were money being received, it would be positive. Figure 3.19 shows the end result.

You may have to adjust your column width to display the full result.

N O T E

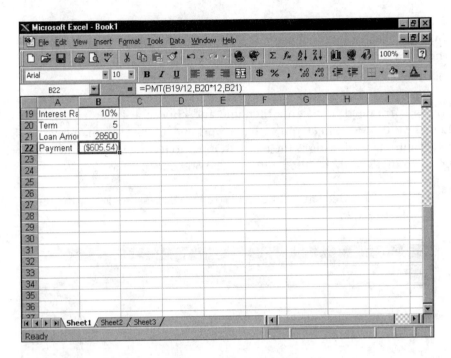

Figure 3.19 *The result of the PMT Function.*

SAVING YOUR WORK

Perhaps the most important habit to develop is saving your work on a regular basis. Until you save, the data you enter or edit is in your computer's temporary memory, called *RAM* (Random Access Memory). Okay, so what's the definition of regular basis? Often enough that, if you lost all the work you had done since the last time you saved, you wouldn't be too upset.

Excel stores worksheets in files called *workbooks*. Within a single workbook, you can have many worksheets, all of which are saved to your computer's disk when you save. You don't need to specify which sheet or portions of a sheet you want to save.

The first time you save a workbook, you are presented with several options. You need to assign a filename and choose a directory to save it in. Let's save the worksheet you've been working on with the name BUDGET. Excel automatically assigns the name BOOK1 to its first blank unnamed workbook, so that's probably the name you see on your title bar right now.

1. Choose **File**, **Save**. The Save dialog box appears, as displayed in Figure 3.20.

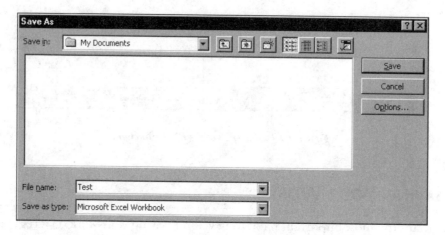

Figure 3.20 The Save dialog box.

2. In the File Name text box, type **budget**. The Save in box tells you which folder your workbook will be stored in. A folder allows you to organize your files on a disk, just as you would in a file cabinet. If you want to save in a folder other than the one specified, click on the drop-down box, scroll to the directory you want to use and click on it.

3. Click on the **Save** button.

As you enter and edit data in Excel, you'll want to save often, perhaps every ten or twenty minutes. The fastest way to do this is to click on the **Save** toolbar button, shown in Figure 3.21.

The saved file on your disk is automatically replaced with the updated version and you won't even have to confirm that you want to replace it.

4. Double-click on the document's control menu box to close the document, and then exit Excel if you aren't immediately continuing on to the next chapter.

*Figure 3.21 The **Save** toolbar button.*

A FINAL THOUGHT

With what you've learned in this chapter, you already know as much as 80% of the spreadsheet users out there and you're now ready to put Excel to productive use. Give yourself a pat on the back.

In the next chapter, you'll explore several of the functions that form the nucleus of Excel's processing capabilities.

CHAPTER 4

Exploring More Excel Functions

MORE ABOUT FUNCTIONS

Excel 97 has functions for just about all your practical needs. In this chapter, you'll learn about the different categories of functions and how to find help using them. You will also get some hands-on experience with a few of the basic functions. Obviously, this chapter can't explain everything there is to know about functions—entire books have been written on the subject. But we will cover enough ground that you'll be able to understand the concepts for putting more complex functions to work.

Function Categories

Although you can recreate most functions by using the mathematical operators we covered briefly in the previous chapter, you'll save time and reduce errors if you track down the function that does the job for you. To help you find the function that will work best, Excel functions are divided into separate categories. Table 4.1 lists the categories by which these functions are classified and gives a brief description of each.

Table 4.1 *Function Categories*

CATEGORY	DESCRIPTION
Database	Functions used to process data.
Date and Time	Functions used to make mathematical calculations on dates and times.
Engineering	Functions used to make calculations on engineering values.
Financial	Functions used to determine values as they relate to such things as loans and depreciations.
Information	Functions that help you determine the type of data in a cell.
Logical	Functions that perform logical and conditional tests.
Lookup & Reference	Functions that analyze tables to help you locate various values utilizing search features.
Math & Trig	Functions that perform simple and complex mathematical and trigonometric calculations.
Statistical	Functions that perform statistical analysis on data.
Text	Functions that analyze or alter text data.

If you're not sure which function to use for a particular task, go ahead and browse through the categories. By clicking on the **Paste Function** button, you can look through the functions in a category that seems to match your needs. Excel will provide a brief description of a selected function at the bottom of the Paste Function dialog box.

Parts of a Function

Every function must have four parts. They are:

❖   Equal sign (=)

❖   Function name

❖   Parentheses (open and closed)

❖   Arguments

The most common error in entering functions manually is the omission of an equal sign. Take a look at the following example of a function and see if you can identify all four parts:

```
= SUM ( F8:F10 )
```

The equal sign and parentheses are easy to locate. SUM is the function name, and F8:F10 is the argument.

The remainder of this chapter will provide you with step-by-step instructions for using and understanding certain functions. With other functions, we will simply explain their use and let you experiment with them on your own. The function categories will appear in parentheses.

Using the NPER Function (Financial)

The NPER (number of payment periods) function lets you calculate how many payment periods are required to amortize a loan. Suppose the Spokane Locks and Bagel Corporation is thinking about purchasing that nifty piece of equipment discussed in the previous chapter, but they can only afford monthly payments of, say, $575.00. You can figure out how long the business will be in hock for this purchase by using the NPER function.

1.   Start Excel if it isn't already running.

2.   If a workbook containing data is on the screen, click the **New Workbook** button on the Standard toolbar to open up a blank workbook (see Figure 4.1).

Figure 4.1 *The New Workbook button.*

The title bar of a new workbook always displays the name Book followed by the number of that workbook. For example, if you were working on the BUDGET workbook in this current Excel session, clicking on the New Workbook button causes the title bar to display Microsoft Excel-Book2.

N O T E

Several of the functions are presented in the context of our example business, the Spokane Locks and Bagel Corporation. However, each is used in a separate worksheet rather than using them to build one huge sheet. Excel 97 automatically assigns three worksheets to a workbook, which won't be enough to follow along in this chapter. To add more worksheets choose **Insert**, **Worksheet** (You'll need a total of eight for this chapter).

For more information on inserting worksheets, see the Inserting Worksheets section in Chapter 5.

3.   Move to cell A1 and type **Interest Rate**.

4.   Move to cell A2 and type **Payment**.

5.   Move to cell A3 and type **Loan Amount**.

6.   Move to cell A4 and type **Number of Payments**.

N O T E

We increased the width of column A to accommodate the longest entries. It isn't necessary for you to do this on these practice sheets, but if you can't wait to learn how you can skip ahead in this chapter to "Using the Now Function."

7.   In cell B1, type **10%**.

8.   In cell B2, type **–575**.

The minus sign is important because this is an expense (money going out) rather than income.

9. In cell B3, type **28500**.

10. Move to cell B4, where the result of the function's calculation will appear, and click on the **Paste Function** button.

    The first Paste Function dialog box appears.

11. In the Function Category list of the Paste Function dialog box, click on **Financial**.

12. In the Function Name list, click on **NPER**, and then click on the **OK** button.

    The Paste Function dialog box for entering arguments appears, with text boxes for the NPER function, as shown in Figure 4.2. If the dialog box covers up the entries you just made on the worksheet, move it out of the way by clicking anywhere within the dialog box and dragging.

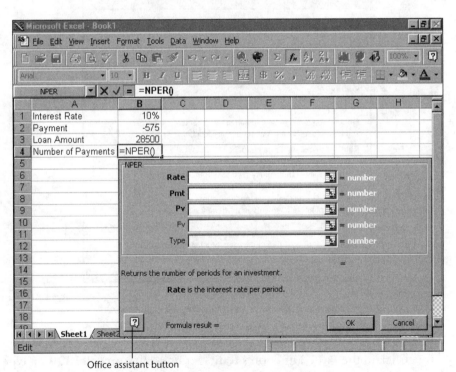

Office assistant button

Figure 4.2 The Paste Function dialog box for the NPER function.

You can get more detailed information about the use and proper syntax of a function by clicking on the **Office Assistant** button in the lower left corner of the Paste Function dialog box.

13. Click on the **Office Assistant** button.

The Office Assistant will appear in the corner of your screen, asking you what you need help with.

14. Click on **Help with this feature**, and then click on **Help with this function**.

The help screen appears, as shown in Figure 4.3. Remember, you can click on the **Maximize** button located on the right side of the title bar to enlarge this box.

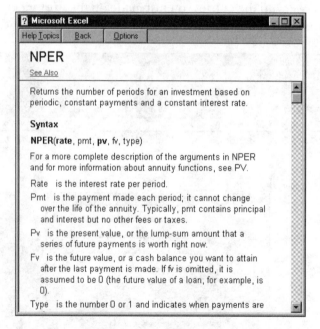

Figure 4.3 *The help screen for the NPER function.*

15. After you finish looking over the Help screen, click on the **Close** button.

16. Click in the Paste Function's **Rate** text box, click on cell **B1**, then type **/12** to convert the annual interest rate to a monthly rate.

17. Press the **Tab** key to move the insertion point to the Pmt text box, then click on cell **B2**.

18. Press the **Tab** key, then click on cell **B3**.

   Now that the three required values are entered, the answer appears at the bottom of the Paste Function dialog box after Formula result =. It is going to take a little more than 64 months to amortize this piece of equipment.

NOTE As you probably noticed, we did not use the two optional parameters—future value and type. You can use *future value* to enter a dollar amount you want to reach at the end of the amortization period. The *type* parameter determines whether the payments are made at the beginning or end of each payment period.

19. Click on the **OK** button to accept the entries you have made in the Paste Function.

Using the PV Function (Financial)

The PV (Present Value) function helps you determine what future cash flows are worth in today's dollars. Suppose Spokane Locks and Bagels is considering investing $10,000 of its cash reserves in a fixed rate annuity that returns three annual payments of $4,000.

   Sounds good, doesn't it? After all, $4,000 multiplied by 3 is $12,000. That's a two thousand-dollar profit. But if the Spokane Locks and Bagel Corp. could get an 8% return by just parking the money in CDs, then how do the two investments compare? The PV function will show you.

1. Click on the **Sheet2** tab to bring up a blank worksheet.

2. In cell A1, type **Initial Investment**.

   The initial investment is not used as one of the arguments in the PV function. It's just helpful to have it on the worksheet for reference.

3. In cell A2, type **Interest Rate**.

4. In cell A3, type **Number of Payments**.

5. In cell A4, type **Payment**.

6. In cell A5, type **Present Value**.

7. In cell B1, type **$10,000**.

8. In cell B2, type **8%**.

9. In cell B3, type **3**.

10. In cell B4, type **4000**.

11. Move to cell B5, where the result of the function's calculation will appear, and click the **Paste Function** button.

12. Be sure Financial is highlighted in the Function Category list, then click on **PV** in the Function Name list, then click on the **OK** button.

13. Click on cell **B2**, which is the cell containing the interest rate.

14. Press the **Tab** key and then click in cell **B3**, the cell containing the number of payments.

    Notice the name of the argument for the number of payments is Nper (for number of periods), just like the NPER function discussed in the previous section.

15. Press the **Tab** key again and click in cell **B4**, the cell containing the annual payment amount.

16. Click the **OK** button.

NOTE

As in the previous examples, if you use the default column widths, some of the text in column A is truncated. Even worse, the result of the formula in cell B5 is too wide to fit and is therefore represented by number signs (#####). You can adjust the column width by positioning the mouse pointer on the right column heading border and then dragging to the right (see Figure 4.4). For more information about changing column widths, take a look at the next chapter.

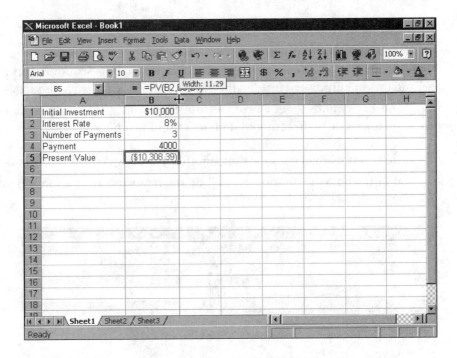

Figure 4.4 Adjusting the column width.

The fixed rate annuity appears to be the better investment, as you can see from the results shown in Figure 4.4.

17. Save the workbook by clicking on the **Save** button on the Standard toolbar. Enter **FUNCPRAC** (for function practice) in the File Name text box and then click **OK**.

Using the MIN and MAX Functions (Statistical)

In the group of statistical functions, two of the more common functions are MIN and MAX. These functions return the smallest or largest number in a range, and the only argument needed for these functions is the range or ranges.

Spokane Locks and Bagel Corp. can use these functions to determine which is the lowest or highest priced item in a list of products.

1. Click on the **Sheet3** tab to bring another blank worksheet into view.

2. Enter the data in columns A and B on the new worksheet, as shown in Figure 4.5.

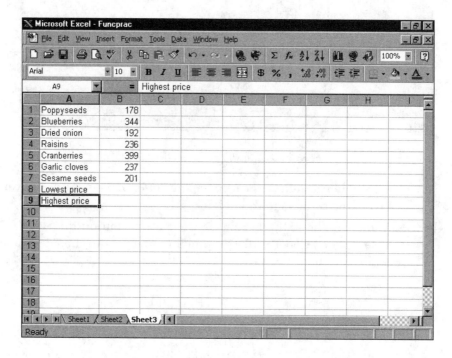

Figure 4.5 *The data for the MIN/MAX worksheet.*

3. Click on cell **B8**, which is where the result of the MIN function will appear.

4. Click the **Paste Function** button.

5. In the Paste Function dialog box, click on the **Statistical** Function category.

6.   Scroll down the Function name list until MIN is visible.

7.   Click on **MIN** and then click the **OK** button.

The argument dialog box now appears with the range B1:B7 selected, as shown in Figure 4.6.

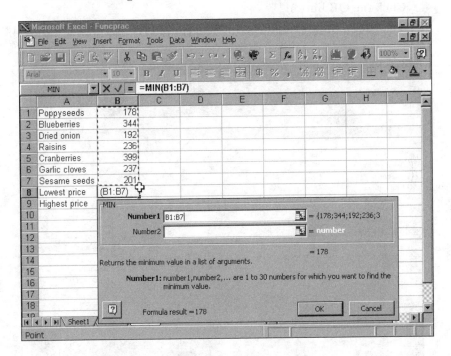

Figure 4.6 Selecting a range of cells for the MIN function.

8.   Click the **OK** button.

The smallest number in the list is displayed in cell B8. Obviously this would be a much more useful function with a larger list, but at least you can see how it works.

9.   Now click on cell **B9**, which is where the MAX function will be applied.

10. Click the **Paste Function** button and make sure Statistical is highlighted in the Function Category list.

11. Scroll down the Function name list until MAX is visible.

12. Click on **MAX**, then click the **OK** button.

The range B1:B8 will automatically appear in the Number1 argument field, but those aren't the correct cells for this argument.

13. Drag over cells **B1** through **B7** to include those cells in the function's argument.

14. Click the **OK** button.

The largest number in the list appears in cell B9, as shown in Figure 4.7.

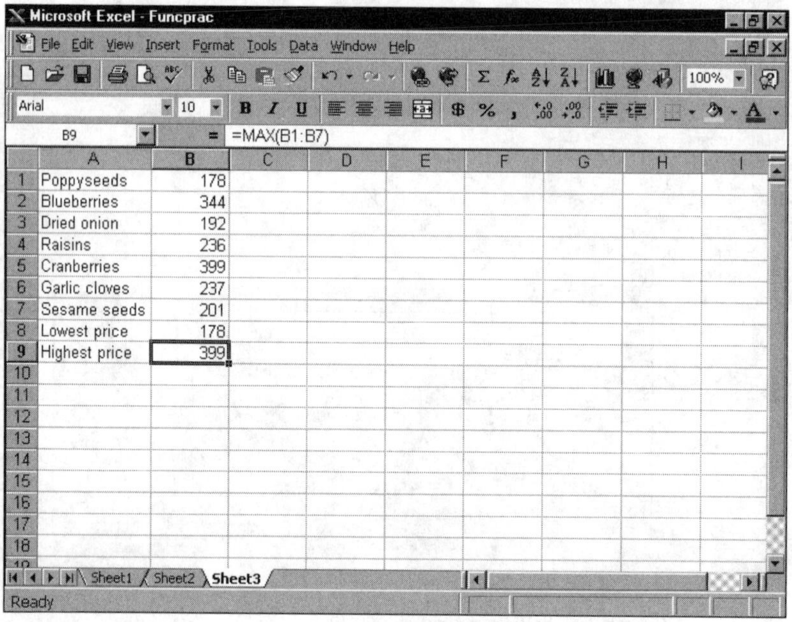

Figure 4.7 *The results of the MIN/MAX worksheet.*

15. Save the additions you've made to the workbook by clicking the **Save** button.

Using the NOW Function (Date and Time)

Excel uses a variety of functions to facilitate date and time calculations. One of the common uses for date calculations is for aging an accounts receivable report. For example, the Spokane Locks and Bagel Corp. might use an aged receivable report to determine how long credit customers are taking to pay their bills. This can be important information, because the longer an account remains past due the less likely it will ever be collected. Calculating the length of time an account is past due could also allow Spokane Locks and Bagel Corp. to tack on late fees.

When you enter dates and times in Excel, they are displayed as (drum-roll, please) dates and times. If you want to change the way these entries are displayed, check out the section on cell formatting in Chapter 6.

As you may remember from Chapter 3, Excel keeps track of dates and times by using a system of numbers. Dates are tracked as serial numbers based on the year 1900, and times are stored as decimal fractions.

1. Click on the **Sheet4** tab.
2. In cell A1, type **=now()** and press the **Enter** key.

At this point, you should be looking at today's date and time. If you see a row of number signs (######), your column width needs to be adjusted. In the next chapter you'll learn all about column width adjustments. For now, in order to see the value of your NOW function, perform the following steps, shown in Figure 4.8:

1. Click on cell **A1**.
2. Select **Format, Column**.
3   Click on **AutoFit Selection.**

You should now be able to see the date and time value from the NOW function.

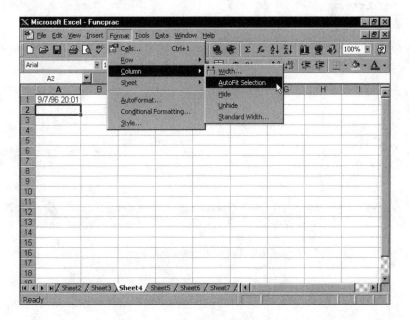

Figure 4.8 *Adjusting the column width.*

The NOW function uses the time and date on your computer's internal clock/calendar. The parentheses are required, although no arguments are entered between them. As with all functions, you can use **Paste Function** to apply the NOW function. However, since NOW doesn't require any arguments, it's just as easy to enter it manually.

NOTE If the wrong date or time appears, you need to reset your computer settings. Many computers use a special method for setting the time and date, so you should check your computer's documentation for instructions.

Now let's have Excel calculate what the date 45 days from now will be. Figure 4.9 displays the results.

❖ In cell A2, type **=now()+45** and press **Enter**.

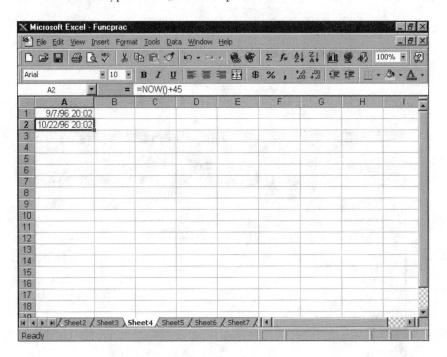

Figure 4.9 *The NOW function worksheet.*

The date displayed in A2 is 45 days later than the date displayed in A1. When looking at Figure 4.9, don't forget that your dates and times will differ according to the time and date set on your computer.

Using the IF Function (Logical)

Of all the functions in Excel, the IF function rates triple-A for power. In fact, it's the IF statements in most software programs that really give computers logic and power. The IF function performs tests to determine whether a condition is true or false. If true, the IF function returns a certain value or takes a certain action. If false, the IF function will return a different value or action. Table 4.2 shows the syntax for the IF function:

Table 4.2 *The IF function*

IF(CONDITION,VALUE_IF_TRUE,VALUE_IF_FALSE)

condition	a mathematical expression as a test condition (e.g., A1=C2).
value_if_true	the value of the tested condition if it is true.
value_if_false	the value of the tested condition if it is false.

As shown in Table 4.2, in order for a condition to be evaluated as true or false it must contain one of the logical operators. In the example A1=C2, the equal sign is the logical operator used to compare the two values. You can use any of the following logical operators to perform comparisons in your IF functions:

Table 4.3 *Logical operators*

OPERATOR	DEFINITION
>	Greater than
<	Less than
=	Equal to
> =	Greater than or equal to
< =	Less than or equal to
< >	Not equal to

In order to get a sense of how the IF function works, let's create a simple table. At this point it's probably best not to create too elaborate a scenario. Once you have a sense of how this function works, you can use it with more complex applications. For now, click on the **Sheet5** tab and enter the data shown in Figure 4.10.

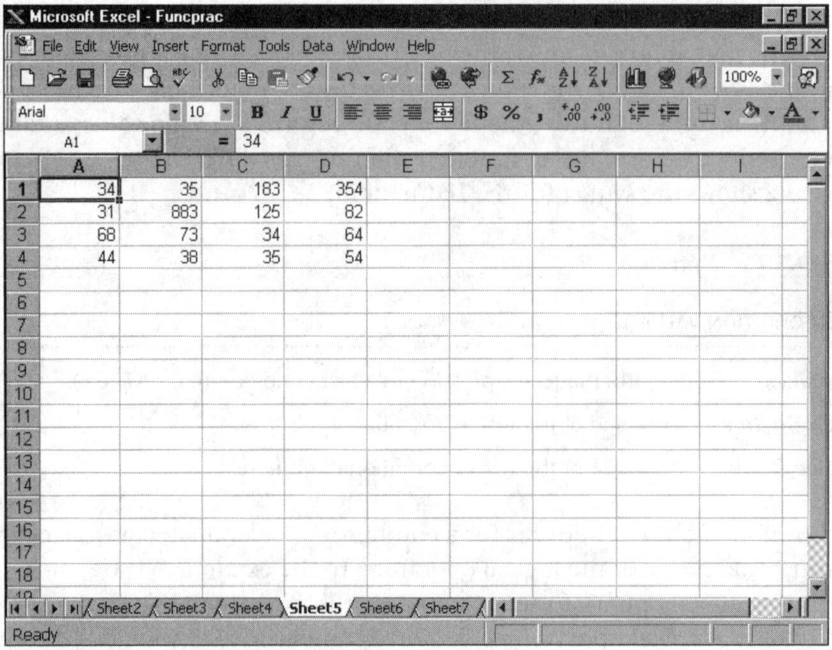

Figure 4.10 *The data for the IF worksheet.*

You'll be using this table to test some basic IF conditions. You'll also see how the IF function returns a value based upon the tested results.

1. Click on cell **A5**, which is where the IF function will be placed.

2. Click the **Paste Function** button.

3. Click on **Logical** in the Function category.

4. Click on **IF** in the Function name box, and then click the **OK** button.

5. Click on cell **A1**, which is consequently entered in the logical_test window.

6. Type =.

7. Click on cell **C3**.

You have just entered the condition for the IF function using the equal sign (=) as your logical operator.

8. Press the **Tab** key and type "**Good.**" This is the value you want returned if the condition is true.

9. Press the **Tab** key again and type "**Bad.**" This is the value you want returned if the condition is false.

Notice the Formula result at the bottom of the dialog box (shown in Figure 4.11) reads Good.

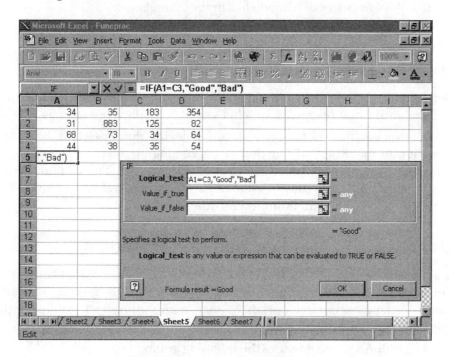

Figure 4.11 The IF function dialog box.

10. Click the **OK** button.

Cell A5 now reads Good. This is because the IF function tested to see if the value in cell A1 equaled the value in cell C3. Because the value in both cells is 34, the formula is true and you see the word Good. If the value in cell A1 didn't equal the value in C3, the formula would be false and you would see the word Bad.

Try changing the value in cell C3 and see what happens.

1. Click on cell **C3**.
2. Type **45** and press **Enter**.

What happened? If the word Bad replaced Good in cell A5, your IF function was entered properly. If it didn't, that's not the type of bad we were hoping for and you might want to recheck the formula in cell A5. Seriously though, let's look at another example.

1. Move back to cell A5 and click in the formula bar.
2. Delete the second equal sign (=) and replace it with the less than operator (<).
3. Press **Enter**.

Because the value in cell B1 is less than the value in cell D3, the formula is true and the word Good reappears. In other words, 35 really is less than 64.

You can continue practicing with this table, but don't delete it. You'll be using it with the ISBLANK function that is coming up next. Try out some of the other logical operators to see what results you get. The IF function is worth understanding because it's one of Excel's most powerful functions and can be used in conjunction with several others.

Using the ISBLANK Function (Informational)

It's probably obvious what this function does. That's right, it finds blank cells. On a small worksheet it's pretty easy to spot a bunch of empty cells, but when you're working with a large worksheet you can save yourself a lot of time with the ISBLANK function.

The ISBLANK function uses the following syntax:

```
ISBLANK(cell)
```

The ISBLANK function is usually used in conjunction with the IF function as a condition. For example, you could write an IF function that says if the value in cell B3 is blank, then type "missing data", and if the value in cell B3 isn't blank, then do nothing.

Let's test the ISBLANK function. Use the same table you made for the IF function. Some of your numbers may have changed, but that's okay. You're going to be testing for blank cells, which won't involve the cell values.

1.   Move to cell E1 and type **Message=**.

2.   In cell F1 type the following IF function using ISBLANK:

```
=IF(ISBLANK(B3)=FALSE,"","Missing Data")
```

This IF function will test to see if the result of the ISBLANK test is true or false for cell B3. If the formula is false, a blank string will be returned. If it's true, a Missing Data message will appear. Since there's data in B3 right now, a blank string was returned. Now remove the data and watch what happens (see Figure 4.12).

1.   Click on cell **B3**.

2.   Press the **Delete** key and then press **Enter**.

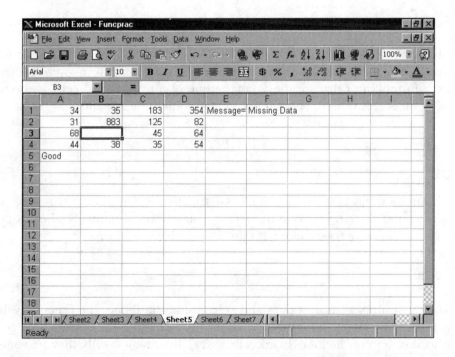

Figure 4.12 *Using the ISBLANK function.*

Now that the ISBLANK test is true, your Missing Data message is present.

The IF and ISBLANK functions may not seem like much now, but as your expertise with Excel improves you'll be able to use both in a variety of ways. For example, when used in conjunction with macros (which are discussed later in the book), you'll be able to conduct a complete search of your database for blank cells.

Using the Average Function (Statistical)

The AVERAGE function calculates the mean of a series of numbers by totaling their values and then dividing this total by the number of values. For example, if you wanted to know the bowling average of a person who bowled three games, you would total the scores of the three games and then divide by the number of games played (3). You can also use the AVERAGE function to achieve the same result.

The correct syntax of the AVERAGE function is simply:

```
=AVERAGE(numbers)
```

One of the best reasons to use the AVERAGE function is to avoid having to type in long formulas that are prone to error. For example, if you were to create a formula to calculate the average value of a range of 13 cells, without using the AVERAGE function, it would look something like this:

```
=(C1+C2+C3+C4+C5+C6+C7+C8+C9+C10+C11+C12+C13)/13
```

Not very pretty is it?

Another reason to use the AVERAGE function is that if there are changes in the range of cells you want to average, you'll have to manually adjust your formula. All things considered, it's just a lot easier to enter:

```
=AVERAGE(C1:C13)
```

Then if you insert more values and cells inside the range, the function will automatically incorporate the new values in calculating the correct average. Also, if your range includes blank cells, text cells, or logical cells, they are completely ignored and will not affect the true average of your range.

Let's do some averaging of our own. Do you remember the bowling example mentioned earlier? Let's calculate the bowling average of five bowlers who compete on a team ("Cutting the Mustard") that is sponsored by the Spokane Locks and Bagels Corp.

1. Click on a new worksheet tab and enter the scores of the five bowlers, as shown in Figure 4.13.

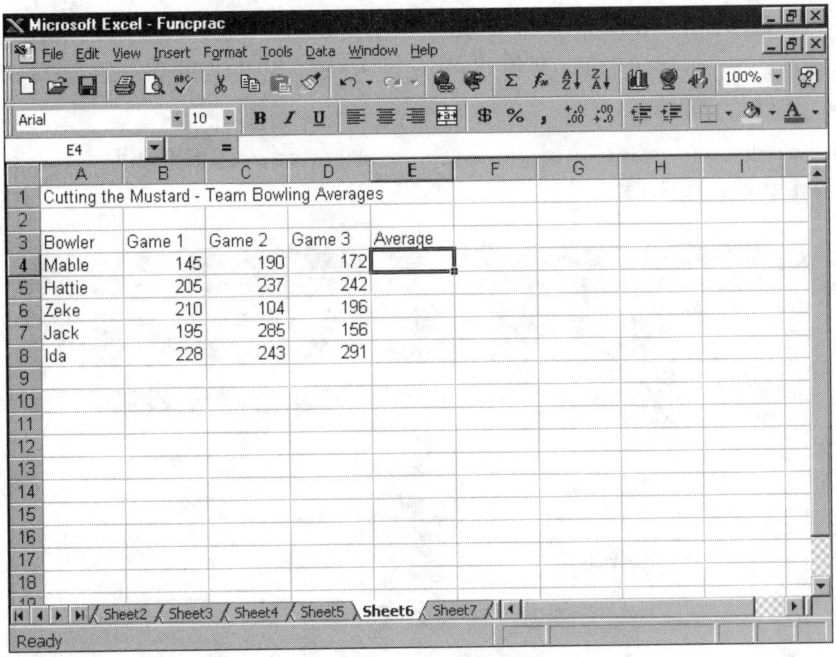

Figure 4.13 *Bowling scores.*

2. Activate cell E4.

   This is where we'll enter the AVERAGE function to compute Mable's bowling average. The formula is actually short enough to be typed in, but try using the Paste Function to get some more experience with it.

3. Click on the **Paste Function** button. You may have to occasionally move the Paste Function dialog box out of the way throughout this exercise.

4. Click on the **Statistical** function category.

5. Click on **Average** in the function name box, and then click the **OK** button.

6. Select the range of cells B4 through D4 by clicking and holding the left mouse button on **B4**. While still holding down the left mouse button, drag down to **D4**.

7. The range is now entered in the dialog window, so you can click on **OK**.

    You can see that Mable's average score has been calculated at 169. Now you can copy the formula in cell E4 to cells E5 through E8.

8. Click on cell **E4**.

9. Position your mouse pointer over the cell's fill handle until the pointer turns into thin cross-hairs. Then drag the mouse pointer to cell E8.

Your worksheet should now show the average scores of all five bowlers, as shown in Figure 4.14.

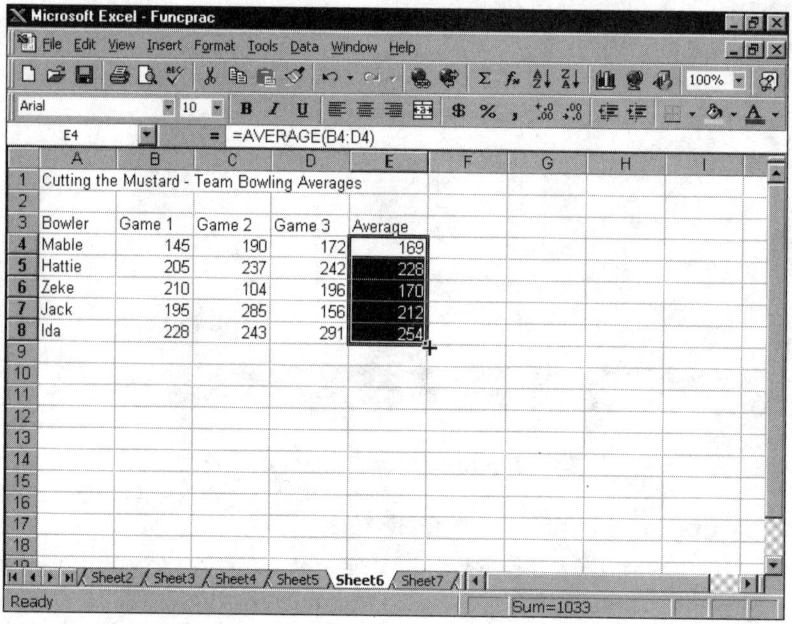

Figure 4.14 *Results of using the AVERAGE function.*

You'll be using the data in Figure 4.14 with our next exercise with the AND, OR, and NOT functions. If you don't plan to continue at this point, click on the **Save** button to avoid having to reenter everything later.

Using the AND, OR, and NOT Functions (Logical)

Now that you've got some of the basics down, it's time to get a little bit more fancy and use the IF function in conjunction with other functions. The AND, OR, and NOT functions are used to create compound conditional tests. You may remember that the IF function evaluates whether a condition is true or false. Using the AND, OR, and NOT functions, we can evaluate whether compound conditions are true or false. The AND, OR, and NOT functions use the logical operators =, >, <, >=, <=, and <>.

Let's suppose the five members of "Cutting the Mustard" are attempting to qualify for a bowling tournament in Seattle. The only requirements to enter the tournament are that participants' bowling average must be equal to or greater than 200 *and* each person must be under 50 years old. Suppose further that you want Excel to return the text value of Yes for those people who meet both conditions, and No for those who don't.

Type in the data shown in Figure 4.15. You'll notice two new columns have been added to the AVERAGE function worksheet used in the previous section—one for the bowlers' ages and the other to indicate whether or not they can enter the tournament.

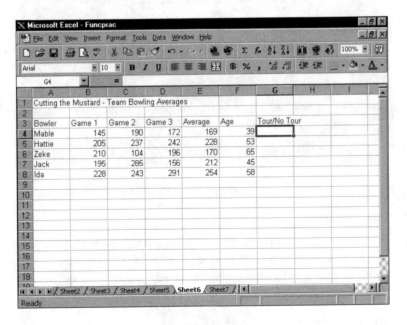

Figure 4.15 Bowler's Age and Average Score.

Follow these steps to create a compound conditional test using the AND function:

1. Click on cell **G4**.

2. Click the **Paste Function** button.

3. Click on the **Logical** function category.

4. Click on **IF** in the function name window of the Paste Function dialog box, and then click on **OK**.

5. Type **AND(** in the Logical_test text box.

6. Click in cell **F4** and type **<50,**.

   This argument stipulates that a bowler's age must be less than 50.

7. Now click in cell **E4** and type **>=200)**.

   This argument requires a bowler's average to be 200 or higher.

8. Press the **Tab** key and type **"Yes"** in the Value_if_true text box.

9. Press the **Tab** key and type **"No"** in the Value_if_false text box. The IF Paste Function dialog box should look like Figure 4.16.

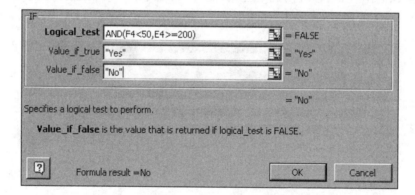

Figure 4.16 The IF Paste Function dialog box.

10. Press **Enter**.

11. Click on **G4** and copy the formula to cells G5 through G8 by using the fill handle. Position your mouse pointer over the fill handle until the pointer changes to thin cross-hairs and drag the mouse pointer down to G8.

Your worksheet should now resemble Figure 4.17.

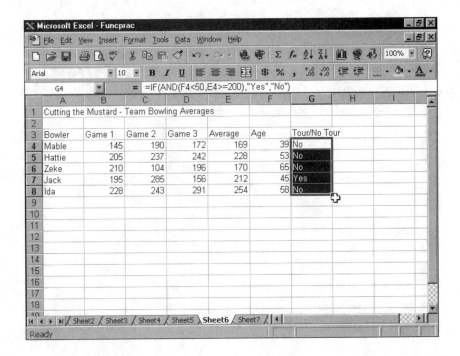

Figure 4.17 *Conditional test of which bowlers cut the mustard.*

Look at the formula in the formula bar. This says that if the bowler's age is less than 50 *and* the bowler's average is not equal to or greater than 200, then the condition is true and the text value Yes should be returned. However, if either the bowler's age is greater than 50 *or* their average is not equal or greater than 200, the condition is false and the text value No will be returned. Pretty neat don't you think?

The OR function uses the same arguments as the AND function, but the results are dramatically different. Let's add one more column to your table.

1. In cell H3 type the following column heading: **Avg or Age**.

2. In cell H4, type the following formula. Notice that it's the same formula used in Column G, but we're changing the AND to OR:

```
=IF(OR(F4<50,E4>=200),"Yes","No").
```

3. Using the fill handle, copy the formula into cells H5 through H8. Notice the difference in results, as shown in Figure 4.18.

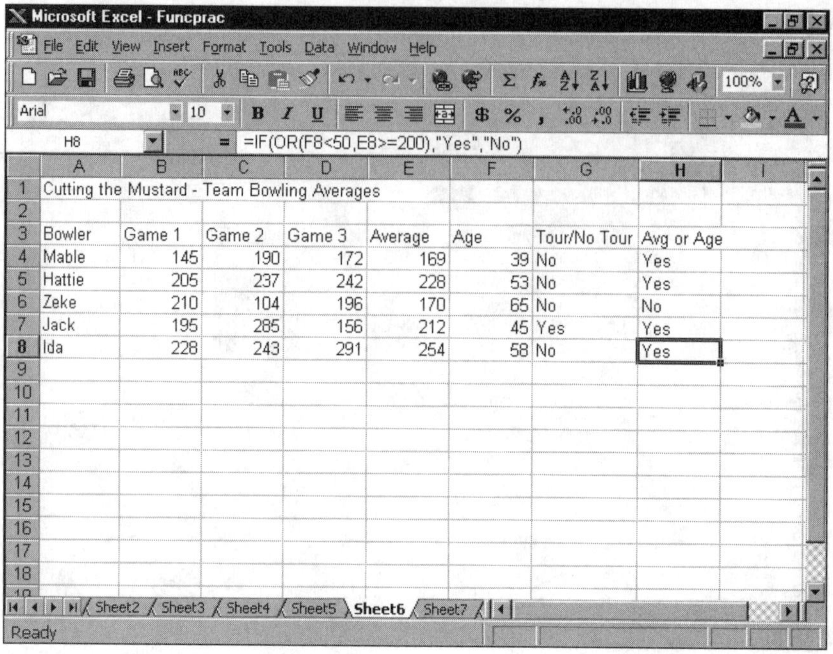

Figure 4.18 *Comparison of the AND and OR functions.*

Compare the differences between the results of the two functions. Notice that Mable, Hattie and Ida did not qualify for the tournament because they didn't pass the average score *and* age tests. But with the OR function conditions, they only needed to pass either the average score test (equal to or higher than 200) or the age test (less than 50). As a result, they could compete in the bowling tournament if selections were based upon the OR function.

The NOT function is used in the context of when a condition is not true. If an argument is false, the NOT function returns a logical value of true. If an argument is true, the NOT function returns a logical value of false. Does this make any sense to you? Probably NOT yet, but it will. Take a look at the following formula:

```
=IF(NOT(C1=5),"Pass","Skip")
```

This formula instructs Excel to return a text value of Pass if the value in cell C1 does not equal 5. If it does equal 5, then the NOT function will return the text value Skip instead.

Using the Round Function (Mathematical)

Guess what this function does? If you said rounding, you should consider writing instruction manuals! The ROUND function rounds a value to a chosen number of digits. Of course, you could also format a cell to cause a number to be rounded to a specific number of digits. However, the ROUND function is different in one primary way.

When numbers are rounded with the ROUND function, they are permanently changed to the rounded value. When numbers are rounded via cell formatting, they can be reformatted so the original value reappears. With the ROUND function, the original value is permanently replaced by the rounding action.

Since the ROUND function permanently changes a value, this has consequences for how the rounded value is calculated. When calculations are performed on values that have been rounded by the ROUND function, the rounded value will be calculated, not the original value. Conversely, when calculations are done on values that have been rounded with cell formatting, the original value will be calculated and not the rounded value.

For example, if cell A1 contained the value 1.5431, and then was rounded by the ROUND function to a whole number, the result would be 2. If you were to multiply the result of 2 by 3, you would have a product of 6. On the other hand, if you rounded the same value, 1.5432, by formatting the cell to display whole numbers, the result would also be two. But when you multiply this result by 3, you would have a product of 4.6296 and not 6. This is because the original value (1.5432) was not permanently changed when it was rounded.

Table 4.4 shows the correct syntax for using the ROUND function:

Table 4.4 The ROUND function

=ROUND(VALUE, PRECISION)

....

value   is the number to be rounded.

precision   is the number of places the number is to be rounded.

Now you can try this out for yourself. Following the steps below, you're going to take the value 1.5432 and round it as a whole number using cell formatting. Then you'll use the same value and round it to a whole number using the ROUND function. Afterwards, you'll perform some simple multiplication on both rounded values to see the different results.

1. Click on a new worksheet tab.

2. Click on cell **A1** and type **Original Number**.

3. Move to cell A3 and type **Rounded by Formatting**.

4. Move to cell A5 and type **Rounded by Function**.

5. Move to cell D1 and enter **1.5432**.

6. Move to cell D3 and enter **1.5432**.

7. Move to cell F3 and type **Multiplied by 3 =**.

8. Move to cell F5 and type **Multiplied by 3 =**.

   Your worksheet should now look like Figure 4.19.

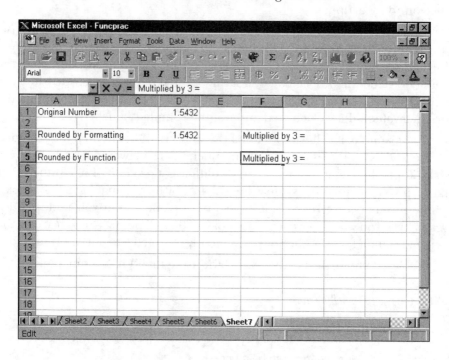

Figure 4.19 *ROUND function vs. cell formatting.*

9. Now let's format the value in cell D3 so that it is rounded to a whole number.

❖ Click on cell **D3**.

❖ Click the right mouse button to bring up a shortcut menu, shown in Figure 4.20.

Figure 4.20 *The cell shortcut menu.*

❖ Click on **Format Cells....**

❖ Click on the **Number** tab if it's not already showing.

❖ Click **Number** in the Category box.

❖ Change the Decimal Places value from **2** to **0**.

❖ Click **OK**. Figure 4.21 shows the dialog box.

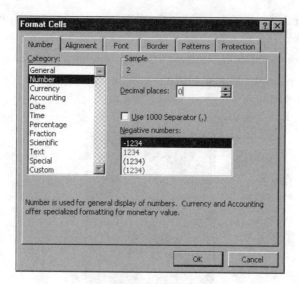

Figure 4.21 *The format cells dialog box.*

Notice that 1.5432 has been rounded to the whole number of 2.

10. Move to cell H3, type **=3*D3**, and press **Enter**.

11. Move to cell D5, type **=ROUND(D1,0)**, and press **Enter**.

    The zero in the formula indicates to round to a whole number. If you wanted to round to one decimal place, you would type =ROUND(D1,1).

    You have just used the ROUND function on the value in cell D1 and placed the result in cell D5. Note that the result appears to be identical to what we achieved by formatting cell D3.

12. In cell H5, you need to enter the same basic formula used in cell H3. Type **=3*D5** and press **Enter**.

Your worksheet should now look like Figure 4.22.

You can now see how looks can be deceiving. There will probably be occasions when you want your original values permanently changed to a rounded number. Moreover, you may want mathematical calculations done on the rounded values and not on the original values. This is where the ROUND function will be of great use you.

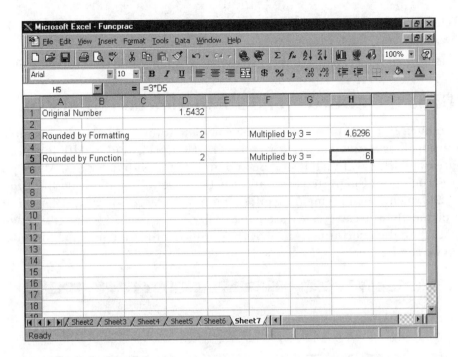

Figure 4.22 *Results of the ROUND function vs. cell formatting.*

Using the ABS Function (Mathematical)

The ABS function returns the absolute value of a number, formula, or cell reference. The correct syntax of the ABS function is:

```
ABS(value)
```

The value can be any expression that results in a value. Here are a few examples of the types of values that can be used with the ABS function:

- ❖ ABS(-45)
- ❖ ABS(C1)
- ❖ ABS(Range_Name)
- ❖ ABS(Range_Name+(G3*8))

The ABS value of a number is neither positive or negative. For example, if −45 was in cell C1, the formula =ABS(C1) would return the value 45.

If the number was positive (45), the same value would be returned (45).

Using the COUNTIF and SUMIF Functions (Database)

No discussion on functions would be complete without referring to a couple of functions in the database category. The COUNTIF and SUMIF functions are two fairly easy functions to use and understand with databases. Although we won't go through step-by-step instructions, we will be referring to Figure 4.23, which contains employee information such as age, salary, and gender. If you want to, you can create the database table in Figure 4.23 (cells A1 through D13) and then perform the analyses by producing the functions and formulas as we come to them.

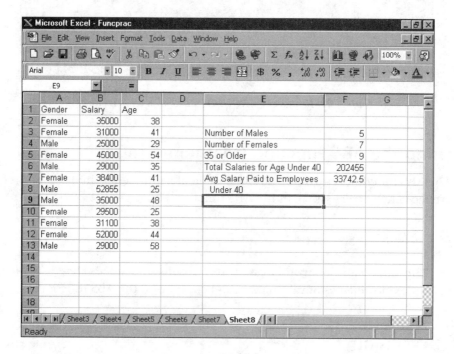

Figure 4.23 Employee data.

The COUNTIF syntax is shown in Table 4.5.

Table 4.5 *The COUNTIF function syntax*

=COUNTIF(RANGE,CRITERIA)

....

range   the range of values to be counted

criteria   a text value identifying the criteria

Suppose you want to count the number of male employees in the Spokane Locks and Bagels Corp. list in Figure 4.23. You would use the formula:

```
=COUNTIF(B3:B14,"Male")
```

This formula instructs Excel to look at ranges B3 through B14 and count the number of cells containing the text value Male. This formula returns the value 5 as the number of males counted. You can instruct Excel to count the number of female employees with a similar formula:

```
=COUNTIF(B3:B14,"Female")
```

This formula returns the value of 7 for the number of female employees.

The COUNTIF function is not case sensitive. This means that if you entered the word "MALE" with all uppercase letters in your formula, Excel would still count all the "Male" or "male" entries in the database range.

NOTE

To count the number of employees in the list who are 35 years of age or older, you can use the following formula

```
=COUNTIF(D3:D14,">=35")
```

The formula returns the value of 9 as the number of employees 35 years of age or older.

Unlike the COUNTIF function, the SUMIF function totals or sums values in a designated range. The syntax for the SUMIF function is shown in Table 4.6.

Table 4.6 *The SUMIF function*

=SUMIF(RANGE, CRITERIA, SUM_RANGE)

criteria	an argument applied to a range
sum_range	the range of data whose value will be added

Referring again to Figure 4.23, if you want to calculate the total salaries of employees under the age of 40, you would use the formula:

```
=SUMIF(D2:D13,"<40",C2:C13)
```

The formula returns $202,455 as the amount of salaries paid to employees under the age of 40.

A FINAL THOUGHT

In this chapter, you learned how to put several basic functions to work. You also learned more about how Excel handles dates and times.

In the next chapter, you'll learn how to make some changes to your worksheet, including inserting and deleting data. You'll also learn more about copying formulas and formatting cells.

CHAPTER 5

Modifying a Worksheet

FINDING AND OPENING AN EXISTING WORKSHEET

One of the biggest fears of new computer users is that they'll put a lot of time and energy into creating a spreadsheet, dutifully save it to the disk, close the spreadsheet, and never be able to find it again. It will be lost forever, as though sucked into a black hole.

Relax! Your spreadsheet is there and Excel makes it easy to find. You did save it, didn't you?

Let's explore some of the ways to open a spreadsheet.

1. Start Excel, if it isn't already running.

   Unless you've been doing some work with Excel behind our backs, the last two workbooks you had on your screen were FUNCPRAC and BUDGET. Even if you have been working on a couple other documents, Excel will display the four most recently opened files at the bottom of the File menu.

2. Choose **File**.

   Notice the group of four file names at the bottom of the menu, just above the Exit command, in Figure 5.1. Your File menu may only display one or two file names, if those are the only files you've worked with.

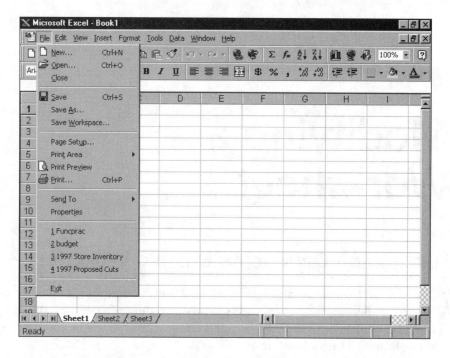

Figure 5.1 *The File menu with the four most recently opened files displayed.*

You could open one of the workbooks by clicking on it or pressing the underlined number in front of its name. Instead, let's examine some other methods for finding and opening a file.

3. Click on any cell outside the menu to clear the menu, or press the **ESC** key twice.

4. Click on the standard toolbar's **Open** button, shown in Figure 5.2.

Figure 5.2 *The Open button.*

Choosing the **Open** toolbar button is the same as choosing **File**, **Open...**, and calls up the Open dialog box, as displayed in Figure 5.3.

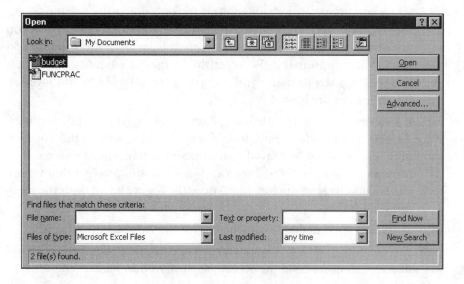

Figure 5.3 *The Open dialog box.*

5. If BUDGET isn't displayed in the list of files and directories, use the Look In drop down list to locate the appropriate directory (folder) that contains the file. See the "Saving Your Work" section of Chapter 3 to move to the folder that contains the file.

    Once you find the folder that contains the file you're seeking, you can use the various options at the bottom of the Open dialog box to locate the file within the folder. This is useful when your folder contains too many files to sort through quickly. You can enter a name into the File

Name box to locate the specific file. You can also narrow the list to files of a specific type (this is automatically set to look for Excel files), or files that contain specific data within their names. Finally, you can narrow the list by selecting just those files that were modified within the last day, week, month, or year. The more selections you establish, the fewer files will appear in the listing. You should be able to locate any file in the active folder using just one of these criteria. Use the **New Search** button to reset these options if desired.

You're probably anxious to open the file, but there's one more method we're going to take a look at first. Bear with us for just a few more minutes.

So far, the methods we've explored for opening a file are fine if the file you want to open is one of the last four you worked with, or if you know its name and the directory where it is located. But suppose you haven't worked on the file recently. In fact, it's been so long that you've forgotten its name and even the directory where you saved it. It happens to the best of us.

It's still easy to find the file using Excel's advanced Find File facilities. As long as you know something about the file, such as the approximate date when it was saved last, some information you entered into the Summary Info dialog box, or even some unique text that is contained anywhere in the file, Excel does the legwork and finds the long-lost file for you.

6.   With the Open dialog box in view, click the **Advanced...** button.

The first time you use Advanced Find File options, the Advanced Find dialog box appears on the screen, as displayed in Figure 5.4.

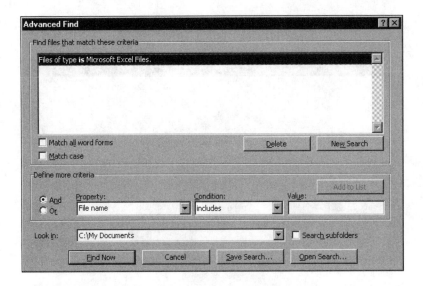

Figure 5.4 *The Advanced Find dialog box.*

This dialog box lets you search for files based on their file name, location, or other information. You can use the Define More Criteria options to establish criteria that appear at the top of the dialog box.

7. Click on the Property drop-down list and choose **Author**.

8. Click on the Condition drop-down list and highlight **includes words** (it may already be selected).

9. Click inside the Value box and type your name.

10. Click the **Add to List** button. The criteria is added to the list at the top of the dialog box, as shown in Figure 5.5.

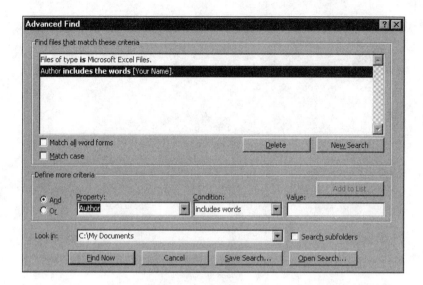

Figure 5.5 *The Advanced Find dialog box with author information identified.*

11. Use the Look in: drop-down box to select the directory where you want to search for this file. If you're not sure where the file is located, choose **Desktop** or a specific disk drive, and then click the **Include Subdirectories** option. This tells Excel to look in all subdirectories within the disk you specified. Of course, the more you narrow down the search, the faster Excel will be able to find the file.

At this point, you can add more criteria to the list by repeating steps 7 through 10 after clicking the **And** or the **Or** option to indicate whether you're adding additional conditions (and) or expanding the search to more possibilities (or). Now you can begin the search by clicking the **Find Now** button, but first let's save this search criteria for future searches.

12. Click the **Save Search...** button, and then enter a name for the search, such as **Files created by [your name]**.

13. Click **Find Now** to begin the search. The desired file, if found, will appear in the Open file listing, where you can select it for opening. If you are still in any doubt, you can click the **Preview** button in the Open dialog box to see a preview of the file before opening it. Figure 5.6 illustrates this option.

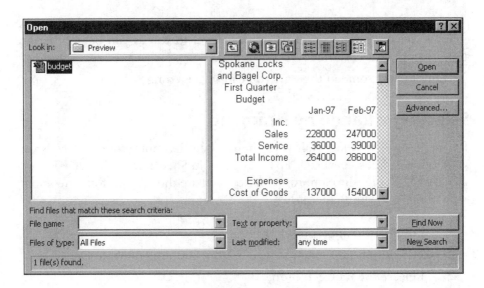

Figure 5.6 *Showing a preview of the file you are about to open.*

Since you saved this search, the same search can be made again with having to retype all the criteria. Just use the **File Open** command and click the **Open Search** button to view the searches you have saved from the Advanced Find options.

You can only search one drive at a time, so you may need to perform separate searches on each drive if you don't know which one contains the file you're looking for.

Using the Include Subdirectories option can dramatically increase the amount of time required for your computer to complete the search. The amount of time depends on the size and speed of the hard disk, the number of files it contains, and the overall speed of your computer. If you know where your file is located, you'll save time by specifying a directory in the Location portion of the Advanced Find dialog box.

SELECTING RANGES

So far, you've only been manipulating one cell at a time. However, Excel lets you select more than one cell, or a *range* of cells, in which you want to perform some action. For example, when a range of cells is selected, you can copy it to another area of your worksheet. Or you can move an entire range from one place to another. We'll be talking more about copying and moving later in the chapter. Selecting ranges will be quite helpful to you as you begin creating and revising your worksheets.

Let's look at some of the ways you can select a range of cells.

Selecting a Range by Dragging

The easiest way to select cells is to simply drag the mouse over the cells you want to select. Let's select cells E5 through E7 in Sheet1 of the BUDGET worksheet, and use the AutoSum function to calculate the quarter total income in each of the cells simultaneously.

1. Position the mouse pointer in E5.

2. Press and hold the left mouse button, and drag down to E7.

3. Release the mouse button.

    The selected range is highlighted as you drag the mouse and when you release the mouse button. The cell you started with, E5, is the active cell as shown in Figure 5.7.

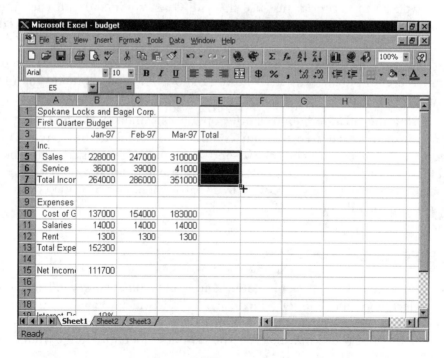

Figure 5.7 Selecting a range of cells.

4. Click on the **AutoSum** button, which will add the function to all the selected cells at once.

Selecting Non-Contiguous Ranges

There may be times when you want to select non-contiguous ranges of cells—which is like selecting several ranges at once. For example, suppose you wanted the sum for the quarter totals of the expenses and the net income/loss at the same time. No problem. Just use the **Ctrl** key to add to a selection.

1. Position the mouse pointer in cell E10.

2. Press and hold the left mouse button, and drag down to cell E12.

3. Release the mouse button.

4. Hold down the **Ctrl** key and click on cell E15.

   Cells E10 through E12 and cell E15 are selected, as displayed in Figure 5.8. The last cell, E15, is the active cell.

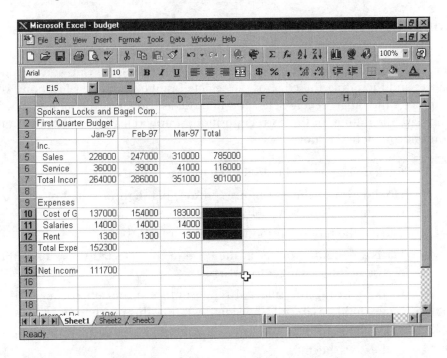

Figure 5.8 *Two non-contiguous selected ranges.*

5. Click on the **AutoSum** button to add the function to all the selected cells.

If you need to select a rectangular range, the Shift key can make the task more efficient. Just click on one corner of the range you want to select, then hold down the **Shift** key and click on the opposite corner of the range. You can also use the GoTo dialog box to select a range. Instead of typing a single cell address in the Reference text box, you can enter two cell addresses separated by a colon (:). When you click on **OK**, the range is selected.

When you're finished, select cell **B15** and press the **Delete** key to clear the contents for future calculations.

MOVING DATA

Now that you know how to select a range of data, you can perform operations on the data such as moving in from one location to another. There are two basic methods of moving data: drag-and-drop, and cut and paste. Let's take a look at both methods.

Moving with Drag-and-Drop

The simplest way of moving data from one location to another is by the drag-and-drop method. You first select and highlight the range of cells you want to move, and then drag the edge of the selected range to the new location. An outline of the range of cells selected will move as you move the mouse. Once you have the outline in the correct position, simply releasing the mouse button will complete the move.

1. Click on cell **A1** and hold the left mouse button down.
2. Holding down the left mouse button, highlight a range of cells by dragging the mouse to cell E15.
3. Release the mouse button to select the range.
4. Place the mouse pointer at the edge of the selected range until the mouse pointer changes to an arrow.
5. Click and drag the selected range until the top left corner of the range outline is in cell C3. Figure 5.9 show this procedure.
6. Release the mouse button to complete the move to the new location of the worksheet.

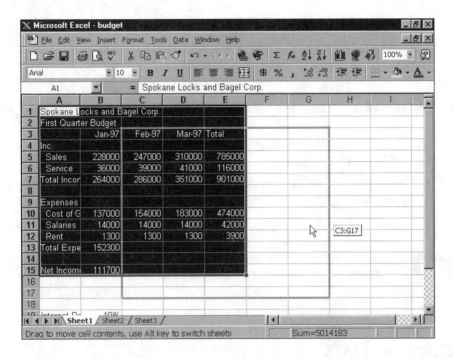

Figure 5.9 Moving a range by dragging its border.

When you are finished moving the range of cells, try moving them back again. This will leave the worksheet in the same condition it was in before you started.

Moving Data with Cut and Paste

When using the combination Cut and Paste commands of Excel, you accomplish the same results as moving data by the drag and drop method. You first select the range of cells you want to move. Select the **Cut** command from the Edit menu, or click on the **Cut** button on the Standard toolbar (see Figure 5.10).

Figure 5.10 The Cut button on the standard toolbar.

Place the cursor at the location where the move is to be accomplished. Finally, select the **Paste** command from the Edit menu or click on the **Paste** button (see Figure 5.11) on the Standard toolbar.

Figure 5.11 *The* **Paste** *button on the standard toolbar.*

Use the following steps to move your data via the cut and paste methods.

1. Select the range of cells you want to move.

2. Click the **Cut** button.

3. Move the cell pointer to the first cell of the new location where you want to move the data.

4. Select the **Paste** command on the standard toolbar, or just press **Enter**.

After selecting the cell range you want to move, you can press the right mouse button inside the range to display the shortcut menu and perform the cut.

N O T E

COPYING DATA

To save yourself from having to type and retype the same formulas, functions, or data in more than one area of your worksheet, use Excel's copy feature. Unlike moving data, when you copy data in Excel, you don't alter the original data; you simply duplicate it in another area of your worksheet.

There are three basic ways you can copy data. You can use either the drag-and drop method or copy and paste method. You can also copy certain data by using the AutoFill method. Let's take a brief look at these techniques.

Copying Data with Drag-And-Drop

The same procedures for moving data using the drag-and-drop method are employed when copying data. The only difference is that when you select the highlighted cells to copy, you must hold down the **Ctrl** key prior to dragging. Try these simple steps to copy cells:

1. Click on cell **A1**.

2. Press and hold the **Ctrl** key.

3. Position your mouse pointer on the border of cell A1. Your mouse pointer will turn into an arrow with a plus sign above it (As shown in Figure 5.12), which indicates you are copying the contents of the cell.

4. Click the mouse button again and drag the cell to G5.

5. Release the mouse button.

Delete the duplicate of cell A1 before proceeding to the next section.

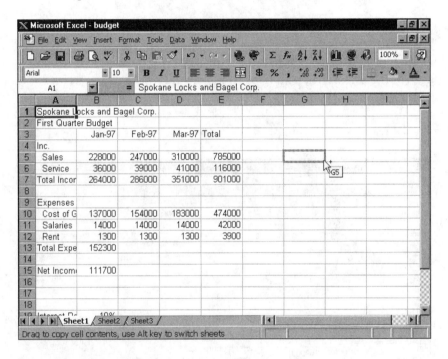

Figure 5.12 Copying a cell with Drag-and-Drop.

Copying Data with Copy and Paste

When using the combination Copy and Paste commands, you accomplish the same results as copying by the drag-and-drop method. One advantage to the Copy command is that you're not limited to creating one duplicate—you can copy a cell and paste into many different cells. First, you have to select the range of cells you want to copy. Select the **Copy** command from the Edit menu or click on the standard toolbar's **Copy** button (see Figure 5.13).

*Figure 5.13 The **Copy** button.*

Then place the cursor at the location where you want the copy and select the
Paste command from the Edit menu or click on the **Paste** button.

1. Click on cell **E5**.

2. Click the **Copy** button.

3. Highlight the range E10 through E12 (Don't worry about the figures
    in these cells, you can copy right over them).

4. Click the **Paste** button.

Figure 5.14 shows the result.

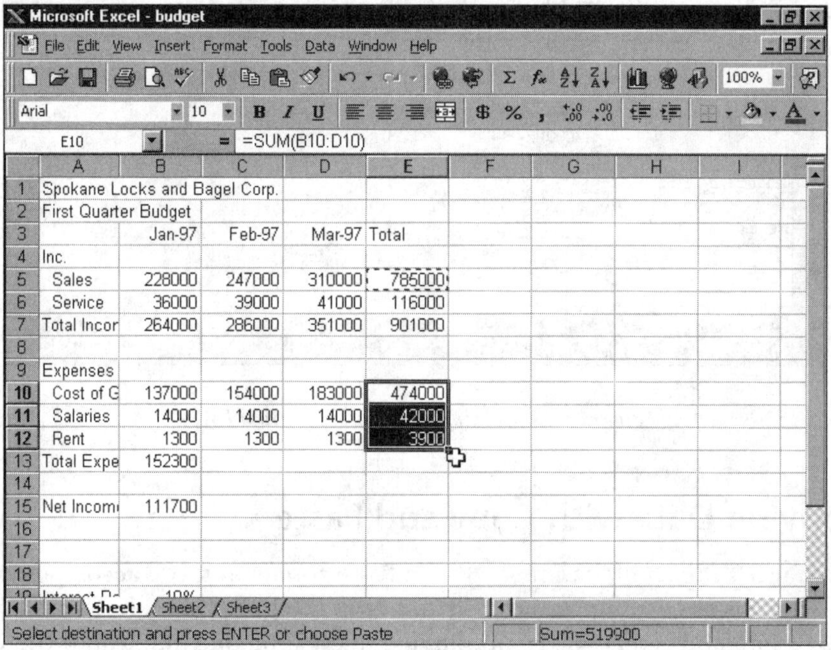

X Microsoft Excel - budget

Figure 5.14 Using the Copy and Paste commands to make multiple copies.

Notice that when copying formulas, the copied information adjust to
show the results of the appropriate columns. Excel's built-in intelligence

knows you want the copied formulas to reflect the appropriate rows or columns of data.

Copying Data with AutoFill

On occasion, you will need to copy data from a cell or from a range of cells to adjacent cells. The quickest way to do this is by using the AutoFill feature. Simply highlight the cell or range of cells you want to copy. Then drag the fill handle of the selected cells to the new adjacent cells. Excel automatically copies the data from the selected cells into the new adjacent cells. Follow these step-by-step directions for practice.

1. Click on cell **B13**.
2. Drag the fill handle across to cell E13.
3. Release the mouse button. The formula in the original cell is now repeated in the adjacent cells of the extended range. See Figure 5.15.

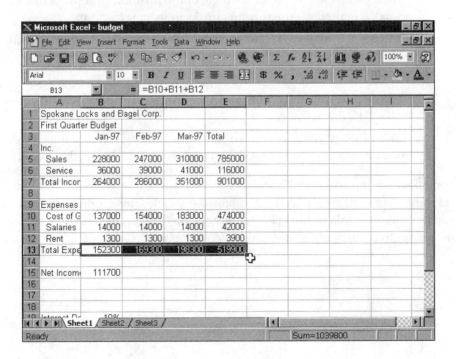

Figure 5.15 *Copying formulas with AutoFill.*

Copying Formulas and Functions

With all the Total Income and Total Expenses calculations in place on your spreadsheet, you're ready to add the formulas for calculating the Net Income/Loss for February and March. Instead of creating separate formulas, we'll copy the formula for January's Net Income/Loss to February and March.

1. Click on cell **B15**.

    If you look in the formula bar, the formula appears to be *=B7-B13*. Well, appearances can be deceiving. Excel and other spreadsheets employ a type of cell referencing called *relative referencing*. By using relative references, cells containing formulas or functions can be copied and they are automatically adjusted to perform properly in their new location.

    Relative reference logic sees the formula in B15 as *subtract the value in the cell that is two rows up from the value in the cell that is eight rows up*. When you copy a formula, the logic of the formula (not the actual formula) is copied, so the formula works in its new location.

    Let's use the fill handle to copy the formula to cells C15 through E15.

2. Position the mouse pointer over the fill handle and drag three cells to the right.

3. Release the mouse button and then press the **Right Arrow** key to make C15 the active cell.

    Take a look at the formula bar to assure yourself that the logic of the formula was correctly copied. You can check D15 for further proof.

Sometimes, when you copy formulas in a cell, you don't want the cell being referenced in your formulas to be relative. Instead, after copying a formula, you want the formula in the cell to reference the exact same reference found in the original cell. This is called *absolute referencing*.

Excel will not adjust cell and range references if the cell in question is set up correctly. When using an absolute reference in a cell, it will never change to a relative reference no matter where you copy the cell to. But you must follow the ensuing format to make a cell reference absolute.

To make a cell reference absolute, place dollar signs ($) in front of both the letter and number address of the cell. For example, if you wanted to make the reference to cell E8 absolute, you would place dollar signs in front of the letter and number, thereby producing *$E$8*.

Formulas can also use both absolute and relative references simultaneously. For example, if the formula *=SUM(A1:A8)*$E$8* is copied from one cell to another, the range reference *A1:A8* will be relative, while the reference *E8* will be absolute.

DEFINING NAMES

So far, we've only referred to cells by their addresses. Naming ranges can make your worksheets much easier to understand. Using names in formulas instead of ranges of cell addresses can make it instantly clear what the formula does. For example, *B7-B13* is meaningless until you look at the worksheet and determine what these cell addresses represent. However, if the formula read *Total Income-Total Expenses*, you'd know exactly what was going on.

You can name individual cells or ranges of cells. You can also specify the name you want to assign or let Excel do it for you. Generally, an appropriate name is already adjacent to the cell or range of cells you want to name. If this is the case, you can include the name with the range and let Excel use it.

Let's create names for the income and expense categories, including total income and total expenses.

1. Select the ranges A5 through D7 and A10 through D13, as displayed in Figure 5.16. Remember to use the **Ctrl** key to select non-contiguous ranges.

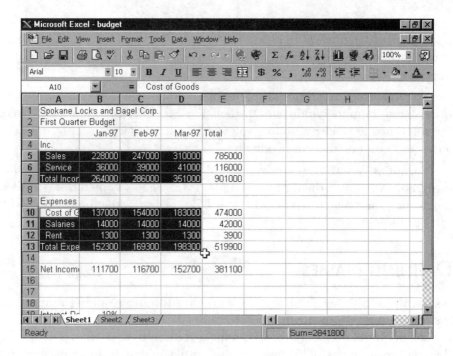

Figure 5.16 *The selected ranges to be named.*

2.   Choose **Insert**, **Name**, **Create…**.

The Insert Names dialog box appears, as displayed in Figure 5.17, with the Create Names in Left Column check box checked.

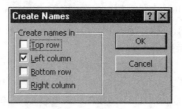

Figure 5.17 *The Create Names dialog box.*

3.   Click **OK**.

Although Excel uses the names in the left column, they aren't included as part of the range. You can use the Define Name dialog box to see which ranges each name is applied to, but the easiest way—and a good shortcut for selecting a named range—is the name list in the cell reference area. Let's use this method to select the Service range.

4. Click on the **Arrow** for the name list, just to the right of the cell reference area.

    The drop-down list, shown in Figure 5.18, displays the names contained in the worksheet.

5. Click on **Service** in the list to select the range B6 through D6.

    Now let's make the formulas in the worksheet more understandable by substituting the range addresses with the range names. To have Excel automatically apply range names, you first need to select the cells that contain formulas or functions. To make sure you don't miss any, select the whole worksheet. A shortcut for selecting the entire worksheet is to click on the **Select All** box (the rectangle in the upper-left corner of the worksheet where the row and column heading intersect).

6. Click on the **Select All** box.

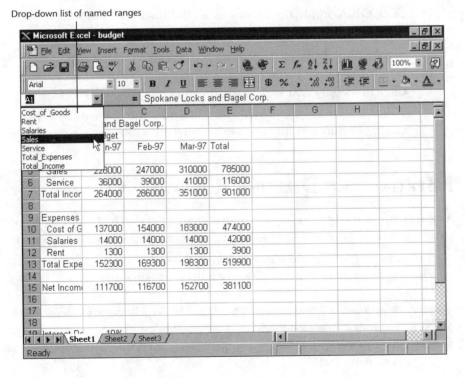

Figure 5.18 *The worksheet's named ranges.*

7. Choose **Insert**, **Name**, **Apply....**

The Apply Names dialog box, with all the range names highlighted, is shown in Figure 5.19. If some of the names aren't highlighted, click on each of them.

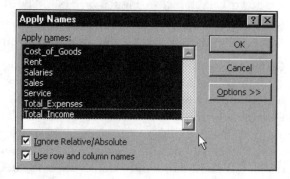

Figure 5.19 *The Apply Names dialog box.*

8. Click **OK** to apply the names to all the formulas and functions that refer to those ranges.

The formula in B7 used to read *=B5+B6*. Let's take a look at how it's changed.

9. Click on cell **B7** and look at the formula bar.

The new formula is *=Sales+Service*. Click on some of the other cells containing formulas or functions to see how the names have been applied.

INSERTING AND DELETING ROWS AND COLUMNS

As you create and edit worksheets, you frequently need to insert or delete rows and columns. Perhaps you want to add or remove categories or time periods.

Let's insert a row to add a new category to your budget worksheet, interest, showing interest income for the company's investments.

Inserting or deleting rows or columns can be very dangerous. You could inadvertently interfere with some data that you can't see on the screen. You could have data off to the side, or above or below the portion of the worksheet that is currently visible.

When inserting or deleting rows or columns, be sure to take into account the effect these actions could have on all portions of your worksheet.

Even though Excel provides an Undo feature to get you out of sticky situations, it's always a good idea to save your work just before making any sort of change that could wreak havoc on your worksheet.

1. Move to any cell in row 6.

2. Choose **Insert**, **Rows**.

   A new row has been inserted and named ranges have been adjusted to reflect their new locations, as have cells containing formulas and functions.

3. Enter the data for the new row, as shown in Figure 5.20.

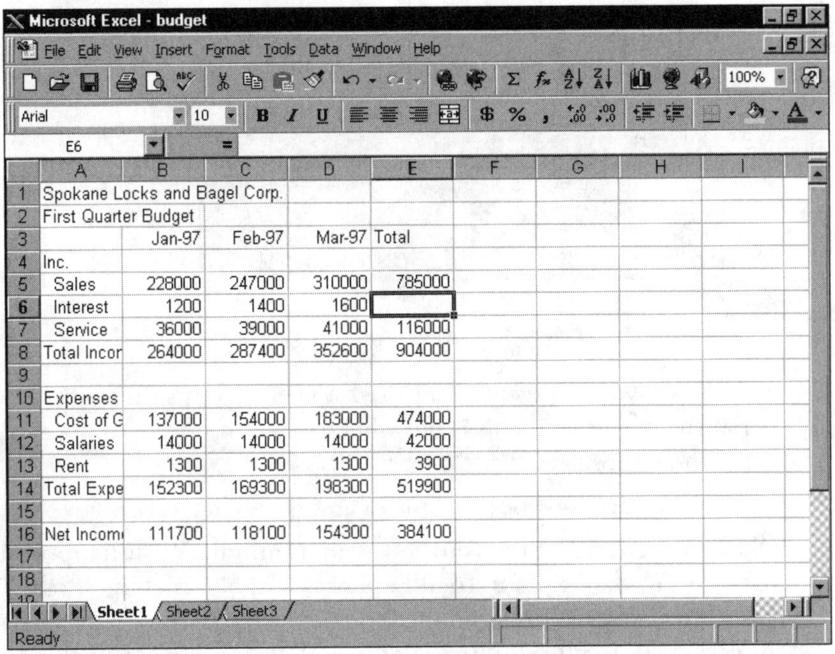

Figure 5.20 *The Budget worksheet with the data entered for the newly inserted row.*

Notice that the January Total Income calculation didn't adjust to accommodate the new cell, but February and March did. What happened? January used a formula that added two specific cells, while February and March used the SUM function to add a range of cells.

When we inserted a row, the new row was included in the SUM function's range, but was not automatically added to the formula.

You can fix this by replacing the formula with the SUM function. You can also use AutoSum to add the calculation for the quarter total interest.

4.   Move to cell B8 and click on the standard toolbar's **AutoSum** button. Press **Enter**.

5.   Move to cell E6 and click on the **AutoSum** button. Press **Enter**.

One way to reduce expenses would be to get rid of the rent. Let's delete row 13 to improve the company's profit picture.

6.   Move to any cell in row 13 and choose **Edit, Delete...**.

The Delete dialog box appears, as displayed in Figure 5.21.

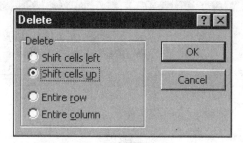

Figure 5.21 *The Delete dialog box.*

Because only a single cell is selected, Excel suggests shifting the cells below the active cell. This is not what we had in mind; we want to get rid of the entire row.

7.   Click the **Entire Row** option button and then click **OK**.

Okay, that got rid of the rent, but wait a minute. What happened to the totals in the rows for Total Expenses and Net Income/Loss? The *#REF!* message that replaced the figures in each of these cells refers to an incomplete cell reference. Because Rent is included in these formulas, Excel is letting you know that it can't complete the equation properly. You could remove +Rent from the formula to eliminate the #REF! errors. Since the Spokane Locks and Bagels Corp. will probably need to pay rent so it has a place to operate its business, you can use Excel's Undo feature to reverse the deletion.

8. Choose **Edit**, **Undo** or click the **Undo** button on the standard toolbar to restore the rent row.

Figure 5.22 *The **Undo** button.*

Changing Column Widths

Finally, what you've been waiting for. When text entries are too long and are truncated or numbers show up as pound signs (#), your column is probably too narrow and needs to be adjusted.

You've probably been anxiously looking at column A since you first entered the numbers and lost part of the text. Well, the time has come to fix the problem and adjust the column.

You can change the column width by entering a new value in the Column Width dialog box by choosing **Format**, **Column**, **Width...**, but there's an even easier, more visual method. You can position the mouse pointer over the right border of the column heading and drag it to the left to reduce the width, or to the right to increase the width. Let's use the dragging method to increase the width of column A.

1. Position the mouse pointer over the right border of the column heading, and drag to the right about half an inch, as shown in Figure 5.23.

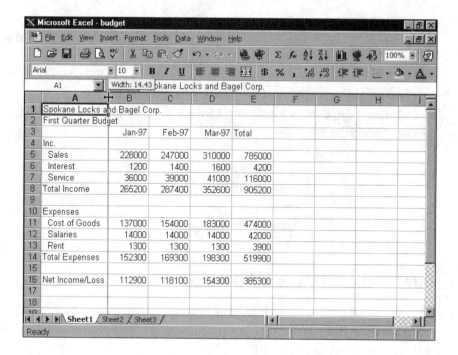

Figure 5.23 *The column width being adjusted.*

2.   Release the mouse button to complete the adjustment.

The column is now wide enough to display all the text in most of the cells. The disadvantage of the dragging method is that you may need to make several stabs at the proper adjustment before you get it right. Also, if there are long cell entries below what you can see, you won't know if you have it right until you scroll down or print the worksheet—and then it's too late.

There is an even better way. When you double-click on the right border of the column heading, Excel adjusts the column so it is wide enough to accommodate the longest cell entry.

But wait a minute. If the column is adjusted for the longest entry, it will be wide enough for the title in cell A1, which would make the column much too wide for the remaining entries.

3.   Select the range A4 through A16 and choose **Format**, **Column**, **AutoFit Selection**. Now the column width is adjusted properly.

Changing Multiple Column Widths

Here's a handy little shortcut for changing more than one column's width at a time. It eliminates the need to go from one column and adjust the width, and then to the next column and adjust the width and so on. Suppose Column A, Column C, and Column F were all the same width and they each needed to be widened by the same amount. One method would be to adjust each column individually. That may not be too bad for 3 columns, but suppose it was 10 or 20 columns with the same situation.

The easiest way to adjust multiple columns is to select each column by pressing the **Ctrl** key and clicking on the column header (e.g., A, B, C, etc.). Holding the **Ctrl** key while clicking on columns allows you to select columns that are not adjacent to each other. Then, by using your mouse, you can adjust one of the selected columns, and all the selected columns will adjust at the same time. Follow these simple steps to adjust multiple column widths.

1. Select the columns whose widths you want to change by holding down the **Ctrl** key and clicking on the appropriate column headers.

2. Place the mouse pointer at the right edge of any of the selected columns in the column header area. The mouse pointer will change from a heavy cross to a double-arrowed column width changing pointer.

3. Press and hold the mouse button down as you move the pointer to the right or left, to either narrow or expand the columns.

4. Release the mouse button. Note that each selected column width has been modified to reflect the change made by the mouse.

Column widths can also be changed by selecting **Column, Width...** from the Format menu. Enter a number (integer or decimal fraction) for the approximate number of characters the column should contain, based on the current font selected.

Changing Row Heights

Although it's less often required, you can also change the heights of rows in an Excel worksheet. Like changing column widths, you can change row heights by dragging on the bottom border in the heading area of the desired row number. You can also double-click on the border to automatically adjust row heights. Try increasing the height of row 3 to make more room between the title and the column headings. Figure 5.24 illustrates this example.

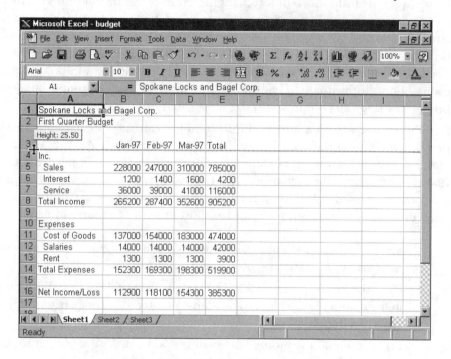

Figure 5.24 *Changing the height of a row.*

GETTING AROUND IN YOUR WORKBOOK

Knowing how to move easily around your workbook is an important aspect of using Excel. One of the chief benefits of using Excel 97 is that you don't have to open 2, 5, 10, 30, or more worksheets at one time. Opening one workbook in Excel 97 give you access to 3 worksheets—and you can add more. This section will teach you how to move between your worksheets, name your worksheet, rearrange your worksheets, and insert and delete worksheets.

Moving Between Worksheets with Page Tabs

When you decide you want to go from one worksheet to another, the easiest way to accomplish this is to simply click on the page tab located at the bottom of the worksheet. For example, if you are working with Sheet1 and want to move to Sheet3, simply click on the **Sheet3** tab. Clicking on the sheet tabs will give you all the mobility you need to move around.

Normally, you can only see 5 tabs at a time. Suppose you wanted to click to, let's say, tab 7, but you can only see tabs 1 through 5. Excel has several easy solutions to this situation. One solution is to slide the horizontal scroll bar to the right. This will shorten the scroll bar, but allow more sheet tabs to be displayed. When you see the sheet tab you're looking for, simply click on it. Figure 5.25 shows how to reduce the size of the scroll bar.

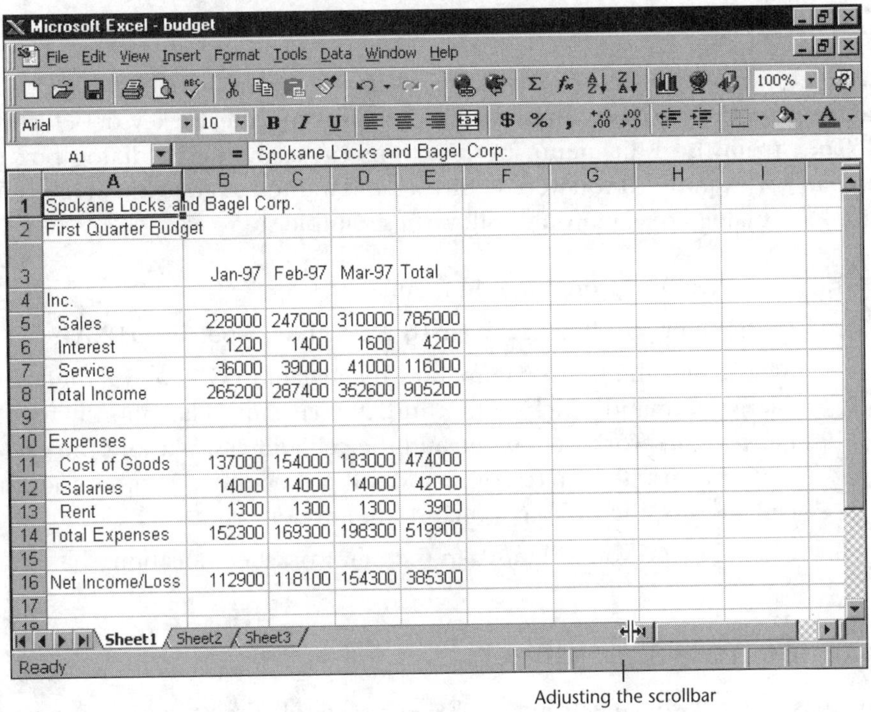

Adjusting the scrollbar

Figure 5.25 *Adjusting the scroll bar to display more page tabs.*

Another solution for selecting sheet tabs hidden from sight is to use the page tab buttons, located on the far left bottom scroll bar of the worksheet. If your worksheets were named Sheet1 through Sheet16, clicking the far right arrow (pointing right) will take you to the last tab sheet or Sheet16 of your workbook. Clicking the far left arrow (pointing left) will take you to the first tab sheet or Sheet1 of your workbook. Clicking the two middle left and right arrows will allow you to move forward and backward through your workbook one sheet at a time, as shown in Figure 5.26.

Figure 5.26   *The page tab buttons allow you to move between tab sheets*

Moving Between Worksheets Using the GoTo Command

Another way to move between worksheets is by using the GoTo command. You can activate the GoTo command by either pressing the **F5** key or selecting **GoTo...** from the Edit menu. Both actions cause the GoTo dialog box to appear. For example, if you were in Sheet1 and wanted to go to Sheet12, using the GoTo dialog box you would follow these simple steps.

1. Select **GoTo...** from the Edit menu.

2. In the reference box of the GoTo dialog box, type: **Sheet12!A1**.

    Sheet12 tells the GoTo command which sheet to visit, and *A1* tells the GoTo command which cell to find. Notice the exclamation mark (!) between the worksheet name and the cell address. Without the exclamation mark, the GoTo command will not operate. Also, without the cell address, the GoTo command will not perform.

3. Click **OK** and you will move to the new worksheet location.

Naming Your Worksheets

If you use several worksheets in your Excel workbook, then the generic names (Sheet1, Sheet2, Sheet3, etc.) may not be descriptive enough for you. You can rename the worksheets to a name that is more meaningful and useful. To rename your worksheets, perform the following steps.

1. Double-click on the worksheet tab you want to rename.

    The Tab name will now appear highlighted.

2. Type in the new name and press **Enter**.

Another way to rename your worksheet is by using the tab shortcut menu, as follows:

1. With the mouse pointer on the sheet tab you want change, press the right mouse button.

    The sheet tab short menu appears, as shown in Figure 5.27.

Figure 5.27 *The sheet tab short menu.*

2. Click on **Rename**.

3. In the rename sheet dialog box, type in the new name and click **OK**.

Moving Your Worksheets

As you begin working with several worksheets in a single workbook, you may decide that the current arrangement of the worksheets does not work well. Fear not. Excel provides you with several methods by which worksheets can be rearranged to better suit your needs. Let's briefly discuss them.

The easiest way to rearrange your worksheets is the drag-and-drop method. Follow these steps to move your worksheets.

1. Click and hold the page tab you want to move.

2. Drag your mouse either left or right across the bottom of your screen to where you want the page to move to. A triangular arrow will appear as you move the mouse.

3. When the triangular arrow is at the location where you want your page to go, simply release the mouse button.

Of course, Excel gives you additional options for moving your worksheets.

1. With the mouse pointer on the sheet tab you want to move, click the right mouse button. The sheet tab short menu appears.

2. Click on **Move or Copy…**.

3. In the Before Sheet window of the move or copy dialog box, click on the worksheet you want to move your worksheet in front of.

4. Click **OK**.

Copying Your Worksheet

At times you may want to copy one worksheet to another worksheet. The procedures are almost identical to the steps of moving your worksheets with the sheet tab short menu.

1. With the mouse pointer on the worksheet tab you want to copy, click the right mouse button. The sheet tab short menu appears.

2. Click on **Move or Copy…**.

3. Click the **Create a Copy** check box.

4. In the Before Sheet window of the Move or Copy dialog box, click on the worksheet you want to copy your worksheet in front of.

5. Click **OK**.

Inserting Worksheets

You may decide you want to create a new worksheet between two existing worksheets. Excel offers an easy way to do this.

1. Select the worksheet tab that you want to insert your new worksheet in front of.

2. Bring up the tab short menu by clicking the right mouse button.

3. Select **Insert…** The Insert dialog box appears, as shown in Figure 5.28.

4. Double-click the **Worksheet** icon. Your new worksheet is inserted and the sheet name assigned to it is the next numerical sheet number of your workbook.

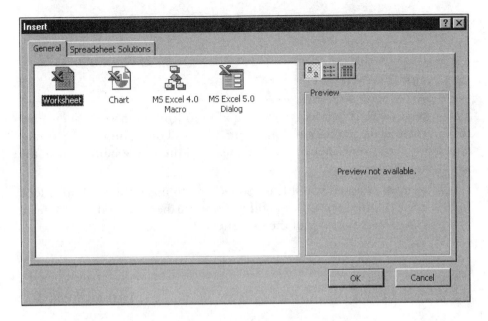

Figure 5.28 *Inserting a worksheet into the workbook.*

Deleting Worksheets

You may decide you want to delete a worksheet you no longer need. Again, Excel offers two methods to achieve this. These are the steps for the first method.

1. Select the worksheet tab you want to delete.
2. Select **Delete Sheet** from the Edit menu.
3. Click **OK** to confirm deleting the selected worksheet.

Of course, you can also use the tab short menu.

1. Select the worksheet tab you want to delete.
2. Bring up the tab short menu by clicking the right mouse button.
3. Select **Delete**.
4. Click **OK** to confirm deleting the selected worksheet.

Save your work and exit Excel if you're not continuing on to the next chapter at this time.

A Final Thought

Now you know that you will always be able to find your worksheets, and this worksheet is starting to shape up nicely. The columns are finally adjusted to accommodate the cell entries, and the range names make the worksheet clearer.

In the next chapter, you'll learn some ways to make the worksheet look snazzier. You'll also learn how to add notes to further clarify the worksheet, and how to protect portions of the worksheet.

CHAPTER 6

Enhancing and Annotating Your Worksheet

This chapter concentrates on aesthetics; adding those nice little touches that make the worksheet more attractive, readable and, perhaps most importantly, persuasive.

Most worksheets are prepared to persuade someone else to come to a particular conclusion. In the case of a budget or forecast, perhaps you're trying to convince your boss, or the board of directors to go along with your assumptions. If you're preparing a business plan, maybe you need to sell your plan so a banker or venture capitalist will provide the needed funds for your new startup or to expand your existing business.

Whatever your worksheet's purpose, the way it looks and how well it's documented does matter and should be given as much consideration as the underlying data. Enhancing the appearance of your worksheet can be as simple as adding dollar signs to the number values or displaying important information in an attractive, bold font. You'll find that Excel has numerous formatting features for your worksheets, including the ability to draw right on the page. Because of the importance of worksheet formatting, you'll probably find that you spend as much time enhancing the appearance of your worksheets as you do creating them.

Don't worry if you think you don't have a good eye for design. This chapter includes some basic tips on making your worksheets more attractive. Plus, Excel even has the ability to format your worksheet for you with predesigned styles, formats, and worksheet templates.

ALIGNING CELL CONTENTS

Choosing the appropriate alignment for the contents of your cells can have an immediate impact on the look of the worksheet. You have seen that, by default, numbers are right-aligned and text is aligned to the left. A variety of alignment options can be applied to a single cell or a range of cells. This includes "pushing" the data to the far left, far right, or center of the cell. Many other content alignment options are available, as the following sections explain.

Left, Right, Center

Let's align the column headings so they are centered over the numbers. Aligning cells falls into the general category of cell formatting. You can reach the cell formatting options through the Format Cells command with the alignment tab, but there is a shortcut.

1. Select cells B3 through E3.
2. Right-click (click the right mouse button) anywhere inside the selected range to display the Shortcut menu, as displayed in Figure 6.1.

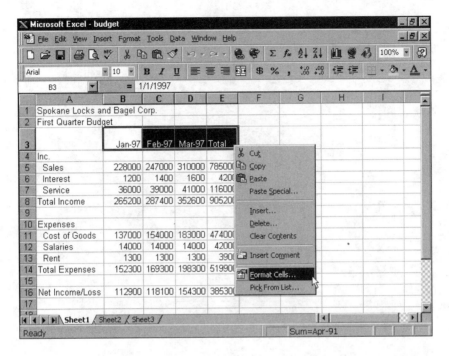

Figure 6.1 *The Shortcut menu for the selected cells.*

SHORTCUT

There are shortcut menus for almost every screen or worksheet element. You can display the shortcut menu by right-clicking on the object you want to manipulate. If you aren't sure what sort of manipulation you can perform on an object, the shortcut menu lets you know. We'll be using shortcut menus for many tasks as the book proceeds.

3. Choose **Format Cells...** from the Shortcut menu.

The Format Cells dialog box appears, as shown in Figure 6.2.

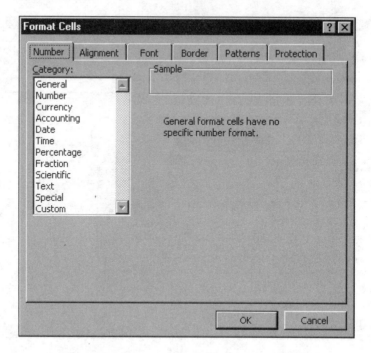

Figure 6.2 *The Format Cells dialog box.*

The tabs in the dialog box let you specify what type of formatting you want to do. You need to get to the Alignment portion of the dialog box.

4. Click on the **Alignment** tab to display the Alignment portion of the dialog box.

This dialog box lets you specify the type of horizontal and vertical alignment you want, the orientation of the text in the cells, and if you want long text entries wrapped (split into several lines). These options are shown in Figure 6.3.

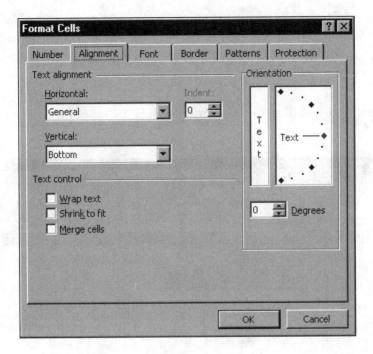

Figure 6.3 *The Alignment portion of the Format Cells dialog box.*

The two alignment types that might need a bit of explanation are Justify and Fill. If the Wrap check box is checked, the Justify option forces the cell entry to spread out so the left and right edges are even (just like the text in this book). The Fill option repeats the cell entry until the cell is filled. These two options are explained in more detail later in this chapter.

5. Click on the **Center** option button in the Horizontal portion of the dialog box and click **OK**.

SHORTCUT

The formatting toolbar has buttons for some of the more common cell formatting options. Instead of using the dialog box, you can simply click on the appropriate toolbar button. In the previous step, for example, you would click on the **Center** button.

Each column heading is now centered over its column, as displayed in Figure 6.4.

	A	B	C	D	E	F	G	H	I
1		Spokane Locks and Bagel Corp.							
2		First Quarter Budget							
3		Jan-97	Feb-97	Mar-97	Total				
4	Inc.								
5	Sales	228000	247000	310000	785000				
6	Interest	1200	1400	1600	4200				
7	Service	36000	39000	41000	116000				
8	Total Income	265200	287400	352600	905200				
9									
10	Expenses								
11	Cost of Goods	137000	154000	183000	474000				
12	Salaries	14000	14000	14000	42000				
13	Rent	1300	1300	1300	3900				
14	Total Expenses	152300	169300	198300	519900				
15									
16	Net Income/Loss	112900	118100	154300	385300				
17									

Figure 6.4 The center-aligned column headings.

Centering Headings Across Columns

The title in cell A1 would look better if it were centered over all the columns in the worksheet. You can't just center it in the cell because it's already longer than the width of column A. So what can you do?

Well, it just so happens that one of the alignment options is to center across a selection. That's the option you'll need.

1. Select cells A1 through E1.

   In doing this, you are highlighting the information you want to center, plus the area in which you want to center it.

2. Click on the formatting toolbar's **Merge and Center** button, shown in Figure 6.5.

Figure 6.5 *The Merge and Center button.*

The title is now centered between columns A and E. Note that the toolbar button is a shortcut method of centering a title. You can also access the Center Across Selection option from the Alignment tab in the Format Cells dialog box.

3. Repeat these steps with cells A2 through E2.

You can adjust the width of any of the columns A through E and the headings will automatically adjust to fit your changes. If you add columns to your table and want to center the heading across a new set of columns, just repeat the steps above and the heading will adjust to the new selected columns. Remember, even though the headings now appear to be centered, the headings still actually exist in Cells A1 and A2 where you typed them.

Justifying and Wrapping Text in a Cell

There may be occasions when you want to have multiple lines of text in a cell. This can be useful for entering notes or extended headings into your worksheet.

Figure 6.6 shows two examples of wrapped text in a worksheet. Note that the heading in cell E3 is wrapped onto two lines within the cell and is centered. The entry in cell F16 is an example of wrapped text with the Justification alignment option. Following are the general steps to achieve these results, although these modifications will not be included in our ongoing sample throughout this chapter.

1. Type the information you want wrapped onto multiple lines, then select the cell containing this data.

2. Right-click on the cell and choose **Format cells...** from the shortcut menu.

3. Click on the **Alignment** tab.

4. Click on the **Wrap Text** option and then choose between any of the Horizontal alignment options. Justify will create the results shown in cell F16 of Figure 6.6; Center will create the results pictured in cell E3.

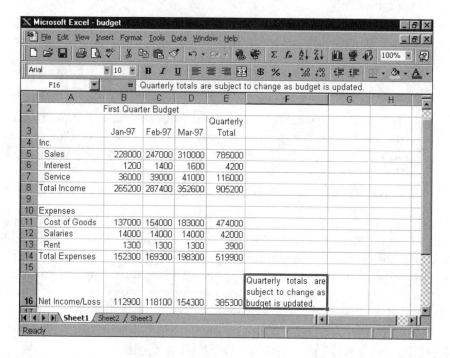

Figure 6.6 *Using the Wrap Text option.*

You can change the column width associated with any wrapped text and Excel will automatically adjust the wrapped data to fit the new column width. You may also adjust the corresponding row height for best results. Refer to Chapter 5 for more information on adjusting column widths and row heights.

FORMATTING NUMBERS

In addition to changing cell alignment, you may also choose to alter the format of the numbers in your worksheet. All of the numbers have been entered using Excel's default formatting. The numbers would look better if they were formatted with commas separating thousands and a decimal point with two decimal places.

1. Select B5 through E16 and click on the **Comma Style** button on the Formatting toolbar (see Figure 6.7).

Figure 6.7 *The **Comma Style** button.*

The number format has been changed as shown in Figure 6.8. Depending on your setup, some of the numbers may have been replaced by pound signs. So what does that mean? It means some of the numbers, with their new commas and decimal places, are now too wide for the column width. Don't worry though, you can fix this.

2. Choose **Format**, **Column**, **AutoFit Selection**—or double-click on the right column border as described in Chapter 5.

    The column widths have been adjusted to accommodate the new number format, as shown in Figure 6.8.

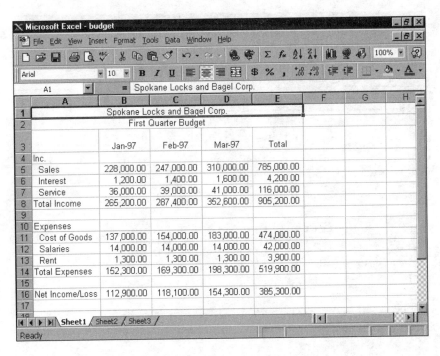

Figure 6.8 *The numbers with the comma format.*

The totals might look a little better if they were formatted with dollar signs, so let's take care of that detail now.

3. Select the ranges B8 through E8, E5 through E7, B14 through D14, B16 through E16, and E11 through E14. Remember to press the **Ctrl** key to select multiple ranges.

   Click on the **Currency Style** button on the Formatting toolbar (see Figure 6.9).

Figure 6.9 *The **Currency Style** button.*

4. Once again, choose **Format**, **Column**, **AutoFit Selection** to adjust the column widths to accommodate the dollar signs.

   Your screen should now look like Figure 6.10.

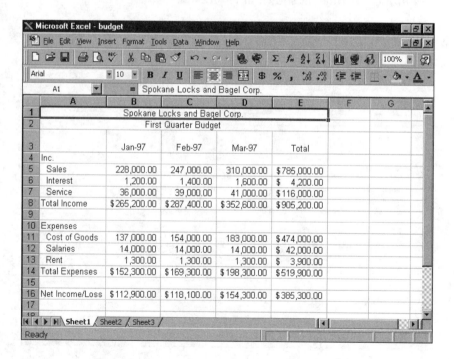

Figure 6.10 *The totals are formatted with the currency style.*

There are many other number formatting options available through the Cell Formatting dialog box, which can be displayed through the Shortcut menu or the Format menu.

N O T E

Since the toolbar buttons offer only a limited selection of number formatting options, let's take a look at all the possibilities available through the Format Cells command. In this case, you'll create a special numeric format that includes the dollar signs for the totals, but leaves out the two decimal places. You'll do the same with the values formatted with the comma style.

1. Select the ranges B8 through E8, E5 through E7, B14 through D14, B16 through E16, and E11 through E14. Remember to press the **Ctrl** key to select multiple ranges.

2. Select the **Cells...** command from the Format menu and click the **Number** tab to see the number formatting options. The screen should look like Figure 6.11.

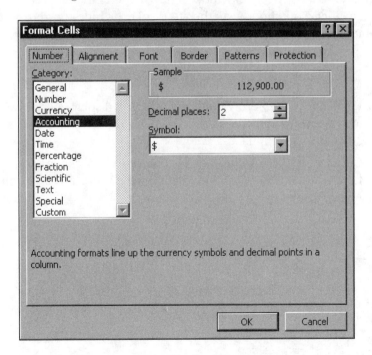

Figure 6.11 *The number formatting options in the Format Cells dialog box.*

Notice that the number format box shows that the current format of the selected cells is an Accounting format using a dollar sign and two decimal places. We can add or remove the dollar sign, change the number of decimal places, or even select a completely different format from here.

3. Click on the number wheel controlling the decimal places until it reads *0*. When finished, click **OK**.

Using steps 2 and 3, change the ranges B5:D7 and B11:D13 to the Accounting format with no dollar sign and no decimal places.

DISPLAYING AND HIDING ZERO VALUES

Although the worksheet example we are using does not contain any zero values in its cells, eventually you will create a worksheet that does. Frequently, these zeros are not input by you on the keyboard, but calculated by formulas. However, your worksheet may look better if the cells with zero values are blank. Excel lets you choose whether to display or hide the zero value cells. Experiment with the following steps to see how this works; you can delete the added cells when finished.

❖ Choose Tools, Options…, View.

❖ If you check the Zero Values option, Excel displays all zero value cells, whether you enter the zeros yourself on the keyboard or they are calculated by a formula.

❖ Click on the **Zero Values** box to remove the checkmark. Now you will have a worksheet with blank cells where there are zero values (see Figure 6.12).

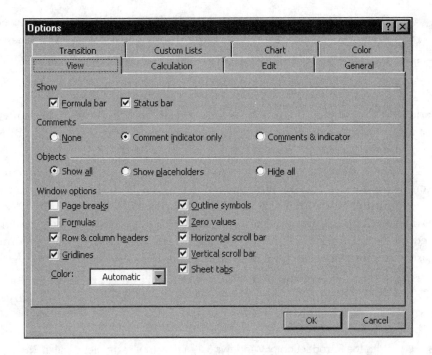

Figure 6.12 *The Options dialog box with View selected.*

FONTS

A *font* is a particular typeface. Windows 95 includes several typefaces from which you can choose to enhance your documents. You can also purchase additional fonts that work with almost any Windows program. Choosing the correct font for a situation can do more to help or hinder your cause than just about any other type of formatting, so choose carefully.

There are many good books available to help you choose and use fonts well. If one of your goals is to produce the most professional-looking and persuasive worksheets possible, learning more about fonts is a worthwhile investment of **N O T E** your time and money.

In addition to changing the font, you can change the style (bold, italic, underline) and the size of the font. Font sizes are specified in points because most fonts these days are proportional fonts.

The fonts used on a typewriter (and even some that are still used on computers) were fixed-width or monospaced, where each character took up the same amount of horizontal space. With proportional fonts, some characters are wider than others. For this reason, using the old method of measurement, based on the number of characters per inch (pitch) no longer works. Points measure the font's height. One point is roughly 1/72 of an inch.

Typical font sizes for the main body of the worksheet are between 9 and 12 points. Anything smaller than 9-point type is considered fine print. Larger than 12-point type is considered large type.

With the introduction of Windows 3.1, a new font technology called *TrueType fonts* became available. TrueType fonts have several advantages over other font technologies. They are scalable to just about any point size you choose **N O T E** and have corresponding screen fonts, so they display very accurately. They work with just about every Windows program in existence. Unless you are a real font connoisseur, you'll probably find the quality of TrueType fonts more than adequate. Keep in mind that TrueType is not a brand of fonts, but rather a *type* of font technology. You can buy TrueType fonts from a variety of manufacturers and the quality can vary.

Changing Fonts

Let's change the font, style and size of the title so that it really stands out. We'll do this using the Font list in the Formatting toolbar.

1. Click on cell **A1**.
2. Click on the font drop-down list **Arrow** to display the list of available fonts, as shown in Figure 6.13.

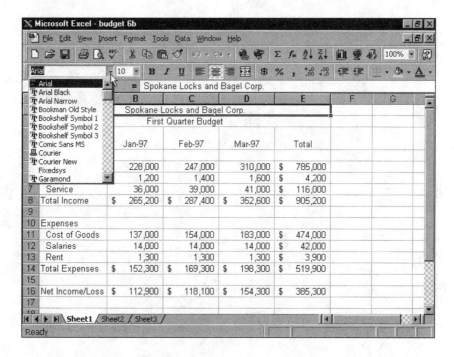

Figure 6.13 *The Formatting toolbar's drop-down font list.*

The fonts in your list may differ from those in the figure. Only those fonts that are installed and available on your system appear on your list. Also, notice that some of the fonts have *TT* in front of them, signifying that they are TrueType fonts.

Let's use a slightly more ornate font called Times New Roman, which is currently out of view near the bottom of the list.

3. Use the scroll bar to scroll down until Times New Roman comes into view and then click on **Times New Roman**.

Notice the typeface of the title has changed. Since this is a title, it should also be larger, so we'll change the size. The current size, as you can see from the Font Size box on the formatting toolbar, is 10 points. Let's change it to 18 points.

4. Click on the **Font Size** arrow on the Formatting toolbar to reveal the list of font sizes, as shown in Figure 6.14.

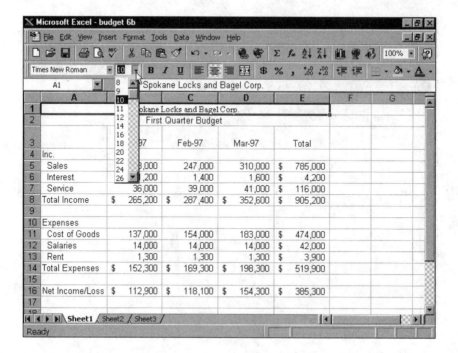

Figure 6.14 *The Font Size drop-down list.*

Unlike the list of fonts, the Font Size list only displays the more common sizes. However, you are not limited to these sizes. You can type in the size you wanted, say 19 points, and the font would change to that size.

5. Click on **18** to enlarge the title, as displayed in Figure 6.15.

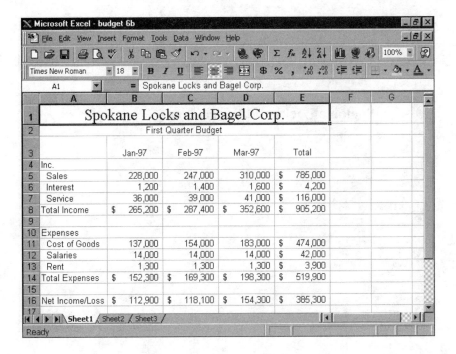

Figure 6.15 *The title in 18-point type.*

Notice that the row height automatically adjusted for the larger size. If your font changes ever cause the heading to exceed the total width of the columns over which it is centered, you may have to use the Left alignment option to fix the problem. On the other hand, it's bad formatting to have a heading that exceeds its columns.

6.   Click on the **Bold** toolbar button.

Your worksheet should look like Figure 6.16.

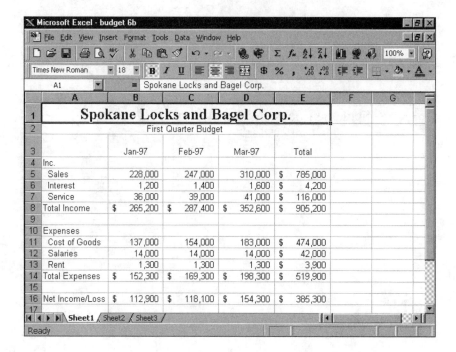

Figure 6.16 *The bold title, completely visible.*

Although the fastest way to change fonts is with the toolbar, it may be advantageous to use the Font portion of the Format Cells dialog box, particularly if you aren't familiar with the way the different fonts look. The dialog box provides a preview of the font, including size and style, so you can see what the font looks like before you apply it.

ADDING BORDERS AND SHADING

To further embellish your worksheet, you can surround cells with borders and fill them with shading. As with fonts, you need to use the appropriate borders and shading or these elements can detract from the look of your worksheet.

Let's add a border and some shading to the column headings.

1. Select B3 through E3.

2. Click on the **Arrow** for the Border drop-down box on the Formatting toolbar.

   The Border drop-down box is displayed, as shown in Figure 6.17.

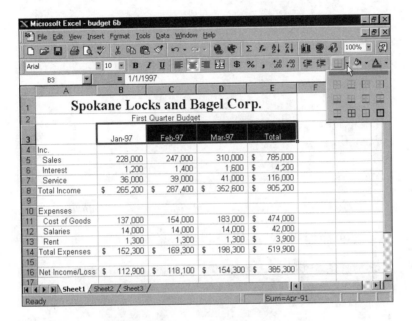

Figure 6.17 *The Border drop-down box.*

3. Click on the border style of your choice. In our example, we're using the thick underline border (the one in the second row, second from the left).

4. Click outside the selection so you can see the border below the column headings, as shown in Figure 6.18.

   Now let's add some shading to the titles.

5. Select B3 through E3 again.

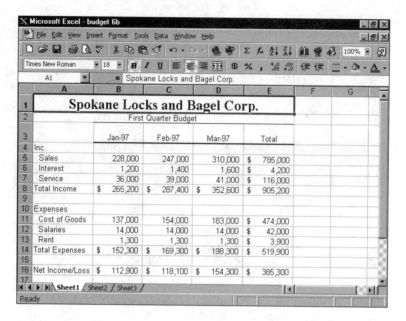

Figure 6.18 *The column headings with a border beneath them.*

6. Click on the **Fill Color** drop-down list, as shown in Figure 6.19.

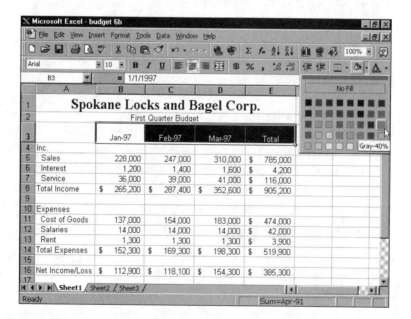

Figure 6.19 *The Fill shades available.*

7. Click on the desired color and shade to fill the highlighted cells.

Our example worksheet uses the eighth pattern from the left in the third row down (it's the one the mouse pointer is pointing to in Figure 6.19). Click outside the selected area to see a color and pattern's effect.

Figure 6.20 exhibits the changes that have been made.

	A	B	C	D	E	F	G
1			Spokane Locks and Bagel Corp.				
2			First Quarter Budget				
3		Jan-97	Feb-97	Mar-97	Total		
4	Inc.						
5	Sales	228,000	247,000	310,000	$ 785,000		
6	Interest	1,200	1,400	1,600	$ 4,200		
7	Service	36,000	39,000	41,000	$ 116,000		
8	Total Income	$ 265,200	$ 287,400	$ 352,600	$ 905,200		
9							
10	Expenses						
11	Cost of Goods	137,000	154,000	183,000	$ 474,000		
12	Salaries	14,000	14,000	14,000	$ 42,000		
13	Rent	1,300	1,300	1,300	$ 3,900		
14	Total Expenses	$ 152,300	$ 169,300	$ 198,300	$ 519,900		
15							
16	Net Income/Loss	$ 112,900	$ 118,100	$ 154,300	$ 385,300		

Figure 6.20 The column headings with a border and shading.

Graphic elements, such as shading, can look very different on the printed page than they do on the screen. Don't decide that a pattern is too dark or light until you print.

T I P

CHANGING THE COLOR OF TEXT

You can use another drop-down list to change the color of the text on the worksheet. This is the Font Color drop down list, as shown in Figure 6.21. Just select the cells containing the desired text, then choose a color from the list.

This is particularly useful for showing certain values in red or blue. Remember that you'll need a color printer to see these enhancements on the printed version of your worksheet. A black-and-white printer will either print the worksheet without the colors or it will convert the colors to shades of gray. See Chapter 7 for more information about printing in color and gray shades.

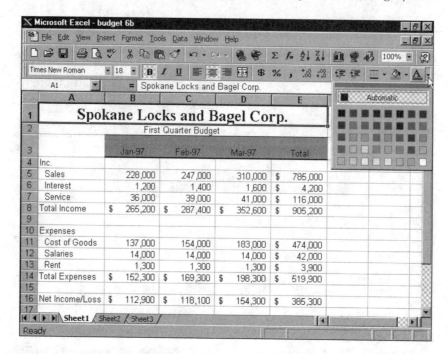

Figure 6.21 The Font Color drop-down list.

SHORTCUT

The Borders, Fill Color, and Font Color lists have a special shortcut feature available. The face of the button changes to the last selected border or shade. This indicates that you can simply click on the button's face to select the same choice again.

USING AUTOFORMAT

Suppose you have as little design sense as we do. Excel's AutoFormat feature will turn your shabby old unformatted worksheet into a work of art.

All you have to do is select the portion of the worksheet you want automatically formatted and choose the most pleasing format style from the list in the AutoFormat dialog box. Let's try it out.

1. Select range A3 through E16 and choose **Format**, **Auto Format...** to display the AutoFormat dialog box, as shown in Figure 6.22.

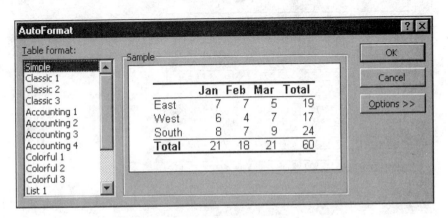

Figure 6.22 *The AutoFormat dialog box.*

The Simple Table Format is highlighted and you can see what that style looks like in the Sample area. The easiest way to check out the various options is with the down arrow key. Each time you press the **Down Arrow** key, you see another format style in the sample area.

We'll use the Classic 1 style. It's simple, yet elegant. After all, we don't want to use anything too overpowering, do we?

2. Click on **Classic 1**, then **OK**, and then click outside the selected area so you can behold the beauty of the newly formatted worksheet, as displayed in Figure 6.23.

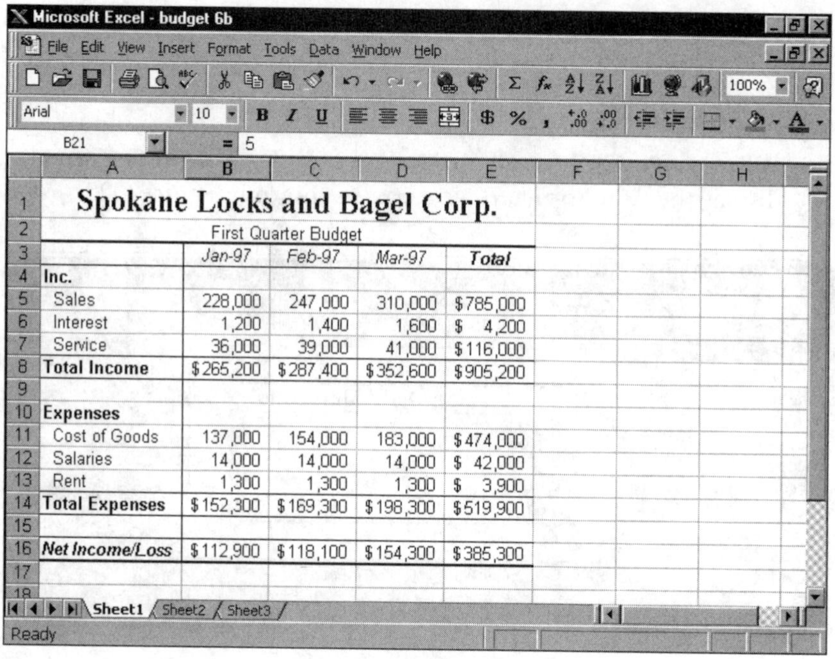

Figure 6.23 *The worksheet formatted with the Classic 1 style.*

REMOVING WORKSHEET GRIDLINES

As your worksheets begin to fill up with data, you might find the gridlines distracting rather than helpful. Removing the worksheet gridlines helps you see the worksheet formatting more clearly. Like removing zero values from cells, you can remove gridlines in the Tools menu.

1. From the Tools menu, select **Options...**, then click the **View** tab.

2. Click on the **Gridlines** box, and then click **OK**.

Now you can view your worksheet without all those distracting lines. Figure 6.24 shows the results.

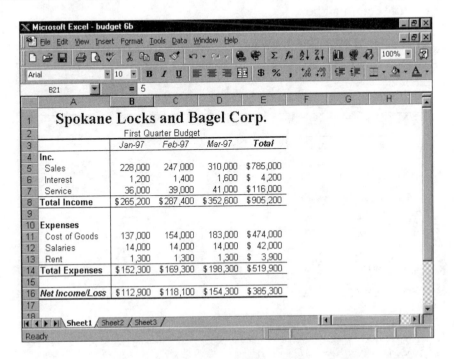

Figure 6.24 The worksheet with gridlines removed.

For the next section we'll need the gridlines again, so just select the **Gridlines** option from the View tab of the Options dialog box.

ADDING COMMENTS

At times, you may want to write yourself a note on a worksheet without having it cluttering up your work area. It could be a note about a formula, a comment about formatting, or anything else. Let's see how this works.

1. Click on cell **B16**.
2. Select **Comment** from the Insert menu.

A comment box will appear to the right of cell B16. As shown in Figure 6.25, a user's profile name is automatically placed at the top of the comment box.

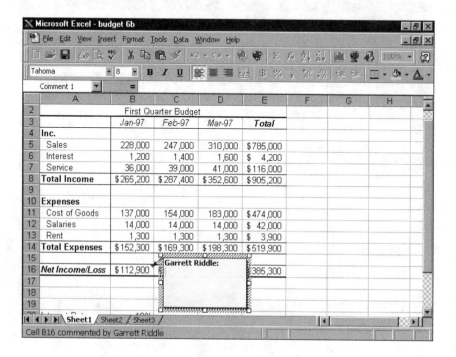

Figure 6.25 *The comment box.*

3. Type **This value equals the total income minus the total expenses**.

4. Click on another cell to complete the entry.

You should now see a red triangle in the upper right corner of cell B15. To view the comment, just move your mouse pointer to the center of the cell. Soon the comment will appear, as shown in Figure 6.26.

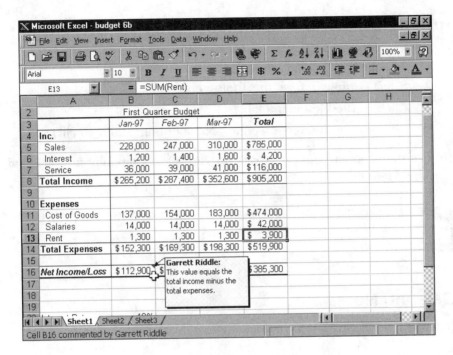

Figure 6.26 *Displaying a cell note.*

If you want to change the note, follow these steps.

1. Right-click on the cell containing the note you wish to edit.

2. Select **Edit Comment** from the Shortcut menu.

3. Now you can edit your note. When you're finished, click on any other cell to complete the entry.

Your changes will now appear in the worksheet when you view the note.

Turning On/Off the Comment Indicator

The red triangle indicating a note can be turned off by following these simple steps.

1. Select **Options...** from the Tools menu.
2. Click on the **View** menu tab.
3. Click on the Comment section's **None** option, and then click **OK**.

To turn the comment indicator back on, just select **Comment indicator only** from the View menu.

NOTE

Turning off the comment indicator won't delete your note. It only removes the note indicator from your worksheet.

Deleting Notes

Deleting a note is just as easy as creating one. Just follow these steps:

1. Right-click on the cell containing the note you wish to delete.
2. Select **Delete Comment** from the shortcut menu.

PROTECTING DATA

If you want to ensure that certain cells in your worksheet can't be accidentally altered (or even seen at all) you can lock or hide them. It's often a good idea to lock cells containing formulas so someone can't accidentally delete or alter them.

If your worksheet contains confidential information, you may want to hide portions of it. You can also require that a password be used to remove the protection you've specified.

Let's protect the formulas in column E.

1. Select cells E5 through E16 and right-click in the selected area to display the shortcut menu.
2. Choose **Format, Cells...** and click on the **Protection** tab to display the Protection portion of the Format Cells dialog box, as displayed in Figure 6.27.

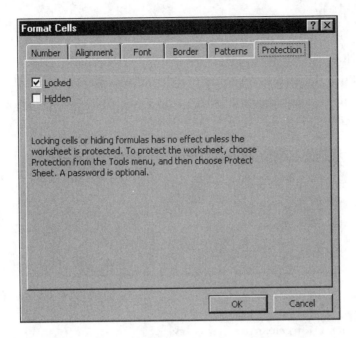

Figure 6.27 *The Protection portion of the Format Cells dialog box.*

3. Click on the **Locked** check box (unless it's already check-marked), and then click **OK**.

    Before the protection actually takes effect, you have to turn on the protection facility.

4. Choose **Tools**, **Protection**, **Protect Sheet...** to display the Protect Sheet dialog box shown in Figure 6.28.

Figure 6.28 *The Protect Sheet dialog box.*

5. After making sure all three check-boxes are checked, click **OK**. (We won't add a password).

   Now let's see if the protection is really working.

6. Press the **Delete** key to try to delete the contents of the selected cells.

   The message dialog box shown in Figure 6.29 lets you know that you cannot mess with locked cells. It works!

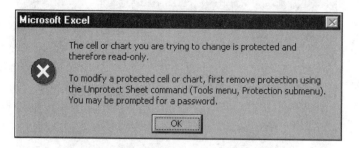

Figure 6.29 *The message dialog box showing that a cell is locked.*

7. Click **OK** to clear the dialog box.

8. Choose **Tools**, **Protection**, **Unprotect Sheet...** to remove protection from this sheet.

COPYING FORMATS

If you spend a lot of time creating the desired fonts, sizes, styles, colors, borders and protection status in the cells of your worksheet, you might want to duplicate your efforts rather than repeat them. You can easily copy the formatting from one cell and apply it to another cell containing different data.

1. Move to cell E3.

2. Select the **Copy** command from the Edit menu.

3. Highlight cells B3 through D3.

4. Choose the **Paste Special...** command from the Edit menu, then click the **Formats** option from the Paste options provided. Click **OK** when finished.

The formatting of the cell you copy is applied to the other cells. A shortcut to performing this task is using the Format Painter button on the Standard toolbar. Just click on the cell you want to copy, and then click on the **Format Painter** button, which is pictured in Figure 6.30. Next click on the cell you want the formats applied to.

Figure 6.30 The **Format Painter** *button.*

USING STYLES

Now that you've made your worksheet look just the way you want it, you may want to create other worksheets that look just like it. Rather than going through all the steps in this chapter, you can save a lot of time by adding the formatting options (fonts, colors, shading, and so on) to the Styles list. This will enable you to duplicate the formatting used in a specific cell or range. The Styles list contains some preset styles, but you can also save your own formatting masterpieces there.

Accessing the Style Tool

To use the Styles list, first you have to add the Style button to your toolbar. Creating custom toolbars is explained in detail in Chapter 15. Here we'll just quickly move through the steps.

1. Choose **View, Toolbars, Customize....**
2. Click on the **Commands** menu tab in the Customize dialog box.
3. Select **Format** from the Categories list, and click on the **Style:** option as shown in Figure 6.31.

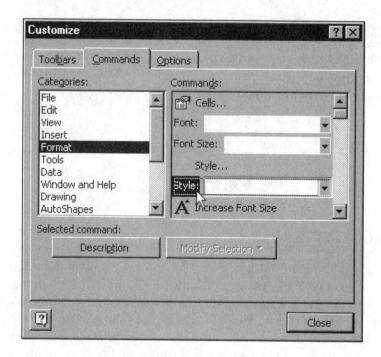

Figure 6.31 *Adding the **Style** button to the Formatting toolbar.*

4. Press and hold your left mouse button.

5. Drag the Style: option over to the Formatting toolbar.

6. Click on the **Close** button.

Now you're ready to start working with Styles. Figure 6.32 shows a toolbar with the Styles list added next to the Fonts list.

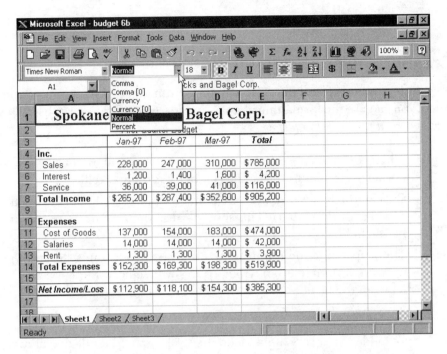

Figure 6.32 *The Styles list added to the Formatting toolbar.*

Applying Styles

You can automatically format all or a portion of your worksheet using the Styles list. The following steps can be applied to any cell or range on any worksheet.

1. Select the cells on your worksheet you want formatted.

2. Click the **Styles** button and choose the style you want from the list.

Excel changes the worksheet to match the style you selected.

Creating Styles

If you want to reuse any of the cell formatting from the worksheet you just finished, you can use the formatting as an example to create your own style. This
is called *creating a style by example.*

1. When you've finished formatting a cell the way you want it (from the
   Format Cells menu), place the cell pointer on that cell.

2. Click in the box where the style name is displayed (don't click on the
   down arrow next to it). This should cause the style name to become
   highlighted.

3. Think up a short, descriptive, and catchy name for your style, and type
   it in the style name box. Your typing will replace the current style
   name in the box.

4. Press **Enter**.

You've now added your very own style to the styles list, and it will appear every
time you choose the Styles list. To reuse the style, simply choose it from the list.

As you become a more advanced Excel user, you may know exactly how
you want to format cells without seeing the formatting first. Then you can create a style from options in the Style dialog box (choose **Format, Style...**). This
is called *creating a style by definition.*

Changing Existing Styles

If you have a change of heart about something in a style that you've already
used in your worksheet, Excel allows you to change it and automatically
applies the changes to all cells that use that style. You can change a style either
by example or by definition. Let's look at how to change a style by example.

1. Select a cell that has been formatted with the style you want to change.

2. Select **Format, Cells** and make the changes you want to the cell format.

3. Pull down the Styles list and choose the name of the style that is
   already applied to the cell.

4.   Excel asks if you want to change the current style to match the cells you selected. Choose **OK** to change the style. (If you choose No, Excel reapplies the old style and all your formatting changes are lost).

All the cells with that style are automatically changed.

To change a style by definition, you access the **Style...** command from the Format menu and select the style you want to change. Click on the **Modify** button and make the changes you want.

As you can see, using styles can be a real time saver. But the benefits only occur when you format using styles. For this reason, you should use styles to format all your worksheets.

Using Templates

Once you begin creating lots of worksheets, you may notice that many of them contain the same elements over and over again. These repeated elements may include formatting (including styles, display settings, and outline settings) and actual data and calculations. You can create a master worksheet (called a *template*) based on these repeated elements, so that you don't have to recreate them with every new worksheet.

A template is actually a certain type of file format in Excel that you use as a starting point for new files. When you create a worksheet using a template, saving the file does not change the template you used to start it.

Creating a Template

You can create a template by making a worksheet that contains all the elements you want to repeat in your worksheets and then saving it as a template.

1.   Make the master worksheet you want to use as a template.

2.   Choose **Save As...** from the File menu.

3.   Choose **Template** from the **Save as type** list.

4.   Think up a name for your master worksheet and type it in.

Excel saves your master worksheet as a template, which you can use over and over again.

DESIGN TIPS

Although you have an almost unlimited choice of fonts, font sizes and font styles, try to avoid cluttering your worksheet with too many different fonts. Stick to two or three fonts, and establish a system that you use throughout your worksheet. For example, you can use one font for headings (with two or three levels identified by size, bold or italics) and another font for text.

A FINAL THOUGHT

You now know how to put together a worksheet so that it is presentable, fully documented, and protected. In the next chapter you'll learn how to transfer your masterpiece to the printed page.

CHAPTER 7

Printing Worksheets

CHOOSING A PRINTER

Windows 95 makes life easy by allowing all your programs to share the same printer files without having to install settings for each one. If you already have one or more printers installed in Windows 95, they are automatically available in Excel. If you don't have a printer installed, refer to your Windows 95 documentation for instructions.

If you have more than one printer connected to your computer, you need to designate the printer you want to use from the Printer Setup dialog box to make sure Excel uses the right one.

NOTE

1. Start Excel and open the Budget workbook if it isn't already on your screen.

2   Choose **File, Print...**.

    The Print dialog box appears, as shown in Figure 7.1.

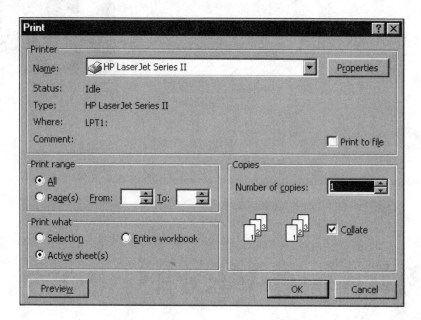

Figure 7.1 *The Print dialog box.*

Later on we'll look at the various options in the Print dialog box. For now, let's concentrate on selecting a printer.

3. Click on the Printer drop-down list to display the Printer list, as shown in Figure 7.2.

    You can choose any printer from this list as the destination for your document. If the highlighted printer is the one you want to use, you're all set. Otherwise you need to select the printer you want to use from the list.

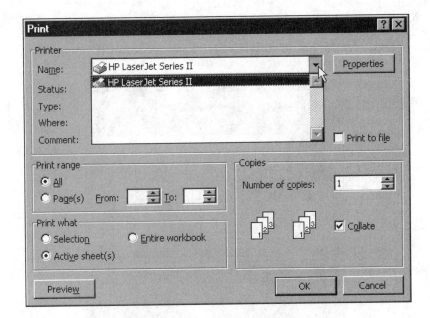

Figure 7.2   *The Printer drop-down list.*

4.   Click on the printer you want to use from the list of available printers, then click **OK**.

If your chosen printer is already selected, click **OK**. Note that under the printer selection list is a summary of details about the printer. Also included is a Properties button to set up different aspects of your printer. Each type of printer has different setup information. Let's take a look.

The list of printers in your Printer Setup dialog box probably looks different than the list in Figure 7.2. Your list reflects the printers installed on your machine. If only one printer is connected to your computer, your list probably has that one printer's name in the list.

5. Click on the **Properties** button to see the Printer Properties dialog box.

Figure 7.3 shows the properties of an HP LaserJet Series II.

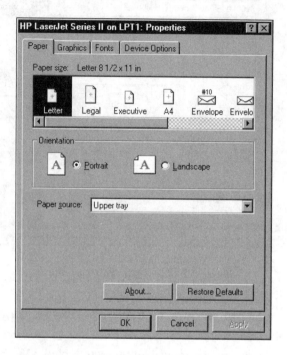

Figure 7.3 *The Printer Properties dialog box .*

6. Click **Cancel** to return to the Print dialog box.

You could click **OK** to print the active worksheet according to default settings, but we're going to explore some of the other printing options before sending the worksheet to the printer.

SETTING UP PAGES

Excel needs some information about how you want your pages printed before you start printing. If you don't provide this information, Excel prints using its current settings, which may not be what you want to use.

Let's take a look at the settings in the Print dialog box on your screen (refer to Figure 7.1). The Print dialog box lets you opt to print the selection (if you've selected a portion of the worksheet), the selected sheet(s), or the entire workbook. You'll see how to print specific ranges in a little while.

You can also choose how many copies you want to print and whether you want to print all the pages, or specific pages. Let's call up the Page Setup dialog box now to start giving Excel some more information.

1. Click **Cancel** to remove the Print dialog box if it's still on the screen, then choose the **Page Setup...** command from the File menu to display the Page Setup dialog box, as shown in Figure 7.4. If the Sheet portion of the dialog box isn't visible, click on the **Sheet** tab.

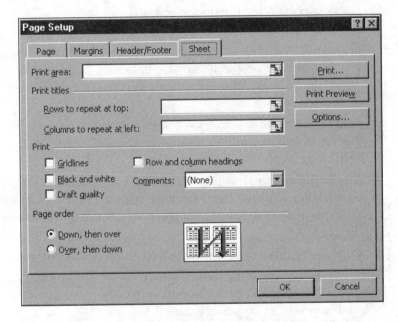

Figure 7.4 The Sheet portion of the Page Setup dialog box.

In the Print Area text box, you can specify a range of cells to print. Let's specify the range A1 through E16.

2. Click in the **Print Area** text box and type **A1:E16**.

You can use the pointing method to specify a print area. Simply point to one corner of the rectangular area you want to print and then drag to the opposite corner and release the mouse button. The range automatically is entered in the Print Area text box.

The Rows to Repeat at Top and Columns to Repeat at Left text boxes let you specify one or more columns or rows to repeat on each page of multiple-page printouts. These can be useful for keeping track of which column and row headings a particular cell entry belongs to. You don't have a multiple-page worksheet to print, so you won't need to use these options now.

The check boxes in the Print area of the dialog box provide several options for customizing the way your pages print.

❖ **Gridlines** chooses whether to print the lines you see separating rows and columns on your worksheet. This option will not affect any borders you've added to a worksheet.

❖ **Black and White** can be chosen if you have used any colors for text or graphics on your worksheet and are printing on a black and white printer. This option may also help your pages to print faster on a color printer, since color printers often print slower in color than black and white.

❖ **Draft Quality** causes Excel to omit any charts or other graphic objects, as well as gridlines, from your printout. Draft Quality often helps your pages to print faster.

❖ **Row and Column Headings** causes the row numbers and the column letters to print. This can make it easier to determine which cell a particular entry is in, but it can also detract from the look of the page.

❖ **Comments** prints any comments you have attached to your worksheet.

3. With the Print Area text box filled in none of the check boxes marked, click on the **Page** tab to display the Page portion of the Page Setup dialog box, as shown in Figure 7.5.

❖ **Orientation** determines whether you want the information printed on the page in the normal upright (portrait) position, or sideways (landscape). Portrait orientation allows you to print more rows but fewer columns on a page. Landscape accommodates more columns but fewer rows. We'll keep Portrait as our orientation option.

❖ **Scaling** adjusts the size of the document you are about to print. The Adjust to option lets you print at 100% (normal size) or a smaller or larger percentage. For example, if you adjust to 200%, all the data (including text, numbers, and graphics) print at twice their normal size. This means that each page only holds half as much data. You can scale pages up to 400% and down to 10%.

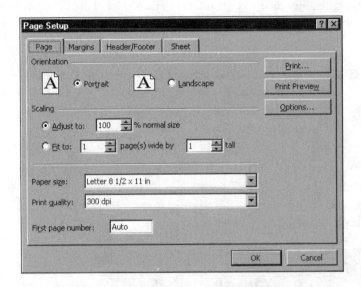

Figure 7.5 *The Page portion of the Page Setup dialog box.*

❖ **Fit to** lets you force the information you want to print to fit on a specified number of pages. This can be useful for shoehorning your data into fewer pages than it might otherwise require. This option does not enlarge the data on the worksheet to fit on the specified pages.

WARNING

Be careful with the Fit to option. You could end up with such tiny print that no one can actually read it. Come to think of it, for some worksheets that might be an advantage!

❖ **Paper Size** lets you choose the paper size you are using in your printer. Some printers are only able to use one or two sizes of paper and the list reflects your printer's capabilities.

❖ **Print Quality** selects the quality of print for your document. The tradeoff here is that choosing a higher quality generally results in slower print speeds. You may want to use a lower print quality for drafts and a higher quality for final prints.

NOTE Some printers don't have print quality options. For others, a change in print quality only affects graphics. The latter is true of laser printers. On a laser printer, the worksheet's text and numbers print at the same quality regardless of your print quality choice in Excel.

❖ **First Page Number** specifies the starting number that is printed on the first page of a worksheet. For example, if you enter 3 as the First Page Number for a three-page worksheet you are about to print, the pages are numbered 3, 4, and 5. This option has no effect if you choose not to have page numbers printed on your pages.

We won't need to change any of the options on the Page portion of the dialog box, so let's take a look at the Margins portion of the dialog box.

4. Click on the **Margins** tab to display the Margins portion of the dialog box, as displayed in Figure 7.6.

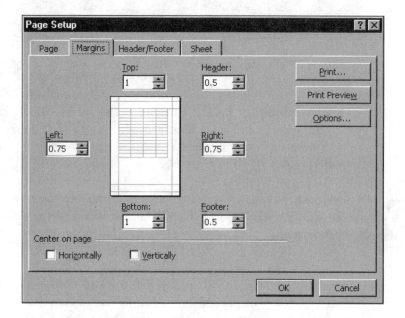

Figure 7.6 *The Margins portion of the Page Setup dialog box.*

Changing the margin setting lets you determine where your document appears on the printed page. The default top, bottom, left, and right margins are generally adequate. You may wish to reduce the margins so you can fit more data on a page, or you may want to increase the margins so you have more breathing room (white space) around your data..

You can also specify how far from the edge of the page your headers and footers appear. You'll learn more about headers and footers in just a bit.

You can use a couple of the option in this dialog box to center the data both vertically and horizontally on the printed page.

5. Click both the **Horizontally** and **Vertically** check boxes in the Center on Page area of the dialog box.

Notice that the Preview area now shows a representation of the data as centered on the page.

Before we finish setting up the pages, let's take a look at headers and footers.

6. Click on the **Header/Footer** tab to display the Header/Footer portion of the Page Setup dialog box, as shown in Figure 7.7.

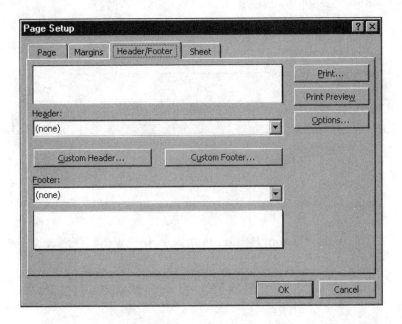

Figure 7.7 *The Header/Footer portion of the Page Setup dialog box.*

Headers and footers are text elements that appear at the top and bottom of your printed documents. A header appears at the top of the printed page and a footer appears at the bottom.

Excel also provides a variety of predefined headers and footers that you can use. Figure 7.8 displays some of the predefined headers (the predefined footers are the same) that can be seen by clicking on the **Arrow** for the Header drop-down list.

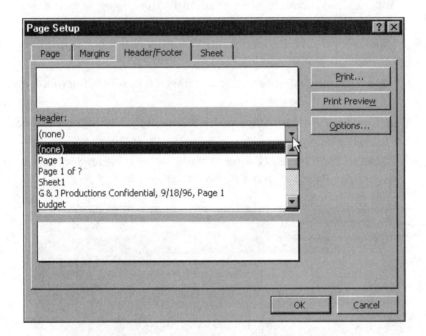

Figure 7.8 *The Header drop-down list.*

Instead of using one of the predefined headers, let's create a custom header.

7. Click on the **Custom Header** button to display the Header dialog box, as shown in Figure 7.9.

Let's type some text in the Left Section.

8. Click in the **Left Section** box and type **Prepared by [Your Name]**.

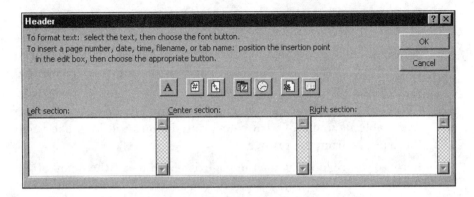

Figure 7.9 *The Header dialog box.*

9. Move to the **Center Section** box and then click on the **Date** icon. (Refer to Figure 7.10).

10. Click in the **Right Section** box and then click on the **File Name** icon. Your screen should now look like Figure 7.10.

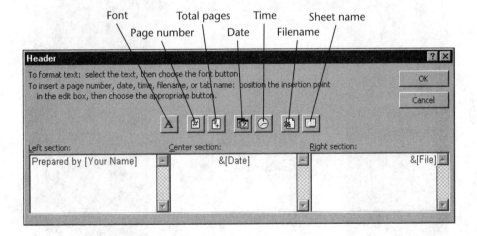

Figure 7.10 *The Header dialog box with the custom header filled in.*

11. Click **OK** to accept the custom header and return to the Header/Footer section of the Page Setup dialog box, where you see what your new header actually looks like.

12. Click **OK** to accept the header and footer and return to the worksheet.

You're just about ready to print, but first we'll preview the page. It's almost always a good idea to preview before sending a document to the printer. It can save time and paper by letting you ensure that everything is just the way you want it.

13. Choose the **Print Preview** command from the File menu to display a reasonable facsimile of what your printed pages will look like when they emerge from the printer.

Because you're looking at a full page, it's hard to see the detail of the worksheet (unless you have a very large screen). Notice that as you move the mouse pointer over the representation of the page, the pointer turns into a magnifying glass. By clicking on a portion of the page, you can zoom in on that area.

Let's zoom in on the January column heading (where the mouse pointer is in Figure 7.11).

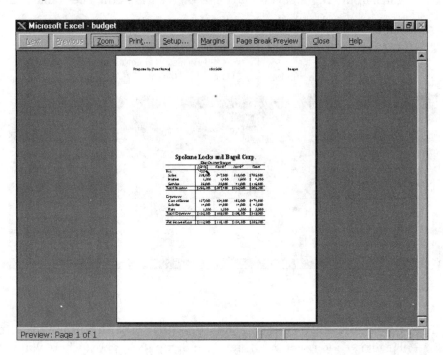

Figure 7.11 *The Print Preview screen.*

14. Point to **Jan** and click. See Figure 7.12 for results.

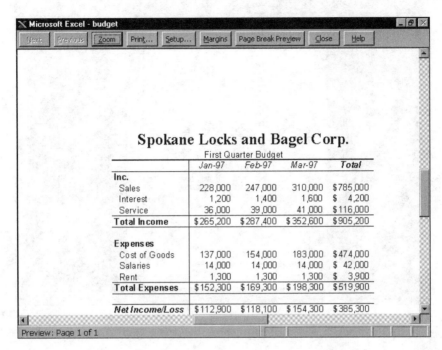

Figure 7.12 *The zoomed preview.*

You can zoom out by clicking anywhere on the page or clicking on the **Zoom** button at the top of the Preview screen. The Next and Previous buttons let you preview the next and previous pages in multiple-page documents. The Setup button takes you back to the Page Setup dialog box.

One unique feature on the Preview screen is the Margins button. Clicking on the Margins button in Print Preview allows you to make changes by dragging margin and column markers so you can see the result prior to printing (see Figure 7.13).

15. Click on the **Margins** button.

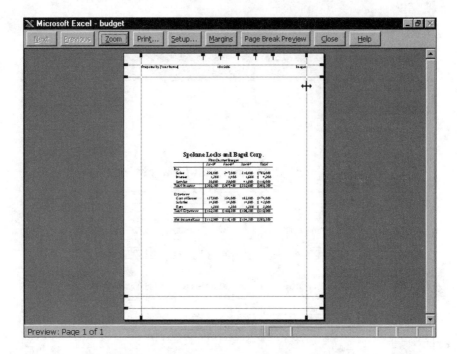

Figure 7.13 *The margin markers displayed in Print Preview.*

By moving the mouse pointer over one of the markers until it turns into a double-sided arrow, as shown in Figure 7.13, you can reposition any of the margins or columns by dragging. The status bar displays information about which margin or column you are changing and its position as you drag.

You don't need to change any of the margins here, so it's time to print. Be sure your printer is properly connected, has paper, is turned on, on line, and ready to print.

16. Click on the **Print...** button to bring up the Print dialog box.

17. Click **OK** to send the worksheet to the printer.

You will briefly see a message dialog box informing you that your document is printing. In a few seconds, your printed worksheet should appear.

The next time you want to print the same worksheet using the same settings, simply click on the Standard toolbar's **Print** button (see Figure 7.14).

Figure 7.14 *The Print button.*

To go directly to Print Preview, click on the Standard toolbar's **Print Preview** button, as shown in Figure 7.15.

Figure 7.15 *The Print Preview button.*

18.   Save your work so the print setting is retained for the next time you want to print, and exit Excel if you aren't moving on to the next chapter.

A FINAL THOUGHT

The process of setting up your pages for printing and sending them to your printer should be a piece of cake by now. In the next chapter you'll learn how to turn your worksheet's text and numbers into beautiful charts and graphics.

CHAPTER 8

Creating a Chart

As the old saying goes, a picture is worth a thousand words. If you have ever thought of a chart as a nice little extra, or even a waste of time and energy, think again!

If the purpose of your worksheet is to increase your readers' understanding of the numerical data and to persuade them to accept your point of view, then adding a chart is much more than a frill. It is an integral part of the information package. A chart can enhance clarity and add strength to your message.

Until now we have been working strictly with numerical data. You can't deny the importance of numbers—just try sending a bunch of pictures to the IRS and see how far you get! But often, numeric data is just a means to an end. A chart can enable you to direct your readers' focus and make your points with pizzazz.

CHART FUNDAMENTALS

Before you start creating charts, you need to understand some fundamental chart concepts and terminology. After all, the world of charts is very different from the worksheet world we have been working with until now. We really are charting new territory here (sorry about that—we just couldn't help ourselves).

If some of the terminology we are about to cover seems a bit murky and arcane, don't worry. As we progress through the steps in this chapter, the fog will lift. Excel makes preparing charts automatic enough that you do not need to master all the details to be able to create good looking charts. However, an understanding of charting basics increases your comfort level and allows you to prepare even more powerful charts.

Chart Elements

A *chart* is a graphical representation of the numeric data in a worksheet. Each cell (piece of data) represented in the chart is called a *data point*. Data points are represented on the chart by bars, columns, lines, or some other graphical device. A group of related data points is called a *data series*. For example, if you were charting the quarter's monthly income compared with expenses, each month's income or expense figure would be a data point. The January, February, and March income figures are one data series and the January, February, and March expense figures are another data series.

Typically, values are plotted along the vertical plane (y-axis) and categories are plotted along the horizontal plane (x-axis). Labels that run horizontally under the various data series and display the categories represented are *x-axis labels*. Labels running vertically and listing the value increments are *y-axis labels*. Tick marks on the axes are the small lines that indicate different data categories or increments of value. The plot area of the chart is the area that includes the axes lines and all the data series.

Chart text is a label that identifies items in the chart. If you attach it to an object (like a data point) in the chart, it is unmovable. If the chart text is not attached to an object, it can be moved. You can also add gridlines to your chart to help identify the values. Notice that the chart consists of data series, which are the two sets of bars in Figure 8.1. In a line chart, the data series would be the lines. Data series are made up of a number of data points, which are the individual bars or points on a line.

Figure 8.1 *A typical column chart with the basic chart elements.*

Most charts include a title, a legend to help clarify what each data series represents, a y-axis title, and an x-axis title. Many other elements can be added to a chart and all of the chart elements can be customized to suit your requirements, but these are the most common elements you find in a chart.

Figure 8.1 shows a typical chart with the data series represented by columns. This is called a *column chart*.

Use Excel's Chart Wizard to step through the chart creation process. You can create charts that are embedded in the worksheet, or place charts on their own chart sheets if you want to print charts on separate pages from the worksheet data to use for handouts. You might want to incorporate chart files in a presentation graphics program such as Microsoft PowerPoint. Embedded charts are placed on the same worksheet as the data they represent. Using an embedded chart, you can see the chart and numerical data at the same time.

Whether a chart is embedded or on a chart sheet, it is linked to the data it represents. This means if the numbers change, the chart changes to reflect the new numbers.

UNDERSTANDING CHART TYPES

Excel lets you choose from a dizzying array of chart types. To add to your decision-making burden, you can also choose from a variety of formats for each of the chart types. So how do you decide which chart type to use for a particular situation? There are no hard and fast rules. However, if you understand the primary intended uses for each of Excel's chart types, the choice is easier.

COLUMN CHARTS

Excel's default chart type is the column chart. *Column charts* are made up of vertical columns representing data series. They are often used for comparing two or more related data series at a specific point in time, or a small amount of data over time. Excel provides options for several column chart formats, including clustered columns, three-dimensional (3D) columns, and stacked columns, as shown in Figure 8.2.

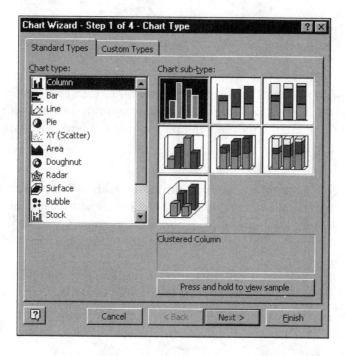

Figure 8.2 *The various Column chart formats.*

The stacked column formats are useful for displaying how much a piece of data contributes to the aggregate. A clustered column is the best choice for column charts representing only one data series, since each series uses a different color or pattern.

In addition to the array of two-dimensional column charts, there are also several three-dimensional column chart formats. Choosing a three-dimensional chart versus a two-dimensional chart is mostly a matter of aesthetics. However, the third dimension gives an additional axis—the Z (value) axis.

Bar Charts

Bar charts are column charts turned on their side—the columns are horizontal instead of vertical. Just as with the column charts, there are clustered bars, 3-D bars, and stacked bars. Figure 8.3 shows the bar chart formats.

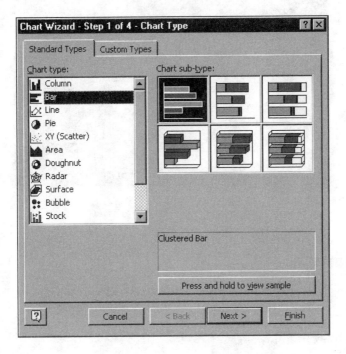

Figure 8.3 *The Bar chart formats.*

Line Charts

Use *line charts* to emphasize the continuity of data over time. They are also a good choice for showing trends. They are especially useful for showing large sets of data, such as the sales of a product over a five-year period. Figure 8.4 shows the line chart formats.

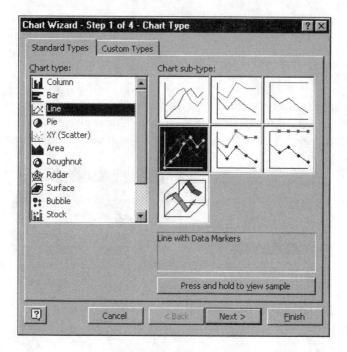

Figure 8.4 *The Line chart formats.*

Pie Charts

Pie charts are great for displaying proportional relationships between data, such as the share each bagel flavor contributes to the hole, er, whole. The pie chart's primary limitation is that it can only display one data series. Figure 8.5 shows the pie chart formats.

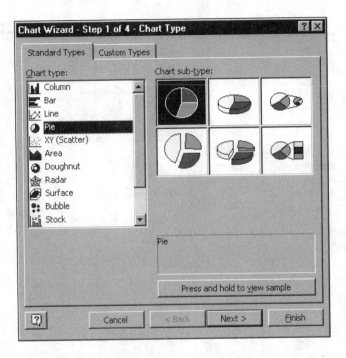

Figure 8.5 *The Pie chart formats.*

Pie charts are also available as 3-D charts. Unlike 3-D column and bar charts, 3-D pie charts do not gain an additional axis. Their only advantage is their different appearance.

XY (Scatter Charts)

Unlike the other chart types discussed so far, *XY (scatter) charts* use both axes for values. This allows you to plot relationships between two data series, such as the effects of temperature on an electronic component's failure rate. Figure 8.6 shows the XY chart formats.

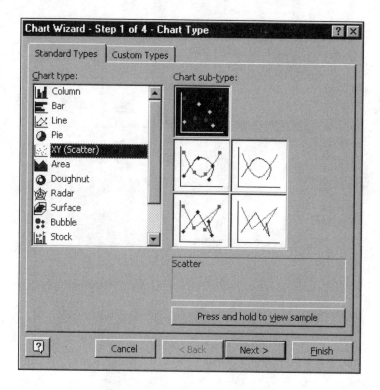

Figure 8.6 *The XY (Scatter) chart formats.*

Area Charts

Area charts are essentially line charts with the space between the lines filled in. Like 3-D column and bar charts, 3-D line charts have an additional axis. Figure 8.7 shows the area chart formats.

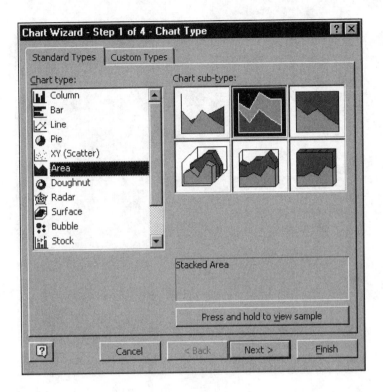

Figure 8.7 *The Area chart formats.*

Doughnut Charts

Doughnut charts are much like pie charts, and both are used for the same purpose. The one advantage of doughnut charts is that they can be used to plot more than one data series. A doughnut chart with more than one data series uses a separate ring for each series. Figure 8.8 shows the doughnut chart formats.

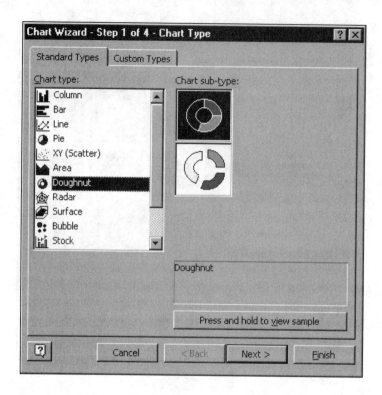

Figure 8.8 *The Doughnut chart formats.*

Radar Charts

Radar charts are similar to line charts, but are often used for comparing the whole value of several data series. Figure 8.9 shows the radar chart formats.

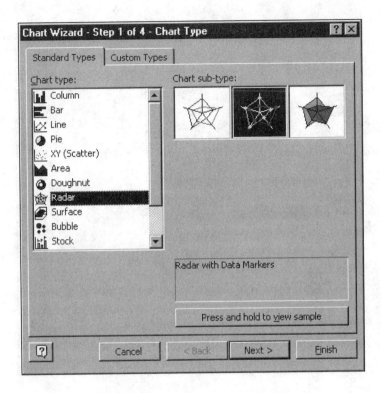

Figure 8.9 *The Radar chart formats.*

Surface Charts

Surface charts are similar to 3-D area charts. Surface charts are useful when searching for optimum combinations between two sets of data. Figure 8.10 shows the surface chart formats.

Figure 8.10 The Surface chart formats.

Bubble Charts

Bubble charts are a type of XY (Scatter) chart. The size of the data marker is used to plot the value of a third value. Figure 8.11 shows the bubble chart formats.

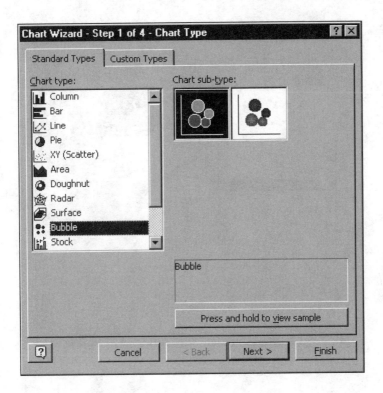

Figure 8.11 *The Bubble chart formats.*

Stock Chart

Stock charts utilize two value axes instead of just one. One axis is used to measure the volume of stock, and the other is used to chart stock prices. Several of the line chart format options are particularly useful for charting highs and lows, such as snowfalls or stocks, and are sometimes referred to as *Hi-Lo* and *Hi-Lo-Close* charts. Figure 8.12 shows the stock chart formats.

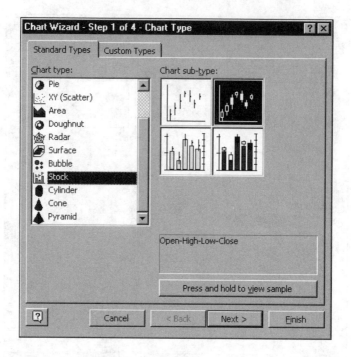

Figure 8.12 *The Stock chart formats.*

Cone, Cylinder, and Pyramid Charts

Cone, cylinder, and *pyramid* charts operate under the same principles as column and bar charts. Cone, cylinder, and pyramid charts are useful when you want a dramatic 3-D chart presentation. Figures 8.13–8.15 illustrate these three chart formats.

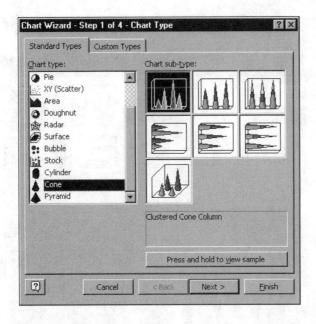

Figure 8.13 *The Cone chart formats.*

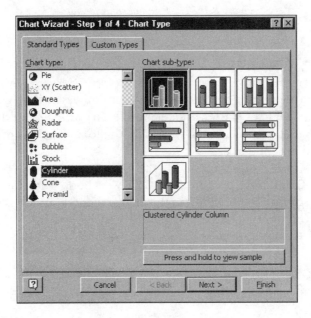

Figure 8.14 *The Cylinder chart formats.*

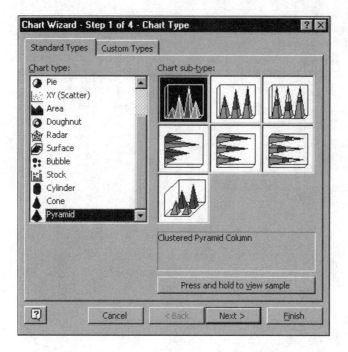

Figure 8.15 *The Pyramid chart formats.*

CREATING CHARTS

Let's start out by creating a chart next to the numbers in the Spokane Locks and Bagels Corp. First Quarter Budget. You'll start with a chart that plots the first quarter's total income. Later, you'll add the total expenses over the three month period for comparison.

1. Start Excel and open the **BUDGET** workbook if it is not already on your screen. The first step in the chart creation process is to select the data you want included in the chart.

2. Select the ranges A3 through D3 and A8 through D8. Don't forget to use the **Ctrl** key to select noncontiguous ranges. We included the empty cell A3 in the first range because the Chart Wizard understands how to deal with selections if each spans the same number of columns.

   Although this example does not show it, you do not have to select complete elements when creating your chart. You can select any element of your worksheet to include in your chart. For example, you might want to create a chart that compares the Sales Income and Salary Expenses for January and February. You can select an entire block of data to chart if you like; the number of columns and rows you choose determines the number of data series and plot points in your chart. For more information on how your data selection affects the data series in your chart, see "Editing Charts" later in this chapter. One caveat: don't include totals in a chart that also plots the values making up the total. For example, if you create a chart that plots the Income lines in our example worksheet (rows 4 through 7) then don't include the total in row 8.

3. Click on the Standard toolbar's **Chart Wizard** button, as shown in Figure 8.16.

Figure 8.16 *The **Chart Wizard** button.*

The first Chart Wizard dialog box appears, as shown in Figure 8.17. This dialog box allows you to choose from among 14 different chart types. From these, you can then choose between numerous sub-types. The default is the clustered column chart, which is a fine choice for the type of data you are plotting. To choose a different chart type, simply click on the one of your choice.

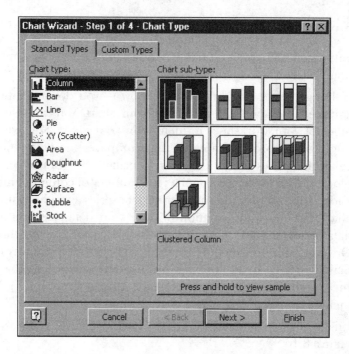

Figure 8.17 *The Chart Wizard's Chart Type dialog box.*

NOTE

As discussed earlier in the chapter, there is no one correct choice when choosing chart types. Fortunately, Excel makes it easy to experiment with various chart types to see how your data is best presented. You may even choose to present the same data with more than one chart type to draw attention to different aspects of the data.

If you want to get a sneak preview of how your chart is going to look, just click and hold the **Press and hold to view sample** button.

4. Click the **Next** button to move to the Chart Source Data dialog box, as displayed in Figure 8.18.

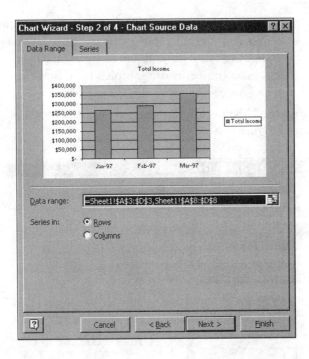

Figure 8.18 *The Chart Source Data dialog box.*

NOTE If you ever want to go back to the previous Chart Wizard dialog box to make a different selection, you can click on the **Back** button. You can click on the **Finish** button to have the Chart Wizard complete your chart based on the defaults for the following Chart Wizard dialog boxes.

The Data Range and Series text boxes display the ranges and series you selected in step two. The dollar sign ($) in front of each column letter and row number indicate that these are absolute references. These references won't change if the data is moved or copied.

The next piece of information the Chart Wizard wants to know is which row or rows to use for the Category axis (the horizontal, or x-axis) labels.

The first row you selected to chart was row 3, which included the column headings *Jan, Feb,* and *Mar*—your category labels—so you don't have to change anything here. If you squint, you can see Jan, Feb, and Mar under the columns in the sample chart. Since everything looks good, you can move on to the next dialog box.

5.   Click on the **Next** button to move to the Chart Options dialog box, as shown in Figure 8.19.

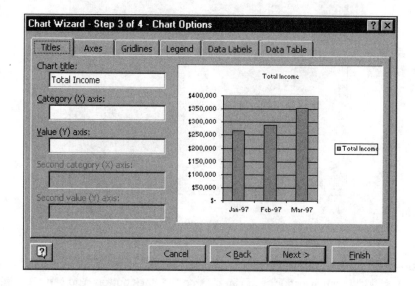

***Figure 8.19** The Chart Options dialog box.*

This box is where you can turn on and off some of the standard options that come with the chart type you selected. By clicking on the tabs, you can work with titles, axes, gridlines, legends, data labels, and data tables. Let's change the chart title.

6. Click in the **Chart Title** text box and type **First Quarter Income vs. Expenses**. If you click in or tab to another text box, the Sample Chart portion of the dialog box will be updated to display the title.

    You can also add titles to the category (x) axis and the value (y) axis. Let's add a value axis title to show that the numbers indicate dollars, which will be helpful when you remove those distracting dollar signs later.

7. Click in the **Value (Y)** text box and type **Dollars**.

8. Click on the **Next** button to move to the Chart Location dialog box, as shown in Figure 8.20. In the Chart Location dialog box, you can choose between inserting your chart in an existing worksheet or creating an entirely new page. You'll need to have this chart in Sheet1, so just go ahead and click on the **Finish** button.

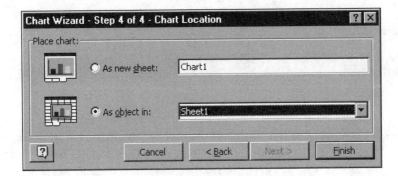

Figure 8.20 *The Chart Location dialog box.*

As shown in Figure 8.21, the chart is now part of your worksheet. Upon placing the chart in the worksheet, Excel automatically displays the Chart toolbar near the chart. If the Chart toolbar doesn't appear, just right-click on the Standard or Formatting toolbar (not on a tool) and then click on **Chart** in the shortcut menu.

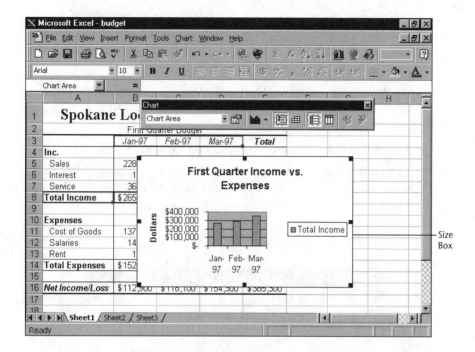

Figure 8.21 The chart and Chart toolbar.

If the Chart toolbar obstructs the chart elements you want to manipulate, you can position the mouse pointer over its title bar and drag it out of the way. You can also remove the Chart toolbar from the screen by clicking the **Close** box in its upper-left corner. For now, you'll need to keep the Chart toolbar around while you manipulate some of the chart's properties.

Moving and Sizing Charts

Now that you've created your chart, you'll need to move it to another area of your worksheet so it's not on top of your data.

1. Click once on the chart. Small black boxes, called *size boxes*, appear. The chart is selected, or activated, when the size boxes appear.

2. Point to the chart area (not the sides) and hold down the mouse button as you drag it to column F.

If you need to move the chart further than you can drag it, use the Cut and Paste commands from the Edit menu. Just click on the chart to select it, choose **Edit**, **Cut**, then click on a cell to mark the destination area and choose **Edit**, **Paste**. This is also a good way to move a chart to a different worksheet inside the workbook.

You can also change the size and shape of the chart by selecting it and using the size boxes.

1. Click once on the chart so the size boxes appear.

2. Click and drag on any of the size boxes, as shown in Figure 8.22.

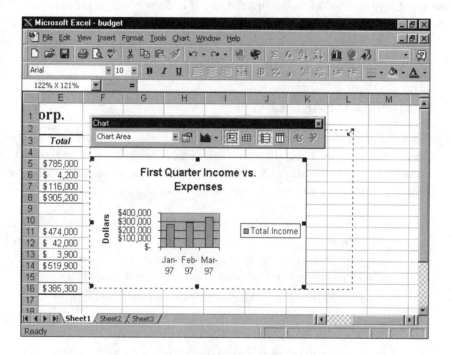

Figure 8.22 *Resizing the chart.*

Dragging on the side or corner size boxes changes the size of the chart. If you hold down the **Shift** key while dragging on a corner box, you can reduce or enlarge the chart size without changing its proportions.

Deleting Charts

If the chart you've created in your worksheet just isn't what you wanted, you can always delete it and start over. Simply select the chart as you would to move or size it, and press the **Delete** button. This will have no affect on your worksheet data; it simply removes the chart from the worksheet. You can start the process over again if you like.

Copying Charts

Copying a chart is also accomplished by first selecting it. Then you can either use the **Copy** button on the toolbar or use the **Copy** command from the Edit menu. Move to the destination range by highlighting a cell in any worksheet, then click the **Paste** button or use the **Paste** command in the Edit menu. The copy will chart exactly the same data as the original chart.

CHANGING CHART DATA

Charts are linked to the underlying data in the worksheet. When you change the values in the worksheet, the chart will automatically update to reflect the new numbers. To prove the chart really is linked to the worksheet data, let's change some of the worksheet data and see how the chart is affected.

1. Click on any of the worksheet cells outside the chart area to deactivate it, and scroll left until column A is visible. The Chart toolbar usually disappears from the screen when the chart isn't selected. Let's change the Sales figure in cell D5 to reflect a more optimistic forecast.

2. Enter **500000** in cell D5 (Mar-95 Sales), and then scroll right until the chart is visible again. Observe the change in the March Total Income column, as displayed in Figure 8.23.

3. Now change cell D5 in the worksheet back to **310000** and see that the chart returns to its original figures.

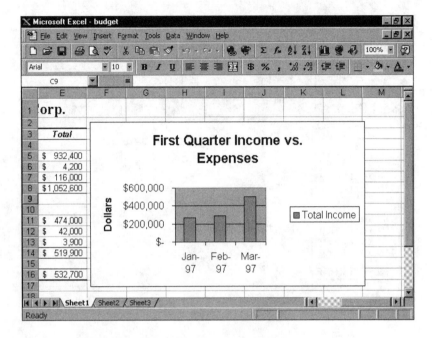

Figure 8.23 *The chart reflects changes to the original data.*

You can also change the March Total Income column directly on the chart by activating it and changing the data elements.

1.   Click the chart frame to select the chart. This brings back the Chart toolbar, and you can now select individual elements in the chart.

2.   Select the **March Total Income** column by clicking on it once, pausing a moment and clicking it again. The selected column has small resizing boxes around its edges, as shown in Figure 8.24.

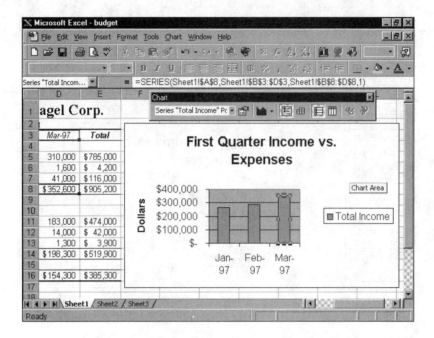

Figure 8.24 Selecting a data point.

3. Move your mouse pointer to the top of the March Total Income col-
    umn, and drag the resizing box to the $500,000 mark (use the box
    that appears above the selected column to track the change in value).

    When you release the mouse button, Excel will display a dialog box
    (Shown in Figure 8.25) asking you how it should modify the resulting
    value on your worksheet. In other words, which cell do you want to
    adjust to achieve your projection?

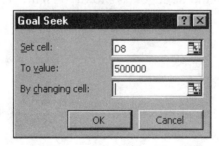

Figure 8.25 Changing chart values by adjusting chart data points.

4. For this example, we want to change cell D8 by changing the value in cell D5. Enter **D5** in the By changing cell portion of the Goal Seek dialog box and click **OK**.

5. Excel will ask if you want to accept the solution it has worked out. Click **OK**, and now look at your worksheet—you'll see that the change has been reflected in the appropriate cells.

CHANGING CHART TYPES

Just to see how easy it is to change chart types, let's use the Chart toolbar to display your data as a line chart. First, make sure the chart frame is selected and the size boxes are visible.

1. Click on the **Chart Type** toolbar button on the Chart toolbar to display the drop-down chart list, as shown in Figure 8.26.

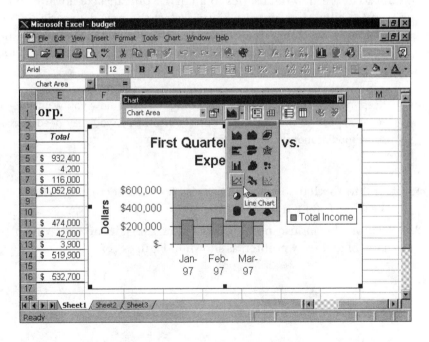

Figure 8.26 The Chart toolbar's drop-down list of chart types.

2. Click on the **Line Chart** button in the drop-down list of chart types
    (The mouse pointer is pointing to this button in Figure 8.26). This
    line chart doesn't show the comparison between income and
    expenses as clearly as the column chart, so you can change it back.

3. Click on the **Chart Type** button and select the **Column Chart** type.

EDITING CHARTS

You've already seen how you can edit a chart by changing the value in a cell of
the worksheet—or by changing the value of the data points in the chart itself.
This section shows some other ways to edit the chart's data, such as adding a
new data series to the chart or removing a data series.

Adding a New Data Series

If you want to add a new data series to a chart, you can take advantage of a
unique feature called *drag and plot*. Simply select the new data series in your
worksheet, drag it onto the chart and release the mouse button. The new
series is automatically added to the chart. Even the data series label is added
to the legend if you include the label in the selection.

NOTE   Keep in mind that Excel makes its best guess as to how you want the data
series applied to the chart. If it guesses incorrectly, you may need to make
some modifications manually.

1. Scroll to the left so column A is visible and select cells A14 through
    D14 (The Total Expenses for the quarter).

2. Position the mouse pointer just below the selection so it is in the
    shape of an arrow pointer, as shown in Figure 8.27.

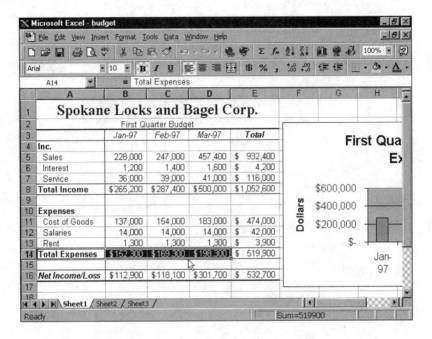

Figure 8.27 *A new data series ready to be added to the chart.*

3. Hold down the left mouse button and drag to the right until the mouse pointer is within the visible chart boundaries, then release the mouse button.

4. Scroll to the right so the entire chart is visible, as shown in Figure 8.28.

WARNING

Numbers formatted using the toolbar buttons, or the Accounting category in the Format Cells dialog box, may not be usable as a data series. If you run into a problem, reformat the numbers using the Number, Percentage, or Currency categories in the Number tab of the Format Cells dialog box.

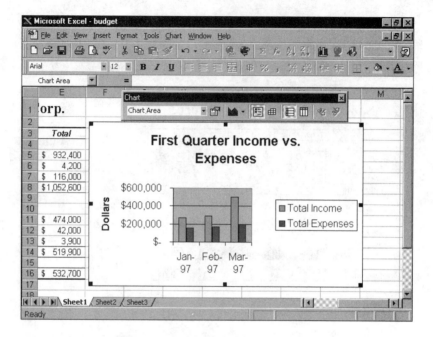

Figure 8.28 *The chart with a new data series added.*

Removing a Data Series

Let's remove the data series you just added. As you're about to see, removing a data series is as simple as a click of the mouse.

1. Click on the chart frame to select the chart. The heavy outline and size boxes should be visible.

2. Select one of the Total Expenses columns by clicking on it once. The selected column should now have a size box in the middle, as do the other columns in this data series.

3. Press the **Delete** key and all the Total Expenses columns will be removed from the chart.

Data Series Orientation

You've already seen how the chart type you select can affect the impact of your data. Now let's experiment with how the orientation of the chart data affects its interpretation. When you select chart data, it's important to keep in mind whether you want to use the rows or columns on your worksheet to represent the data series on your chart. This is called *data orientation*. As you found out earlier in the chapter, you can present a data series in a column, line, pie chart, and so on.

Figure 8.28 shows how rows of your worksheet became a data series in a column chart. The data series is from the Total Income row, with columns for the categories of January, February and March. Now let's change that data series orientation so the categories (Jan, Feb, Mar) become the data series, and the Total Income row becomes the categories.

1. Click on the chart to select it (if it's not already selected) and then click on the **Chart Wizard** button.

2. Step 1 of the Chart Wizard dialog box appears. Click **Next**.

3. In the Series in portion of the second dialog box, click on the **Columns** option.

4. Click on the **Finish** button.

So, what do you think? Looking at your chart, as shown in Figure 8.29, you can see how the impact of the chart has changed. Notice that the chart now plots the months as a data series within the Total Income axis. You have three bars across one period, rather than one bar across three periods.

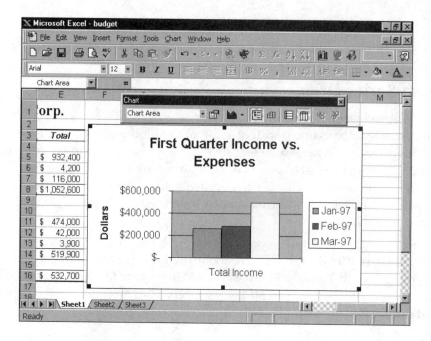

Figure 8.29 *Changing the orientation of the chart.*

For some of the upcoming exercises you'll need to use the rows of your worksheet to represent the data series on your chart. To change things back, follow these steps:

1. Click on the chart to select it, and then click on the **Chart Wizard** button.
2. Click **Next** after the Step 1 of the Chart Wizard dialog box appears.
3. In the Series in portion of the second dialog box, select the **Rows** option.
4. Click on the **Finish** button.

CREATING CHARTS IN CHART SHEETS

There may be times when you want to make a separate chart from the data on your worksheet. You can perform the same manipulations on a chart in a chart sheet as in an embedded chart. The only difference is that you can't see the data the chart is based on while the chart is on the screen.

The steps for creating a chart in a chart sheet are essentially the same as those for creating an embedded chart. Let's make a chart comparing the Spokane Locks and Bagel Corp.'s Net Income/Loss for the quarter.

1. Select the ranges A3 through D3 and A16 through D16 and then click the **Chart Wizard** button. The first Chart Wizard dialog box appears, just as it did when creating an embedded chart.

2. Click on the **Pie** chart type and then click the **Next** button. The Chart Source Data dialog box appears.

3. Click the **Next** button to accept the selected ranges and move to the third Chart Wizard dialog box.

4. Click the **Legend** tab in the Chart Options dialog box and deselect the **Show legend** option by clicking on it. The Legend tab is pictured in Figure 8.30.

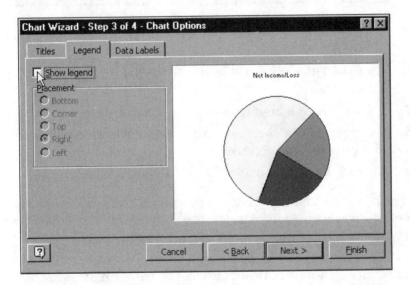

Figure 8.30 *The Legend tab of the Chart Options dialog box.*

5. Click the **Data Labels** tab and select the **Show percent** option. The Data Labels tab is shown in Figure 8.31.

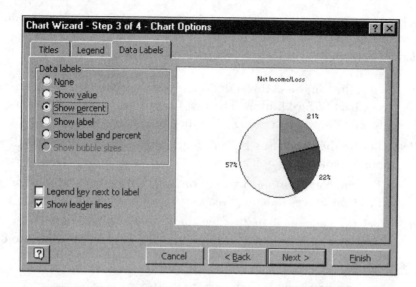

Figure 8.31 *The Data Labels tab of the Chart Options dialog box.*

6. Click the **Titles** tab and enter **Pie in the Sky Projection** in the Chart Title text box.

7. Click the **Next** button to move to the **Chart Location** dialog box.

8. Select the **As new sheet** option and type **Pie in the Sky Projection** in the corresponding text box.

9. Click the **Finish** button.

The completed pie chart appears in a chart sheet that is inserted in front of the worksheet containing the data it is based on (as shown in Figure 8.32).

You can use exactly the same techniques to format any of the chart elements in a chart sheet that you'd use with an embedded chart. The only step you can omit is double-clicking on the chart to activate it. When a chart sheet is visible, the chart is active and you can manipulate the chart elements.

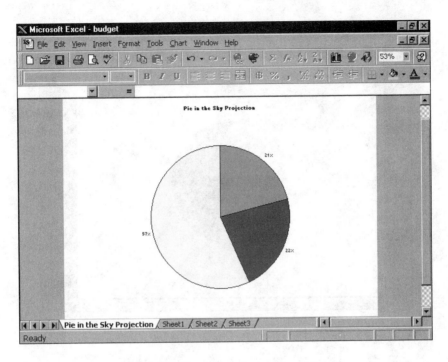

Figure 8.32 The pie chart in its own worksheet.

PRINTING CHARTS

You can print embedded charts in exactly the same way as other portions of a worksheet. Just include the embedded chart in the print range and you're all ready to go.

Printing a chart on a chart sheet is even easier than printing an embedded chart, since there is no range to select. Of course it is still a good idea to use Print Preview before printing a document to make sure everything is set up properly.

1.   Click the **Print Preview** button on the Formatting toolbar to display a preview of the printed page, as displayed in Figure 8.33.

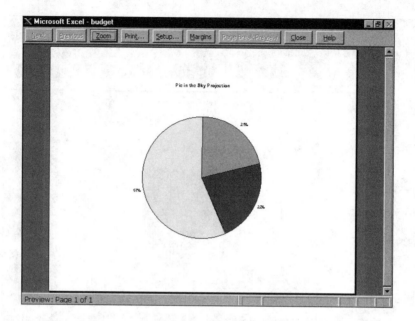

Figure 8.33 *The Print Preview screen for the chart sheet.*

2. When you're ready to print the chart, check to make sure your printer is turned on, on-line, and has paper loaded. Then click on the **Print** button.

3. Click on the **Sheet1** tab to move back to the worksheet containing your original data.

4. Save your work and exit Excel if you're not continuing on to the next chapter at this time.

When you save your work, you're saving the entire workbook, so you don't need to save the chart sheet separately from the worksheet.

N O T E

A FINAL THOUGHT

You have now learned how to turn numbers into dazzling charts that are sure to add punch to your presentations and help you persuade even the most skeptical of people. In the next chapter, you'll learn how to enhance and customize your charts using Excel's powerful chart formatting features.

CHAPTER 9

Enhancing Charts and Drawing

Now that you know how to create a chart, it's time to learn about some of Excel's snazzy chart enhancement features. In this chapter, you'll learn about formatting different parts of a chart, such as changing the color of the chart's background. You'll also learn about using Excel's drawing tools to annotate your charts and worksheets. There are many, many ways to enhance and customize your charts; this chapter will cover some of the main components. Exploration is your greatest teacher in this subject, so have some fun with it.

SELECTING CHART ELEMENTS

Before you can customize the different parts of a chart, you must first know how to select them. The following discussion helps you understand how to select chart elements so you can manipulate and customize them. You've already learned about clicking on a chart once to display the small size boxes around it. By doing so, you can click on any of the elements in the chart to alter them. Let's illustrate.

1. Start Excel and open the Budget worksheet if it isn't already on your screen.

2. Select **Sheet1** and click anywhere inside your chart. Notice the size boxes as shown in Figure 9.1.

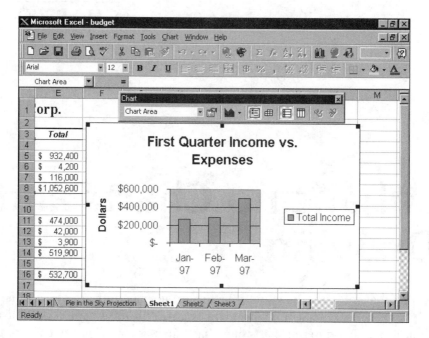

Figure 9.1 *Selecting the chart.*

3. Click once on the **March** column. Notice that when you selected the one bar for March, you selected the entire data series. As a result, the bars for January and February are also selected.

4. Click once more on **March**. Black size boxes now surround the March column, indicating that it is selected, as shown in Figure 9.2.

5. Click once outside of the chart to deselect it. Now let's see what happens when you double-click on your chart.

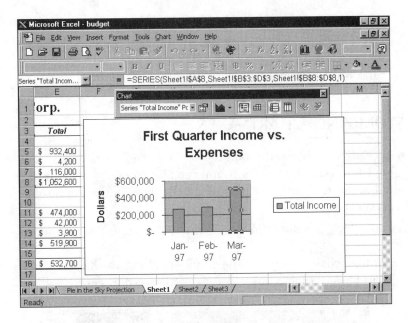

Figure 9.2 *Selecting a single column in the chart.*

6. Double-click on the chart or chart frame. The Format Chart Area dialog box appears, as shown in Figure 9.3.

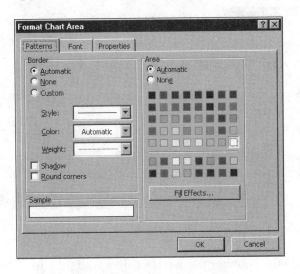

Figure 9.3 *The Format Chart Area dialog box.*

You can change a multitude of chart settings in the Format Chart Area dialog box. This is the place to go when you want to administer formatting changes for the entire chart.

7. Click on the **Cancel** button.

CUSTOMIZING CHART AXES

You've already experienced changing the value (y) axis in the section on Changing Chart Data in Chapter 8. You can also change the way numbers are formatted along the value (y) axis so they make a better representation of your worksheet data.

Let's try changing the values along the value axis and see what happens.

1. Double-click on one of the numbers along the value (y) axis. The Format Axis dialog box will appear, as shown in Figure 9.4.

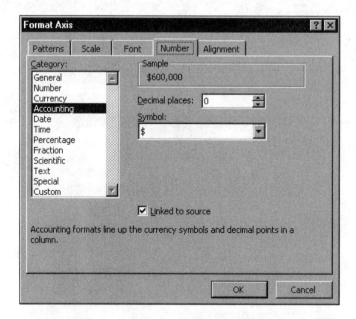

Figure 9.4 *The Number tab in the Format Axis dialog box.*

2. Click on the **Number** tab, if it isn't already highlighted. This dialog box should look familiar to you. It's almost the same as the number portion of the Format Cells dialog box used earlier in the book. The check box

in the lower half of the dialog box tells you that the formatting for the numbers along the value (y) axis are linked to the source.

This means that whatever formatting was applied to the data series being represented is being used here. While this is often a good assumption, you need to make a change here. You don't need to uncheck the **Link to Source** check box because, as soon as you choose another number format, Excel understands the formatting is no longer linked to the source and removes the check mark.

3. In the Category list, click on the word **Custom**.

4. In the Type text box, enter the custom format **##0,** (include the comma at the end). This format will display the numbers in thousands. In other words, the number 200,000 will be displayed as 200.

Now, let's spruce up your chart by changing the font of the value (y) axis labels to italics.

5. Click on the **Font** tab of the Format Axis dialog box. This section (Figure 9.5) should also look familiar to you. It is identical to the Font section in the Format Cell dialog box. Let's keep Arial as the default font and change its style.

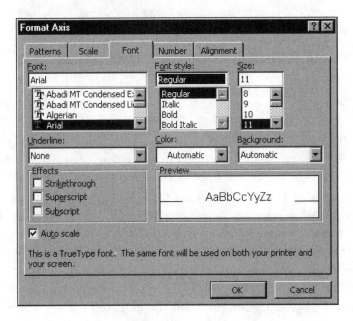

Figure 9.5 *The Font tab in the Format Axis dialog box.*

6. Click on **Italic** as the Font Style. Now let's try adding a few more tick marks, changing the color of your value (y) axis, and changing the increments of the value (y) axis labels.

7. Select the **Patterns** tab from the Format Axis dialog box, as shown in Figure 9.6.

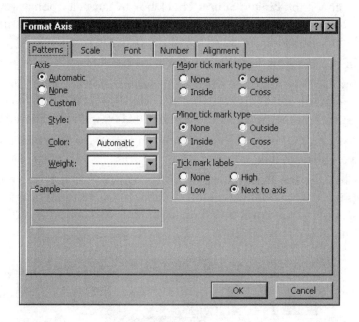

Figure 9.6 *The Patterns tab in the Format Axis dialog box.*

If you preferred not to have a value (y) axis, you could click **None** in the Axis area.

8. Click on the **Color** drop-down menu and select a shade of blue. This action will change the color of the value (y) axis from black to blue.

9. Make sure **Outside** is selected for both Major and Minor tick mark types. Minor tick marks will give you additional hashes on the value (y) axis. If you didn't want to show the tick mark labels, also referred to as the value (y) axis labels, you would select **None** in the Tick mark labels area. If you wanted your tick mark labels on the right side of your chart, you would select **High** in the Tick mark labels area.

Finally, because your chart was incremented on a per 100,000 basis, let's increase the increments so it's not overcrowded with numbers.

10. Select the **Scale** tab from the Format Axis dialog box, as illustrated in Figure 9.7.

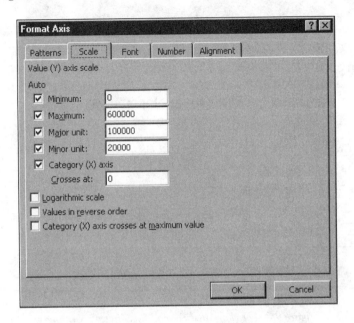

Figure 9.7 The Scale tab in the Format Axis dialog box.

The Scale tab allows you to change the way values are represented on your value (y) axis. It displays the minimum value of zero and maximum value of 400,000. When the Auto text box is activated, Excel selects these values. However, you can customize these options to suit your own needs. For instance, let's have your value (y) axis labels increment by 150,000.

11. Type **150000** in the Major Unit text box. Are you ready to see all the changes you've made to your chart?

12. Click on the **OK** button. Your chart should look like Figure 9.8. See how the value (y) axis labels have been simplified to only three digits? Also, notice they have taken on a fancier, italic look. Moreover, there are now fewer labels because they are being incremented every $150,000. Finally, if you have a color monitor, you can see that your axis is now blue.

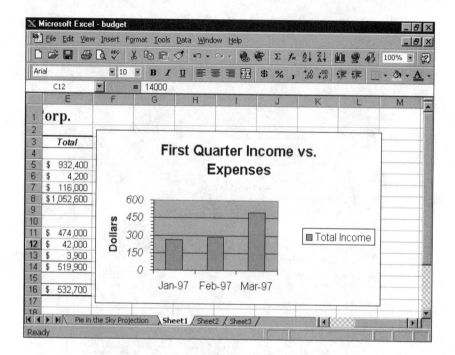

Figure 9.8 *The chart after Format Axis dialog box changes.*

CUSTOMIZING CHART TEXT

Now that you've changed the chart axis values, you need to let people know that the dollar values are shown in thousands. You can change the value axis label to add the appropriate information.

1. Click once on the **Dollars** label along the value axis. Notice that a text box is now visible.

2. Click once again on the **Dollars** label. This time the label changes position and a cursor is available for you to make changes.

3.   Type **(in thousands)** at the end of the label, as shown in Figure 9.9.

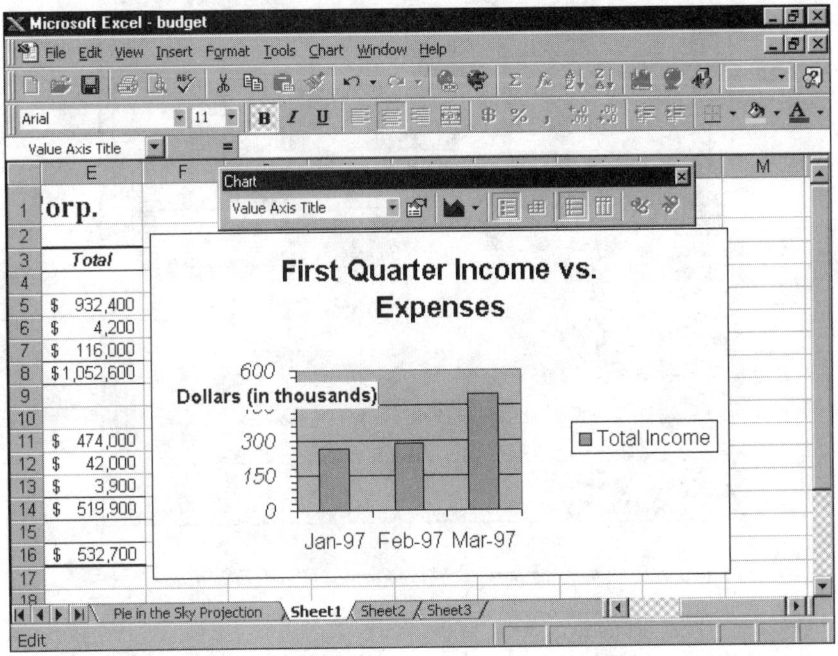

Figure 9.9 *Changing chart text.*

4.   Click outside the chart frame to move the text changes in place.

CUSTOMIZING CHART FONT

Now let's change the font and size of the chart title.

1.   Double-click on the chart title (**First Quarter Income vs. Expenses**) to display the Format Chart Title dialog box, as shown in Figure 9.10. Click on the **Font** tab if it isn't already selected.

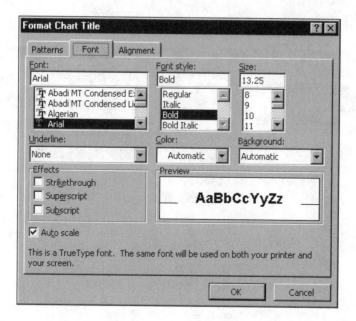

Figure 9.10 *The Font portion of the Format Chart Title dialog box.*

As you can see, this dialog box is the same as the Format Cells dialog box you used in Chapter 6. The default font is Arial, its style is bold, and its size is 12 point. Let's change the title's font to Times New Roman, bold italic, 18 point.

2. Scroll down the Font list and click on **Times New Roman**. Select **Bold Italic** in the Font Style list, and then click on **18** in the Size list.

3. To implement these changes, click the **OK** button. Your screen should now look like Figure 9.11.

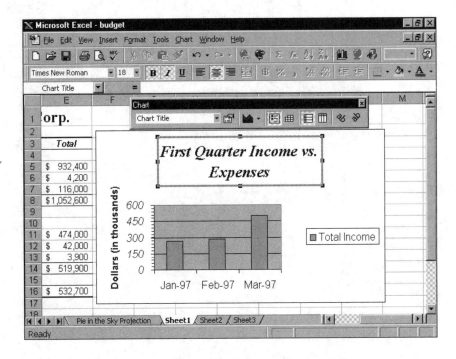

Figure 9.11 *The chart with its newly formatted title.*

Since the title font is larger, it takes up too much room. Let's modify the title to be more concise.

4. Double-click anywhere on the word **Expenses** to highlight it. Press the **Delete** key to remove the word.

5. Double-click on the word **vs.** to highlight it. Remove this word by pressing the **Delete** key. Your chart should now look like Figure 9.12.

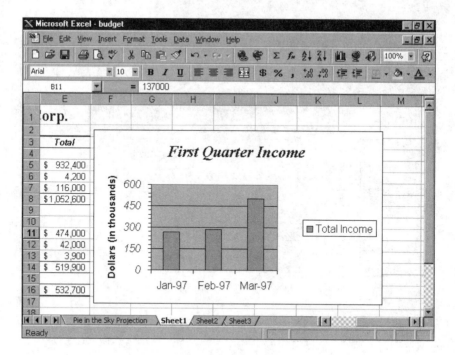

Figure 9.12 *The new title.*

Click outside of the chart area to completely view the changes. Your chart is definitely shaping up, and we're not done yet.

CUSTOMIZING THE PLOT AREA

Notice how the changes you made to the main title reduced the size of the chart. Let's enlarge the chart's plot area.

1. Click once inside the plot area, being careful not to click on any of the gridlines. The plot area should now be outlined with size boxes, as shown in Figure 9.13.

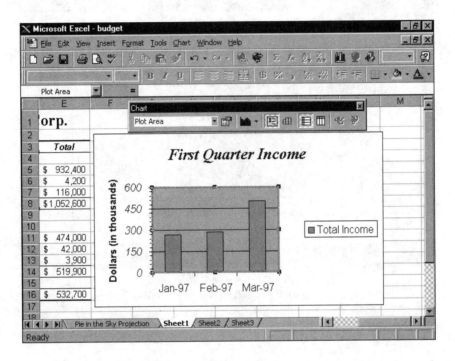

Figure 9.13 *Selecting the plot area.*

2. Move the mouse pointer over the size box in the upper-right corner of the plot area so it transforms into a double-sided arrow.

3. Hold down the left mouse button and drag up and to the right. Your plot area will expand, as shown in Figure 9.14.

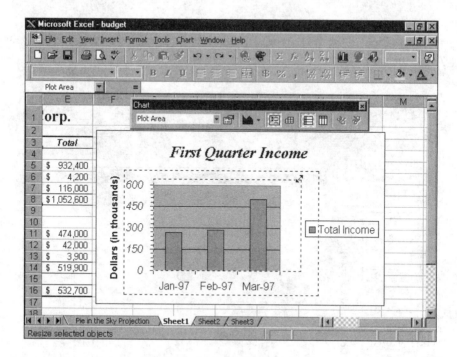

Figure 9.14 Expanding the plot area.

4.   Release the mouse button to view the new plot area.

CUSTOMIZING DATA SERIES

Excel allows you to change the color and pattern of any data series, which is especially useful if you're printing to a color printer. Let's change the color of your Total Income data series to yellow with a red border.

1.   Double-click on one of the **Total Income** columns.

2.   Click on the **Patterns** tab in the Format Data Series dialog box if it isn't already selected. Figure 9.15 shows the Patterns tab.

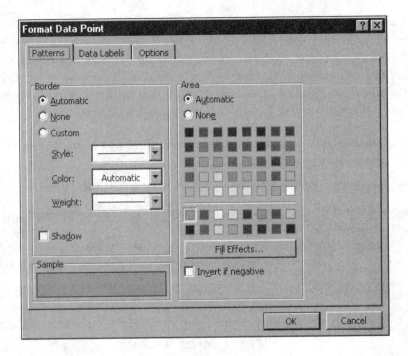

Figure 9.15 The Patterns tab of the Format Series dialog box.

3. Click on the **Color** drop-down menu in the Border section, and select a shade of red.

4. In the Area portion of the dialog box, click on a shade of yellow. Notice that the Sample area in the lower left-hand corner of the dialog box lets you preview how your data series columns will look.

5. Click on the **OK** button to accept the edits.

As you can see, the columns and legend have changed colors in response to your selections.

DISPLAYING DATA LABELS

While most charts use numbers along the value (y) axis to identify values, sometimes it's unclear what these numbers stand for. Excel allows you to place data labels within your chart to make it more descriptive. Let's go back to the Format Data Series dialog box to display data labels on your chart.

1. Double-click on one of the **Income** columns to bring up the Format Data Series dialog box.

2. Click on the **Data Labels** tab, which is shown in Figure 9.16.

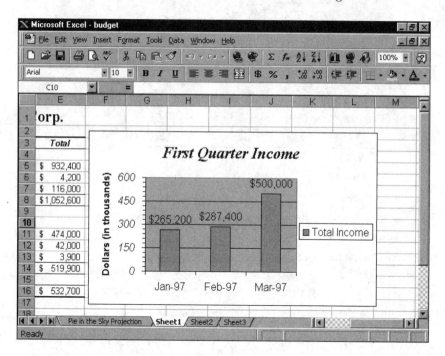

Figure 9.16 *The Data Labels portion of the Format Data Series dialog box.*

3. To show the value of your Total Income columns, select **Show Value** and click **OK**.

Your chart is really looking fancy now. With the data labels added, chart readers will know exactly what the columns represent. This feature could be useful for a wide range of applications.

BASIC DRAWING TECHNIQUES

Excel provides an amazing array of drawing tools for adding lines, arrows, circles and text. These drawing tools (shown in Figure 9.17) can be used in your worksheets as well as your charts.

Each of the tools operates on the same basic principle: you select the tool you want to use, click on the location you want to start drawing the object, and then drag the tool. You can use this technique with several of the tools on the Drawing Toolbar, including auto-shapes, lines, arrows, rectangles and ovals.

Figure 9.17 *The Drawing toolbar.*

If you want to use a drawing tool several times in succession, just double-click on it. Then when you're through using that tool, click on the tool again to turn it off.

N O T E

DRAWING, MOVING, AND SIZING OBJECTS

Let's spruce up your chart with drawings and objects using the Drawing Toolbar. You can draw circles and squares freehand by choosing the appropriate tool and then clicking and dragging. Sometimes, however, you may want to draw perfect circles and perfect squares. This can be accomplished by holding down the **Shift** key as you click and drag the circle or square on your chart or worksheet.

Let's place a freehand oval around March's Total Income.

1. Click on the Standard Toolbar's **Drawing** button, as shown in Figure 9.18.

Figure 9.18 *The Drawing button.*

2. Select the **Oval** tool on the Drawing Toolbar by clicking on it. The Oval button is shown in Figure 9.19.

Figure 9.19 *The Oval button.*

3. Place the mouse pointer above and to the left of the March Income data label.

4. Hold the left mouse button down and drag the mouse pointer over the data label, as shown in Figure 9.20.

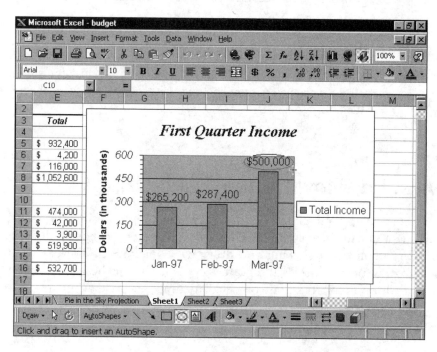

Figure 9.20 *Drawing an oval on the chart.*

5. Release the mouse button. The March data label is now covered by the oval you drew. You can click on the size boxes to resize the oval, and you can drag the oval to adjust its positioning. To view the Income data again, you'll have to change the oval's fill color.

6. Right-click on the oval to display its shortcut menu.

7. Click on **Format AutoShape** to display the Format AutoShape dialog box, and click on the **Colors and Lines** tab if it isn't already selected.

8. Click on the **Arrow** next to the Fill Color drop-down list to display the availble options.

9. Select **No Fill** and click **OK.**

COPYING OBJECTS

When you want to use the same object in separate locations, you can copy the item instead of trying to redraw it. For example, you can copy the oval object you just finished drawing and use it to circle the lowest expense data label. Let's try it.

1. Click on the border of the oval you just created. If you select the chart by mistake, single-click outside the chart area and try again.

2. Right-click the mouse button to display the shortcut menu.

3. Select **Copy**.

4. Right-click the mouse to bring up the shortcut menu again, and select **Paste**. The new oval should appear in the upper-left corner of your chart.

5. Point to the oval's border and then click and drag the object to January's Total Income data label. Your chart should now look like Figure 9.21.

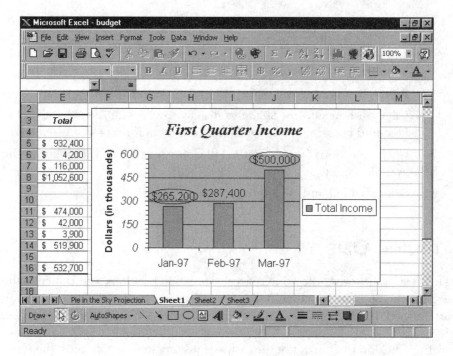

Figure 9.21 *The chart with two ovals.*

DRAWING ARROWS

You can bring even more attention to the highest Income data series. Let's draw an arrow that will slightly overlap your oval and really bring attention to this area. In order to draw an arrow, just follow these steps.

1. Click on the **Arrow** button on the Drawing Toolbar, which is shown in Figure 9.22.

Figure 9.22 *The Arrow button.*

2. Position the mouse pointer, which is now a cross-hair, to the above right of the oval that circles the highest expense in the March column.

3. Hold down the left mouse button and drag the pointer until it is slightly inside the oval.

4. Release the mouse button to create an arrow, as shown in Figure 9.23. The handles on the end of the arrow indicate that it is selected and can be moved or sized. You can also format the arrow, which is what we'll do next.

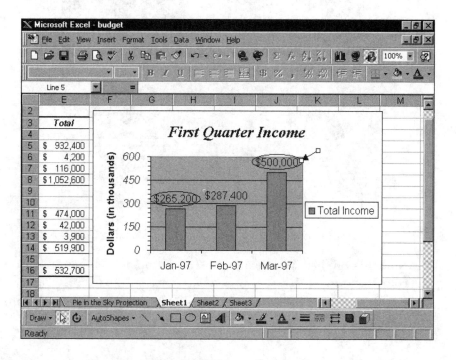

Figure 9.23 *The completed arrow.*

5. Double-click on the arrow to display the Format AutoShape dialog box, as displayed in Figure 9.24.

   The Format AutoShape dialog box is specific to the type of drawing object you are formatting. In this case, you can change the type of arrowhead or line. You can also adjust the line width, which is what we'll do next.

6. Click once on the Weight option's **Up** arrow to make your line 1 pt. wide.

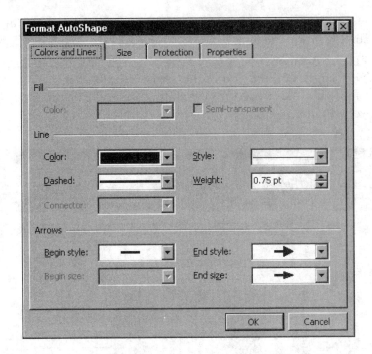

Figure 9.24 *The Colors and Lines portion of the Format AutoShape dialog box.*

7. Now click on the arrow next to the **Color** drop-down list to display the color options.

8. Select your favorite color and click the **OK** button to accept the changes.

CREATING TEXT BOXES

You saw in the last chapter that Excel helps create and place certain text on a chart for you. For example, the Chart Wizard created a chart title, legend, and axes labels. So what happens when you want to add text that isn't included in the Chart Wizard? Let's add a statement at the bottom of the chart to indicate it was prepared by you.

1. Select the **Text Box** button on the Drawing Toolbar. The Text Box button is shown in Figure 9.25.

2. Move your mouse pointer to the lower-right corner of the chart.

Figure 9.25 *The Text Box button.*

3. Hold down your left mouse button and drag out a rectangular text box, as shown in Figure 9.26.

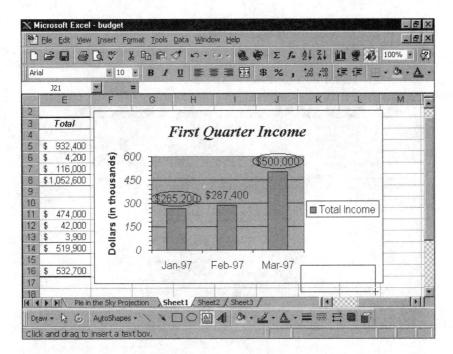

Figure 9.26 *Creating a text box.*

4. Type **Prepared by {enter your name here}**.

5. If all the text won't fit in the text box, you can adjust the size by clicking and dragging one of the size boxes. You can also click and drag the entire text box if you need to reposition it. If the text is too large, you may want to change the font size. The following steps will reduce the font in your text box.

6. Double-click directly on the border of the text box to bring up the Format Text Box dialog box.

7. Click on the **Font** tab if it is not already selected.

8. In the Size list, select **8** and click **OK**. While your text box is still selected, let's add a drop shadow to it.

9. Click on the Formatting Toolbar's **Shadow** button, which is shown in Figure 9.27. Select a shadow format by clicking on it.

Figure 9.27 *The Shadow button.*

10. Click once outside the chart area so you can view the entire chart. Your chart should resemble Figure 9.28.

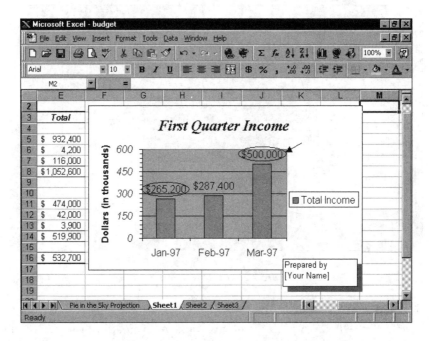

Figure 9.28 *The chart with text box and drop shadow.*

A FINAL THOUGHT

You've now learned how to enhance your charts and worksheets with a few of Excel's basic drawing features. In the next chapter we'll switch gears and look at using Excel to manage and manipulate data.

CHAPTER 10

Managing Data

DATA BASICS

In addition to the worksheet and charting capabilities you worked with in the beginning chapters of this book, Excel provides a powerful facility for creating and manipulating databases.

So what is a database? A *database* is a collection of information (data) organized to make it easy to find and use the data you are looking for. An example of a database you use every day is the phone book. The white pages of the phone book contain several categories of data: Last Name, First Name, Address, and Phone Number.

In database terms, each of these categories is called a *field*. All the field entries for one person make up a *record*. On one page of the phone book, there are four fields and perhaps several hundred records. The phone book makes it easy for you to find the data you want by sorting the records in alphabetical order. With Excel databases, you can sort and search the data in a wide variety of ways. You can even perform calculations on the data in an Excel database, just as you can with any worksheet data.

WHEN TO USE EXCEL AS A DATABASE

How can you determine when or if you need to use Excel as a database? As we discussed in the previous section, if you maintain data with many records and fields, like a phone book does, then you would benefit greatly by using Excel's database management tools. Of course, your data doesn't have to be as massive as a phone book to use Excel as a database.

Let's look at some of the benefits of using Excel as a database and see if a database will fit your needs.

One benefit is that you'll be able to easily add and remove records or data from a data range. In the phone book example, new names and addresses are added and some are deleted. If you find yourself performing similar tasks with your data (adding and deleting records), then you should seriously consider using Excel's database management tools.

Another benefit is the ease with which data can be changed. Again, using the phone book example, sometimes phone numbers change and have to be updated. If you find yourself having to update your data and records, the Excel database management tools will provide you with easy procedures to accomplish the task.

A third benefit in using Excel as a database management tool is if you need to look at subsets of your data. With a phone book, you could print out the entire book, or look at only a subset. For example, you could find just those people who live on a certain street. If you need to see different subsets of your data and records, then an Excel database would work well for you.

One other benefit is that you will have the ability to do statistical analysis on a subset or on all of your database. You'll be able to create charts, pies, and other visual presentations of your data. By using Excel as a database management tool, you can create your data in picture form.

If any of these attributes apply to your tasks, then you should seriously consider using Excel as a database. Excel uses a dialog box called the *data form* that makes adding, removing, changing, sorting, subsetting, and searching your database range very easy and user-friendly. We'll talk more about the data form later in this chapter.

SETTING UP A DATABASE

To create a database, you need to enter field names in the first row you want to use for your list. Each row below the field name or header row is a record. There can't be any blank rows between records, and all the cells in a field should be formatted the same way to facilitate sorting and database manipulation.

In setting up your database, you should follow certain guidelines to assure that your database will maintain integrity:

❖ Make absolutely sure that all field names, which are sometimes called *column headings*, are unique. You'll run into trouble manipulating your data if you use the same name more than once for a field or column heading.

 It's best to keep field names as short as possible, yet descriptive enough that you know what should be entered in the field. If you need to use a field name that is longer than the column width, consider wrapping the text so it occupies multiple lines instead of requiring an inordinately wide column. To wrap text, choose **Format Cell** from the cell's shortcut menu and click in the **Wrap Text** check box.

❖ Remember that your field name has a limited number of characters. No field name can be longer than 255 characters. A good rule of thumb is to try to keep your field names as short as possible, but at the same time descriptive enough so that you know what the name refers to.

❖ Each row should contain a new record. Records are delineated by rows. Also, you should never have a blank row in your database range. Moreover, each row/record should be unique from other rows and records. You should always have at least one field in your record that is unique from any other record.

❖ Format your header row or field names differently from your rows containing data. You may want to change the justification, font type, and font style of the field names to distinguish them from your records. This way, Excel knows automatically where the first row of your data begins.

❖ Give your database plenty of breathing room. Since databases tend to grow, make sure that your database is located on the worksheet where records can be easily added and not run into limitation problems. If possible, use one full sheet for your entire database.

CREATING A DATABASE

Now that you know the basics of a database, how about some hands-on experience in creating one? Once you create your own database and try out some of the neat database management tools, it will be much easier for you to determine if and when you should use Excel as a database. Let's start creating a partial inventory list database for the Spokane Locks and Bagel Corp.

1. Start Excel and open the BUDGET workbook if it isn't already on your screen.

2. Click on the **Sheet2** tab at the bottom of the worksheet to move to a clean worksheet in the same workbook.

NOTE   Keeping related worksheets in the same workbook is one of the reasons Excel uses workbooks in the first place. We could put the inventory list in a new workbook, but then, when we want to work with our various financial data from Spokane Locks and Bagel, we'd have to open two workbooks instead of one.

3. Enter the field names and data for the first record in the appropriate cells, as displayed in Table 10.1. The formula in E2 multiplies the item's cost by the quantity.

Table 10.1 *The field names and data for the first record of the inventory database*

	A	B	C	D	E
1	ITEM	TYPE	COST	QTY	TOTAL
2	Small padlock	Hardware	4.33	42	=C2*D2

NOTE   The fastest way to enter the data in this range is to select the entire range first (A1 through E2) and press **Enter** after each cell entry to move to the next cell in the selection.

Next, you can format the cells containing the field names as center-aligned and the first record cells to display the numbers properly.

4. Select the range A1 through E1 and center the cells. You can right-click on the selection to display the shortcut menu, then choose **Format Cells...**, click on the **Alignment** tab, and select the **Center** option button in the Horizontal portion of the dialog box.

5. Making sure that the range A1 through E1 is still selected, click on the Formatting toolbar's **Bold** button.

6. Format cell C2 with the comma format by clicking on the **Comma** format button on the Formatting toolbar.

7. Format cell E2 with the currency format by clicking on the **Currency** format button on the Formatting toolbar.

8. Double-click on the right border of each of the column headings to adjust the column widths to accommodate the cell entries. You'll need to do this again every time you enter data that is wider than the current column widths. Your screen should now look like Figure 10.1.

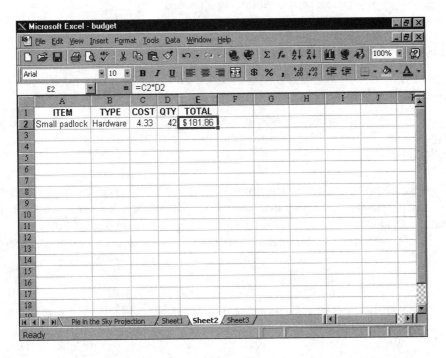

Figure 10.1 *The field names and first record of the database.*

Entering Database Records

You already entered data in a database when you entered the first record. You can enter data directly into the database in the same way to add as many records as needed. However, the following steps show a time- and effort-saving method for entering database records.

1. Approximate the number of records you plan to enter and then high-light the range to accommodate that number of records under the last record in your database.

2. Enter the corresponding data in the first cell of your range and press the **Tab** key when you're finished.

3. Excel will move you to the next cell, horizontally, while keeping the range highlighted. Continue to enter data in the specified field using **Tab** to move between cells. Excel will automatically move to a new line when you are finished entering a record.

Using the Data Form

Excel provides an even slicker method for entering data in a database—the data form.

Once you've started a database, you can use the data form, which includes text boxes for the fields requiring data entry and also displays the results of calculated fields.

 There's no right or wrong way to enter data in an Excel database. You may decide that entering data directly into the database and bypassing the data form is the easiest method for you. One advantage of using the data form to enter data is that the cell formatting in the current record automatically applies to the next record, eliminating the need to format more than one record.

Let's enter the next record using the data form.

1. Be sure one of the cells in the database is active and choose **Data, Form...** to display the Data Form dialog box, as displayed in Figure 10.2.

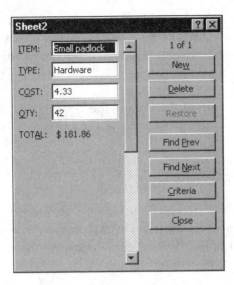

Figure 10.2 *The Data Form dialog box.*

The title bar in the dialog box displays the name of the sheet where the database is—in this case, Sheet2. If the sheet were renamed something more relevant to the database, such as INVENTORY, that name would be displayed in the title bar.

The data for the first record is displayed in the text boxes for each field. Notice that the data for the TOTAL field isn't in a text box since, being a calculated field, it can't be edited. The scroll bar to the right of the text boxes allows you to scroll through each record in the database. The dialog box also displays the number of the record you are currently viewing and the total number of records in the database in the upper-right corner of the dialog box. Let's add the next record in the data form now.

2. Click the **New** button to clear the text boxes for the new record entry. As you enter new records, the dialog box displays the words New Record in the upper-right corner.

3. Type **Bagel dogs**, **Food**, **1.27**, **375** in the ITEM, TYPE, COST, and QTY text boxes. You can press the **Tab** key to move the insertion point from one text box to the next.

N O T E

If you need to correct a typo in a text box you've already completed, you can click directly in the text box you need to edit, or press **Shift-Tab** until the field you need to edit is highlighted, and type the correct data.

4.   Click on the **New** button to add this record to the bottom of the database and clear the text boxes for the next record. The new record is added and you'll notice that the cell formatting was copied from the first record. If the dialog box is obscuring too much of the database, you can drag it out of the way by its title bar.

SHORTCUT

When you finish entering the data for the last field in a record, the fastest way to confirm the entry and clear the text boxes for the next record is to press the **Enter** key. This way you don't need to move your hands from the keyboard as you enter a series of records.

Now you can enter the remaining records for the inventory database.

5.   Enter the data for the records, displayed in Table 10.2.

Table 10.2 The data for the inventory database

ITEM	TYPE	COST	QTY
Plain bagels	Food	.22	456
8 oz. cream cheese	Food	1.33	78
BMW keys	Hardware	.87	26
Mercedes keys	Hardware	.47	73
Ferrari keys	Hardware	.56	37
Garlic bagels	Food	.25	133
Jalapeno bagels	Food	.27	277
Chocolate bagels	Food	.32	76
Large padlock	Hardware	3.42	44

6.   Click on the **Close** button to clear the dialog box from the screen, and readjust the width of column A to accommodate the new entries. Your screen displays all the records, as shown in Figure 10.3.

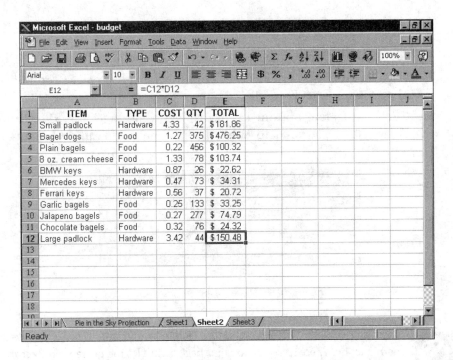

Figure 10.3 All the records in the inventory database.

DELETING AND EDITING RECORDS

As with any other data on a worksheet, you can delete and edit records directly. If you wanted to delete a record directly, you could select a cell in its row and **Edit**, **Delete...**, **Entire Row**. Editing a record's data directly is simply a matter of moving to the cell you want to edit and making the change, just as you would in any cell.

Another way to edit and delete records is with the data form dialog box. An advantage of using the dialog box is that you can combine editing and deleting with the search capabilities we'll cover later in this chapter. For example, if you wanted to edit all the records that matched certain comparison criteria, you could specify the criteria, click the **Find Next** button, perform all the edits in the text boxes, and click on **Find Next** to display the next record you want to edit.

Let's delete one of the records using the Data Form dialog box.

1. Choose **Data, Form...** to display the Data Form dialog box.
2. Click on **Find Next** or **Find Prev** until the Small Padlock record is displayed in the Data Form dialog box.
3. Click the **Delete** button. Excel displays a message box, shown in Figure 10.4, to let you know what you're about to do can't be undone.

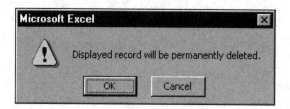

Figure 10.4 *The warning message box.*

WARNING

Excel isn't kidding. When you click the **Delete** button, the record is removed permanently. There's no way to get it back. Don't let the grayed-out **Restore** button in the Data Form dialog box fool you either. That only works for restoring an *edited* record to its original state prior to confirming the edit. So be careful before deleting a record in this way.

There is one safety measure you can take before doing something dangerous like deleting a record—save your work. If you save your work just before deleting the record, you can always close the workbook without saving changes and then open the saved version to get back to where you were before the deletion.

4. Click **Cancel** to close the dialog box without deleting.
5. Click the **Close** button to clear the Data Form dialog box.

SORTING THE DATABASE

At the beginning of the chapter, you saw how the phone book makes it easy to find a particular entry. The records are sorted in alphabetical order. When you add records to the database list, you don't need to worry about entering them in the correct order. Excel makes it easy to sort the list in a variety of ways.

> Your list doesn't even have to be a database for Excel to sort it. Any rectangular area consisting of rows and columns of related data can be sorted in the same manner as database data.

NOTE

One sorting concept that is important to understand is the *sort key*. The key is the basis for the sort, and you can sort by up to three keys. In the phone book example, the first sort key is the last name. A second sort key (the first name) is used as a tiebreaker. If there is more than one entry of a particular last name, those last names are sorted by first names.

Let's perform a simple sort on the inventory database. First, you'll sort the list in alphabetical order by the ITEM field (this is so easy you won't believe it).

1. Click on any cell in column A of the database (the ITEM field).
2. Click on the **Sort Ascending** button on the Standard toolbar (see Figure 10.5).

Figure 10.5 *The Sort Ascending button.*

Voila! The list is instantly sorted, as displayed in Figure 10.6.

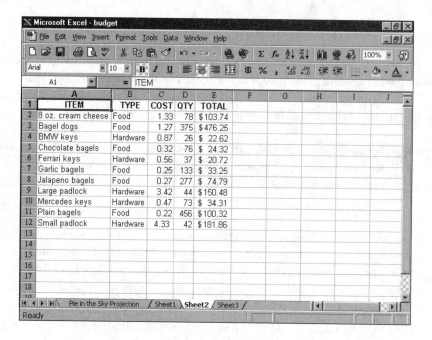

Figure 10.6 *The sorted database.*

The word *Ascending* in Sort Ascending means from lower to higher. For an alphabetical sort such as this, it means A through Z. For a numerical sort, ascending would be 1 through 100. The toolbar button to the right of the Sort Ascending button is the Sort Descending button, which performs a sort from higher to lower. The Sort Descending button is pictured in Figure 10.7.

Figure 10.7 *The Sort Descending button.*

It's a good idea to save your work before performing a sort so you can get back to the original sort order later if you need to.

WARNING

If you perform a sort and want to return the list to its original order, you can choose **Edit**, **Undo Sort** before taking any other actions in

Excel. A trick you can use if you think you will need to return to the original sort order more than once is to add a field for record numbers. In one column of the database, type **1**, and then hold down the **Ctrl** key and use the fill handle to increase the numbers in ascending order down the column. With the records numbered, you can get back to the original order any time you want by performing a sort by the column containing the record numbers.

Let's sort the list in descending order by the COST field.

3. Move to any cell in the database range in column C and click on the **Sort Descending** toolbar button.

Sorting with Multiple Keys

Now that you've mastered a basic sort, it's time to sort the database by two sort keys. Sorting a database by two fields isn't quite as easy as clicking on a toolbar button, but it's still pretty easy.

You can use the TYPE field as the first sort key, which groups the food and hardware items separately. Because there are several records for each of the two types of items, you can use the ITEM field as the second sort key.

1. Make sure that a cell in the database is active, and then choose **Data, Sort...** to display the Sort dialog box, as shown in Figure 10.8.

Figure 10.8 *The Sort dialog box.*

Notice that the entire list is selected, excluding the column headings, and the field name in the Sort By list box is COST (which was the last sort action you performed). This isn't what you want to use for the first Sort By, so you can change it now.

2.   Click on the **Arrow** next to the Sort By drop-down list to display all the field names in the database, as shown in Figure 10.9.

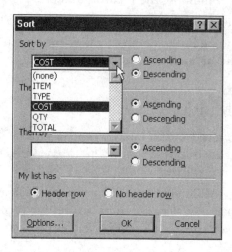

Figure 10.9 *The Sort dialog box displaying the drop-down list of field names.*

3.   Click on **TYPE** in the drop-down list to select it as the first field to sort. Each field you choose to sort can be sorted in ascending (the default) or descending order. You can accept ascending for both of these sort keys.

4.   Click on the **Arrow** next to the Then By drop-down list and click on **ITEM**. Since there aren't any duplicate item names, there is no need for a third sort key, so you can leave the bottom Then By list blank.

5.   Click **OK** to perform the sort. The list is sorted with all the food items at the top and the item names alphabetized within the food group. Next, the hardware items are alphabetized within the hardware group, as shown in Figure 10.10.

Excel can only use three sort keys, which could be somewhat limiting for some complex lists. However, as with most limitations in Excel, there is a way around it. If your sort requires more than three sort keys, simply sort multiple times.

N O T E

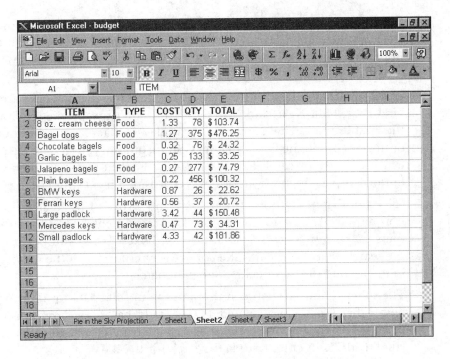

Figure 10.10 *The list sorted by two sort keys.*

SEARCHING THE DATABASE

In the database you just created, there is no need to use any fancy searching techniques because there are so few entries and all of them are visible at the same time. However, as the number of records increases to hundreds or thousands, it can be difficult, if not impossible, to find the records you want by visually scanning the list.

Excel provides several ways to find records that meet certain criteria. Later in the chapter, you'll learn to use Excel's filtering system to display the records that meet your specifications. But the most straightforward way to find records you are looking for is to use the Data Form dialog box.

Using the Data Form dialog box does not change the database in any way. As you perform the search, the dialog box displays the records in the database that meet the search criteria, one at a time. Let's use the data form dialog box to search for some records.

1. Be sure one of the cells in the database is still active, and choose **Data**, **Form…**. The Data Form dialog box displays 1 of 11 in the upper-right corner, indicating that the data for the first of eleven records is presented.

    The three dialog box buttons used for searching the database are: **Find Prev**, **Find Next**, and **Criteria**. If you don't specify any criteria, the **Find Prev** and **Find Next** buttons display the data for the previous or next record in the list. Using the **Criteria** button, you can tell Excel which records to search for, and then the **Find Prev** and **Find Next** buttons display the previous or next records that meet your criteria.

2. Click the **Criteria** button. The upper-right corner of the dialog box now displays Criteria, indicating that you can enter search conditions called *comparison criteria* in the text boxes. When you perform the search, Excel compares the comparison criteria with the records in the list and displays the first one that matches.

    The other difference between this and the normal data form dialog box is that even the calculated TOTAL field has a text box. This is because you can specify search criteria on any field, including calculated fields. Let's enter criteria to search for the BMW keys.

3. In the ITEM text box, type **bmw** and then click the **Find Next** button.

The data form now displays the data for the BMW keys record and, in the upper-right corner, displays 7 of 11 indicating that this is the seventh record in the database. If you click the **Find Next** button, your computer will probably beep at you and won't display any other records. Now, let's try finding records that match the multiple criteria.

4. Click the **Criteria** button again so you can enter new criteria. The ITEM text box is highlighted so you can start typing to enter new criteria for the ITEM field, or delete what's there. You can delete it since you won't be using the ITEM field as part of the next search.

    The first comparison criterion you can use is HARDWARE to locate only records that have HARDWARE entered in the TYPE field.

5. Press the **Delete** key to delete the highlighted text, then press the **Tab** key to move the insertion point into the TYPE text box and type **HARDWARE**. If you enter comparison criteria in more than one text box, the record must meet both conditions. For this example, you'll search for records that fall into the Hardware category and also have a total value of more than $100.

6. Click in the **TOTAL** text box and type **>100**. The greater than symbol (>) can be used by Excel to compare values. The other comparison operators are:

❖ = (equal to)

❖ < (less than)

❖ >= (greater than or equal to)

❖ <+ (less than or equal to)

❖ <> (not equal to)

These operators can be used with numeric values only, not text data.

7. Click the **Find Next** button to display the first record that meets both of the comparison criteria. Only three records match both criteria. You can click on **Find Next** to display the other records.

Filtering the Database

The major limitation to using the data form to find records that meet certain criteria is that you can only display one record at a time. There may be times when you want to be able to view and manipulate a subset of the list. Excel's filter capabilities allow you to do just that.

By filtering the database, Excel automatically hides all records that don't meet your specifications, leaving only the records you want to see displayed on your screen. Just as with sorting, you can have multiple criteria for filtering the database.

Let's use Excel's AutoFilter feature to display only the food records.

1. Make sure one of the cells in the database is active and choose **Data, Filter, AutoFilter**. Drop-down arrows appear at the top of each column next to each field name, as shown in Figure 10.11.

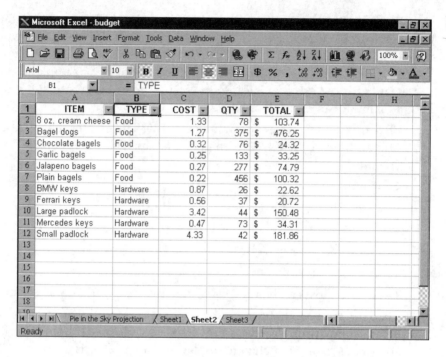

Figure 10.11 The list with the AutoFilter drop-down arrows displayed.

2. Click on the drop-down **Arrow** next to the TYPE field name. The drop-down list provided by the AutoFilter Arrows display all the unique entries for that field, as shown in Figure 10.12.

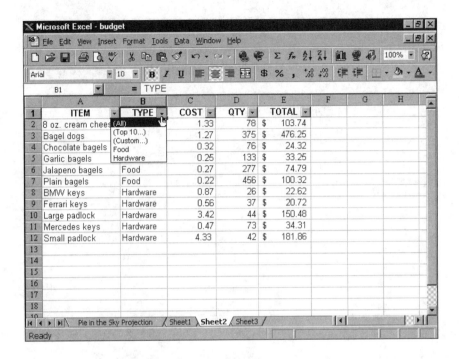

Figure 10.12 An AutoFilter drop-down list.

You would select **All** in the drop-down list to cancel a filter selection for that field. Selecting **Custom...** lets you specify more complex filter specifications, including the use of the comparison operators you use in the data form dialog box. The **Top 10...** option allows you to rank records according to their numerical value.

3.   Click on **Food** in the drop-down list. Instantly, all the records that don't meet the food criterion are hidden, as shown in Figure 10.13.

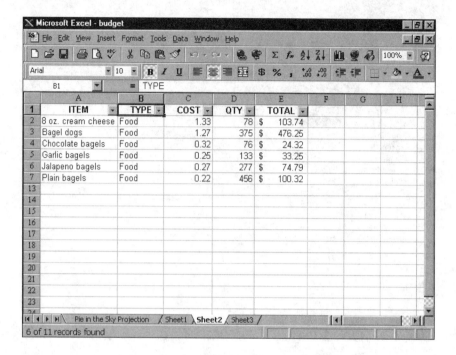

Figure 10.13 The list filtered to show only the food items.

You can't tell from the figure, but if you look at your screen you'll notice that the arrow next to the TYPE heading is blue. This indicates that a filter criterion has been specified for this field. If you display the list again and choose **All,** the hidden records reappear and the Arrow returns to its default appearance.

Using Custom Filters

Let's display a filter criterion for another field. This time you can ask Excel to display records from the filtered list that have quantities of greater than 100 and less than 400.

1. Click on the drop-down **Arrow** next to the QTY heading. You need to create a custom filter for this field to specify the range of acceptable values.

2. Click on **Custom...** to display the Custom AutoFilter dialog box, as shown in Figure 10.14.

    The comparison operators must be chosen from their own drop-down list in the dialog box, instead of being typed in the text box as you did in the data form dialog box.

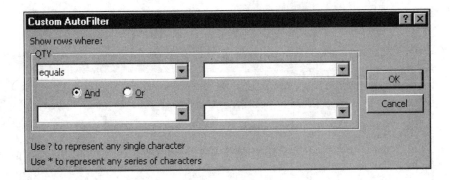

Figure 10.14 *The Custom AutoFilter dialog box.*

3. Click on the drop-down **Arrow** next to the box with equals in it (just below QTY) to display the list of comparison operators, as shown in Figure 10.15.

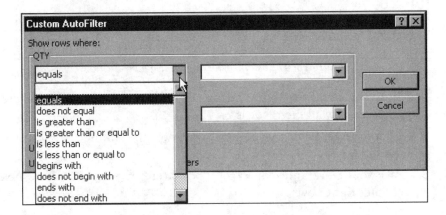

Figure 10.15 *The drop-down list of comparison operators.*

4. Click on **is greater than** in the drop down list, then click in the text box to the right of the comparison operator list and type **100**.

5. Leave the And option button selected and choose **is less than** from the bottom drop-down list of comparison operators and type **400** in the bottom text box.

6. Click on the **OK** button. Your screen should now have three records matching the two filter criteria, as displayed in Figure 10.16.

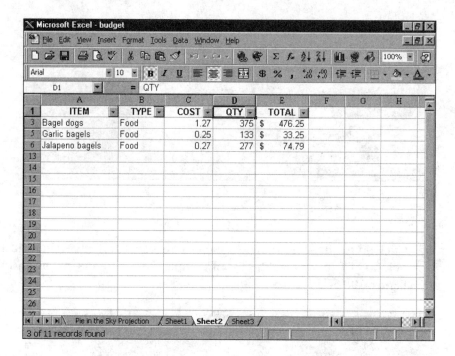

Figure 10.16 *The list after entering the two filter criteria.*

Since you're finished with the filtered list, you can turn off AutoFilter and redisplay all the records.

7. Choose **Data**, **Filter**, **AutoFilter** to turn off the AutoFilter and reveal the hidden records.

8. Save your work and exit Excel if you aren't moving on to the next chapter right now.

A FINAL THOUGHT

As you work with Excel, you'll find yourself using the database creation and manipulation techniques you learned in this chapter more often than you can imagine. You'll also discover that many of these database concepts also apply to the full-featured database programs used for larger database applications. In the next chapter, you'll learn to use some of Excel's worksheet, data proofing, and analysis tools.

CHAPTER 11

Proofing and Analyzing Worksheet Data

You should be sure that the final version of any document is as error-free as possible and presents the data you want to present, whether from a spreadsheet program, a word processor or a database. Excel provides several tools for making sure your worksheet is accurate, and for looking at the data in various ways.

USING THE SPELL CHECKER

The most obvious place to start ensuring accuracy is with Excel's spell checker. Spelling errors can contribute to a perception that your entire worksheet and the logic used to prepare it are sloppy. If you want to convince your readers that the data in your worksheet is accurate and your conclusions are correct, you want to be absolutely sure any spelling errors are corrected.

Many cells in a worksheet contain only values or formulas. You may be wondering how the spell checker deals with these cells. That's easy: Excel ignores the contents of these cells.

So far you've only been entering correctly spelled data in your worksheet, so you shouldn't have to worry about checking the spelling. Of course, it is still a good idea to check the spelling in case there are some typos. Just to be sure you have something to correct, try editing one of the cell entries so it's intentionally misspelled.

1. Start Excel and open the BUDGET workbook if it isn't already on your screen. Make sure Sheet2 (the database sheet) is active. If it isn't, click on the **Sheet2** tab.

2. Change the contents of cell B2 from Food to **Foood**.

3. Click on the **Spelling** button on the Standard toolbar. The spelling button is pictured in Figure 11.1.

Figure 11.1 *The Spelling button.*

The Spelling dialog box appears, as shown in Figure 11.2, with the cell value of the first misspelled word displayed in the lower-left portion of the dialog box above the two check boxes.

Spelling		? ☒
Not in Dictionary: Foood		
Change to:	Food	
Suggestions:	Food	Ignore / Ignore All
	Foods / Fool / Foot	Change / Change All
		Add / Suggest
Add words to:	CUSTOM.DIC ▼	AutoCorrect
Cell Value: Foood		
☑ Always suggest		Undo Last / Cancel
☐ Ignore UPPERCASE		

Figure 11.2 *The Spelling dialog box.*

Because the **Always Suggest** check box is checked, the dialog box offers suggestions for correcting the misspelled word. The word in the Change to box is the suggestion Excel thinks is most likely the correct spelling of the word you had in mind. In this case, the Change to box does, in fact, contain the correct spelling. If the spelling of the mis-spelled word had been mangled too badly, Excel might not have been able to make a correct guess. In such a case, you could click on one of the other suggestions in the Suggestion list, or edit the word in the Change to box.

NOTE Having Excel make suggestions every time it stops at a misspelled word can slow down the process, so you might consider clicking in the **Always Suggest** check box to remove the check mark. If Excel stops on a particular word and you want suggestions, you can click on the **Suggest** button.

If you find that eliminating suggestions doesn't noticeably improve the speed, it might be more convenient to have Excel always provide you with suggestions.

You may also want to use the **Ignore UPPERCASE** check box to have the spell checker ignore any word that is in all uppercase letters. This option might be useful if, for example, you had a list of names or other words that would not be in the dictionary, all in uppercase.

The Add Words To box displays the name of the custom dictionary where you can add the word if it is correctly spelled, but isn't found in the normal dictionary. The default dictionary for adding words is CUSTOM.DIC, but you can create other dictionaries for use with various types of documents. If you add a word to the dictionary, the spell checker won't stop on that word as a misspelled word in other documents. Examples of the kinds of names you might want to add to the dictionary are your name, your company's name, or other special names or terms you use in your business.

4. Click the **Change** button to replace the cell contents with the word in the Change To box. Excel stops stops next on Jalepeno, which is spelled correctly but is not in the regular dictonary. You have several appropriate choices. The **Add** button would add the word to the custom dictionary. If you're sure the word is spelled correctly, this might be the best choice. The **Ignore** button will leave the word as is. **Ignore All** will leave the word as is and any other occurances of the word in this document.

5. Click on the **Ignore** button. Excel continues checking the spelling until it reaches the bottom of the worksheet and then displays the message dialog box, shown in Figure 11.3, asking if you want to continue checking from the beginning of the sheet.

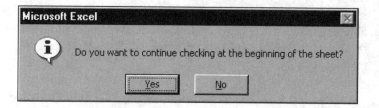

Figure 11.3 *A spelling message dialog box.*

6. Click **Yes**. If there are no errors in your document, Excel displays the message dialog box shown in Figure 11.4.

Figure 11.4 *The end of spell check message.*

7. Click **OK** in the message box to end the spell check session.

WARNING

A common error some people make is to assume that if the spell checker doesn't find any errors, everything is spelled correctly. Wrong! What the spell checker does is to make sure each word in your worksheet matches a word in its regular or custom dictionary.

If there is a word in your document that is a correctly spelled word, but just not the word you intended, the spell checker won't catch it as a misspelled word. For example, if you type the word *pane* but you mean *pain*, the spell checker won't catch your error.

To be safe, even when you use the spell checker you still need to proof-read your document. Better yet, have someone else do it—it's hard to spot your own errors (just ask our copy editors).

WORKING WITH PIVOTTABLE WIZARD

The PivotTable command lets you analyze and view data in a list or database by producing tables that are easy to understand. Your database may contain hundreds of pieces of raw data in the form of records and fields. One way to analyze your database is by viewing one record at a time (or even one field at a time). But this could take days, if not years, depending on the size of your database. Furthermore, you can never gain an *overall* summary of your data in this manner.

The PivotTable command allows you to summarize your database results in a nice presentation that will be useful to you. A company, for example, may use a database for keeping various data relating to their sales, products, sales-persons, buyers, etc. However, the marketing, sales, and warehouse departments all must have reports and tables tailored from this one database that will suit their particular needs. A useful summary table for the marketing department, for examples, may not be useful for the warehouse department.

This is why the PivotTable is such a powerful database tool. It allows you to easily manipulate and create tables that are relevant for different needs. It doesn't matter that the raw data is the same for various departments. The PivotTable concerns itself with how you want your data summarized and presented to provide meaningful and useful tables.

Now that you understand the concept behind PivotTables, let's get to work creating the data for your PivotTable. Let's start fresh with a new sheet.

1. Click on the **Sheet3** tab.
2. Type the information in Table 11.1 so your worksheet looks like Figure 11.5. Center your column headings (field names) within the cell and, if needed, expand the column widths so you can see all your data.

Table 11.1 *The field names and data for current and past year inventories*

A ITEM	B TYPE	C COST	D QTY	E YEAR
Small padlock	Hardware	4.33	42	1997
Bagel dogs	Food	1.27	375	1997
Plain bagels	Food	0.22	456	1997
8 oz. cream cheese	Food	1.33	78	1997
BMW keys	Hardware	.87	26	1997
Mercedes keys	Hardware	.47	73	1997
Ferrari keys	Hardware	.56	37	1997
Garlic bagels	Food	.25	133	1997
Large padlock	Hardware	3.42	44	1997
Small padlock	Hardware	4.01	34	1996
Bagel dogs	Food	1.31	55	1996
Plain bagels	Food	0.44	834	1996
8 oz. cream cheese	Food	0.99	75	1996
BMW keys	Hardware	0.87	22	1996
Mercedes keys	Hardware	0.40	80	1996
Ferrari keys	Hardware	0.51	5	1996

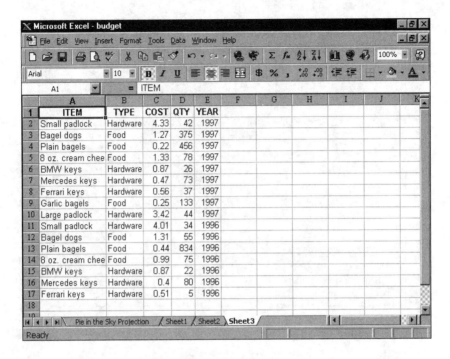

Figure 11.5 *The field names and records of the inventory database.*

3. With one of the cells in the list as the active cell, choose **Data**, **PivotTable Report...** to display the first of four PivotTable Wizard dialog boxes, as shown in Figure 11.6.

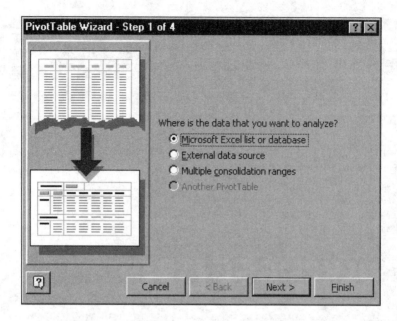

Figure 11.6 *The PivotTable Wizard dialog box—step 1 of 4.*

Because the data source you're using is from an Excel worksheet, **Microsoft Excel List or Database** is the correct and default option. Otherwise, you would select a different option according to your data source.

4. Click **Next** to move to Step 2 of the PivotTable Wizard.

5. The PivotTable wizard places a dashed line around the data it thinks you want to use for the PivotTable and asks you to confirm or modify the range (See Figure 11.7).

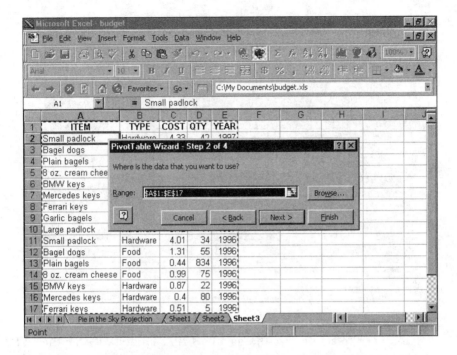

Figure 11.7 *The PivotTable Wizard dialog box—step 2 of 4.*

One way to modify the range is to type the range in the range box. Or you can click on the worksheet and highlight a new range which places the range automatically in the range box. Accept the range the PivotWizard selected by clicking **Next** to move to Step 3.

6.   Figure 11.8 shows the third dialog box. You can drag field names from the right edge of the dialog box into the ROW, COLUMN, DATA, and PAGE portions of the dialog box to determine which data is summarized. This will produce the layout of the PivotTable.

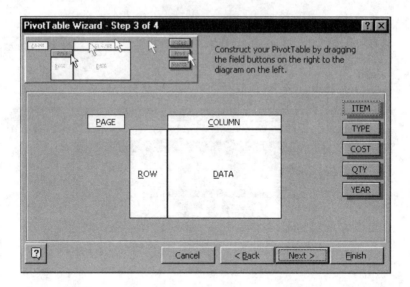

Figure 11.8 *The PivotTable Wizard dialog box—step 3 of 4.*

You need to summarize the data by TYPE. Therefore, drag the **TYPE** field name button into the ROW portion of the dialog box, and then drag the **YEAR** field name button into the Column portion of the dialog box. Finally, drag the **COST** field name button into the DATA box.

7. When your dialog box is displayed, as shown in Figure 11.9, click on the **Next** button.

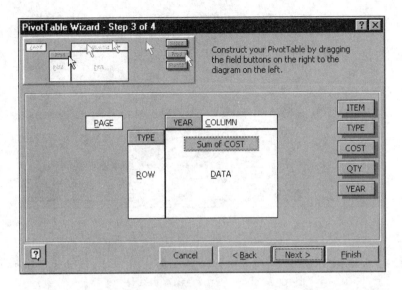

Figure 11.9 The field buttons in place for the PivotTable Wizard.

8. Figure 11.10 displays the final PivotTable Wizard dialog box. Select the **Existing Worksheet** option for where you want to put the PivotTable. Type **A19** in the Existing Worksheet text box, so the Pivot Table will be placed a couple of rows below your list. Note that you can also choose to have your table housed on its own sheet.

WARNING

If you don't specify a starting cell in this dialog box, the PivotTable replaces the database, which may not be what you have in mind.

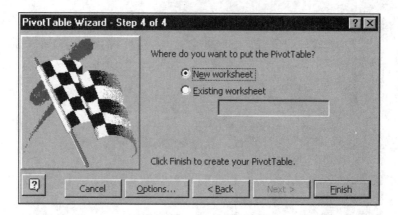

Figure 11.10 *The PivotTable Wizard dialog box—step 4 of 4.*

9. Click the **Finish** button when you're done, and the table will be placed in your worksheet as shown in Figure 11.11.

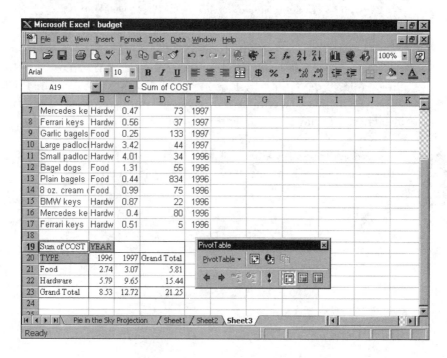

Figure 11.11 *The PivotTable displayed below the list.*

The PivotTable toolbar also appears with the PivotTable. You may want to drag the PivotTable toolbar to a new location if it obscures part of the PivotTable or is too far away from the PivotTable.

You have just created a simple table from your database which summarizes and compares the cost of the items in your inventory from the current year to the previous year. Let's add another piece to the puzzle. Suppose the hardware department wants to see a summary cost of the hardware items over the past two years, and the food department wants to see a summary cost of the food items over the past two years. Let's create one table that will work for both departments.

1. First, let's copy your data into a new worksheet. Create a new worksheet by right-clicking on the **Sheet3** tab and choosing **Insert**, **Worksheet**.

2. Highlight your database (cells A1 through E17). Press the right mouse button to bring up the short-cut menu and select **Copy**.

3. Click on the new workbook sheet (**Sheet4**). Place the mouse pointer in cell A1, click the right mouse button to display the short-cut menu again, and choose **Paste**. While the database is still highlighted, double-click between the column header labels to adjust the columns. You've now copied your database into a new sheet.

4. With one of the cells in the list as the active cell, choose **PivotTable Report...** from the Data menu to display the first of the PivotTable Wizard dialog boxes.

5. Because the data source you're using is from an Excel worksheet, **Microsoft Excel List or Database** is the correct option. Click **Next**.

6. The PivotTable Wizard has correctly placed a dashed line around the data you are going to use for the PivotTable. Click **Next**.

7. Drag **TYPE** and then **ITEM** into the ROW portion of the dialog box. Then drag **YEAR** into the COLUMN portion of the dialog box. Finally, drag **COST** into the DATA portion of the dialog box. When the dialog box is displayed as shown in Figure 11.12, click the **Next** button.

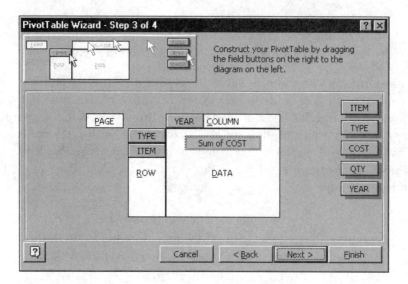

Figure 11.12 *Another PivotTable setup.*

8. In the final PivotTable Wizard dialog box, select the **Existing Worksheet** option for where you want to put the PivotTable. Type **A19** in the Existing Worksheet text box, so the PivotTable will be placed a couple of rows below your list.

9. Click the **Finish** button when you are done. Use the scroll bar to see your new table. It should look like the table in Figure 11.13.

You have just created a table that summarizes and categorizes both the food and hardware items. The table can now be given to both the hardware and food departments, because the data is arranged to be meaningful for each department.

Save your work before proceeding with the next section.

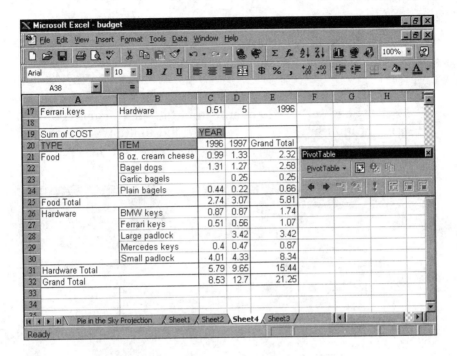

Figure 11.13 *The completed PivotTable—ready for rearranging.*

Rearranging the Table

Rearranging and altering the PivotTable is very simple. You may decide that you want your table to have a slightly different look. All that is needed to alter an existing PivotTable is to drag the field heading markers in the existing PivotTable to different locations. Excel automatically updates the changes and produces the new table. Let's try a pretty basic rearrangement so you can get a feel for it.

1. Using the table you just created, click on the **YEAR** file heading button and drag it until it is on top of the TYPE file heading button. Notice that the rectangular icon changes from a horizontal shape representing column headings to a vertical shape representing row headings.

2. Release the mouse button; Excel automatically rearranges the table. You may have to select **Zoom...** from the View menu, choose **75%** magnification in the custom window, and then press **OK** to see the whole table. Your table should look like Figure 11.14.

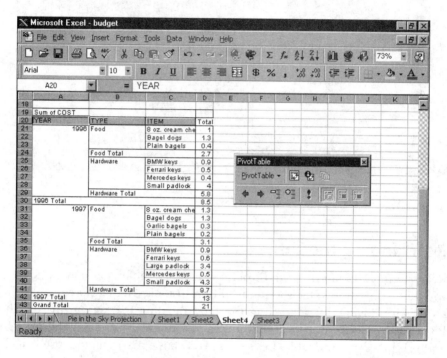

Figure 11.14 *Rearranging the PivotTable.*

Try creating other PivotTables and rearranging them from the sample database you've created. The concepts of the PivotTable will become clearer the more you practice them.

Using "What If"

One of the main reasons people enjoy using Excel worksheets is that they allow you analyze your data by doing *what if* tests on variable data. For example, you may have a savings account and want to know the future value of the account in 5 years if you systematically deposited a certain amount. But suppose you want to play *what if* with the amounts you deposit? Suppose you want to test depositing $100 a month, or $125 a month or $75 a month. What would the future value be in five years for each amount?

There are a number of powerful tools in Excel that you can use to play *what if* to determine the results of different scenarios. You'll have to determine the *what if* tool that is right for your analysis. Following is a brief outline and description of these tools.

Single-Variable Data Tables

The single-variable data tables will help you analyze how a variable will change the result of a formula. For instance, suppose you know your bank is paying .75% interest. You also know that you want to make an equal deposit each month for the next 3 years. This would equal 36 deposits. How much would you earn if you deposited $100 a month, or $125, or $150, or $175? Let's create a single-variable table using the Future Value function (FV) to find out. The following steps create the single-variable table using the Function Wizard.

1. Create a new worksheet by right-clicking any of the existing sheet tabs and choosing **Insert**, **Worksheet** from the shortcut menu.

2. Enter the data shown in Figure 11.15.

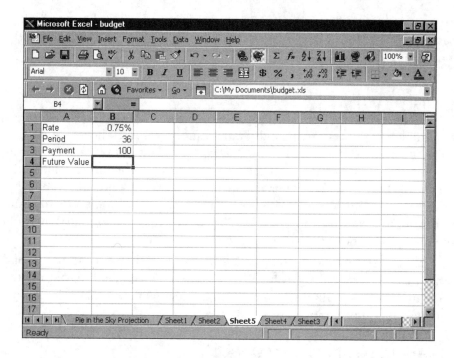

Figure 11.15 Setting up the data table worksheet.

3.   Click on cell **B4** and go through the following procedures:

   ❖ Click the **Paste Function** button.

   ❖ Choose **Financial**, **FV**.

   ❖ Click the **OK** button.

   ❖ Click on cell **B1** for the Rate and press the **Tab** key.

   ❖ Click on cell **B2** for the Nper (Number of Periods) and press the **Tab** key.

   ❖ Click on cell **B3** for the Payment and click on the **OK** button.

   Basically, you just used the Paste Function to create the FV formula in cell B4. The complete details of using the Paste Function are provided in Chapter 4.

4.   Click in cell **D2** and type **=B4**. This is the first cell of the table you are going to create. The starting cell will be the same as the result of the FV function.

5. Starting in cell C3, let's list the *what if* variables. In cell C1 type **Test Values**. Then enter the values shown in Figure 11.16. Adjust the column widths as necessary.

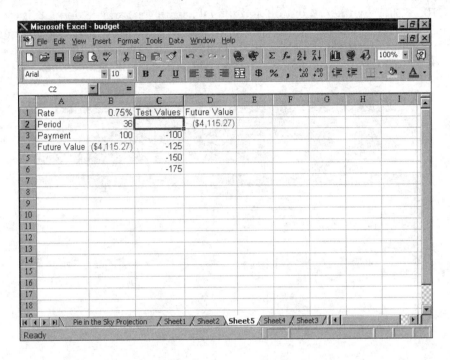

Figure 11.16 *Entering test values for the table.*

6. Highlight cells C2 through D6, which will make up your table.

7. Select the **Table...** command from the Data menu. The Table dialog box appears, as shown in Figure 11.17.

Figure 11.17 *The Table dialog box.*

8. Since we want data to appear in a column format, click in the **Column input cell** dialog box.

9. Click in cell **B3** because this is the variable data you're using (an absolute reference to the cell will be displayed in the Column Input Cell window).

10. Click on the **OK** button and the table with the variable deposits is created, which shows you how much you would earn depending on your monthly payment. Your table should look like Figure 11.18. You can format the cells using the **Currency Style** button on the Formatting toolbar.

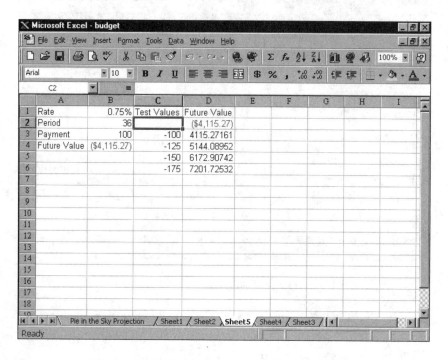

Figure 11.18 *The completed single-variable data table.*

Double-Variable Data Tables

Sometimes you may want to use the *what if* test when you have more than just one variable. Excel can produce data tables using double variables. In order to create a double-variable table, you must enter variable amounts in both rows and columns. Suppose you want to analyze different numbers of payments AND different payment amounts. Let's use the previous example to demonstrate double variable tables.

1. Select cells A1 through C6. Click on the **Copy** button, then move to cell A10 and click on the **Paste** button.

2. Proceed with the following entries (Each of the following represents the number of months):

   ❖ Click on cell **D11** and enter **36**.

   ❖ Click on cell **E11** and enter **42**.

   ❖ Click on cell **F11** and enter **54**.

3. In cell C11 you need to duplicate the Future Value Function in cell B13. Simply type **=B13**. Your screen should now look like Figure 11.19.

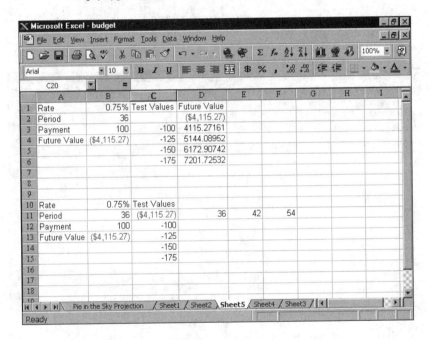

Figure 11.19 Setting up a double-variable table.

4. Highlight the entire table (cells C11 through F15).

5. Choose **Data**, **Table**. Click on cell **B11** (Nper) for the Row input cell. This indicates that the number of periods are listed across the top row of the table. Click on cell **B12** (payment amount) for the Column input cell. This indicates that the payment amounts are listed down the column of the table. Figure 11.20 shows the completed dialog box. When you're finished click **OK**.

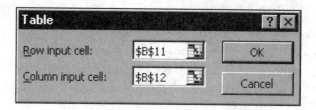

Figure 11.20 *The double-variable setup.*

6. To format your data, highlight cells D12 through F15 and click on the **Currency Style** button on the Formatting toolbar.

7. Expand the width of your columns to see the data. Your table should look like Figure 11.21.

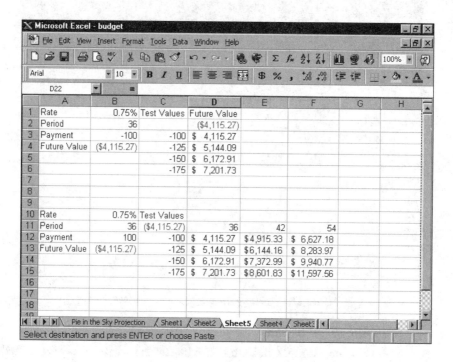

Figure 11.21 *The finished double-variable table.*

You have just created a double-variable table for finding the future value using the number of payments as one variable and the amount of payments as another variable.

Using Scenario Manager

Playing *what if* is one of the spreadsheet's most useful functions. You can change values in various cells of the worksheet to see the effect the changes will have. For example, what would happen if January sales increased by $100,000? You could just enter the new value in the January sales cell. But you'd have to keep re-entering values to switch between the scenarios.

You could use a data table as described earlier in this chapter. But data tables are only useful when you're inserting different variables into a formula to change the result of a single formula. There may be times when you want to experiment with many values on your worksheet—setting up scenarios for best-case budgets, or worst-case projections.

Excel's Scenario Manager makes switching between various what-if scenarios a breeze by letting you name the scenarios and then choosing the one you want to see from a list in the dialog box. Let's create scenarios for your BUDGET worksheet to allow you to switch among a couple of sales possibilities.

1. Click on the **Sheet1** tab to make the budget worksheet data visible and then choose **Tools**, **Scenario** to display the Scenario Manager dialog box, as shown in Figure 11.22.

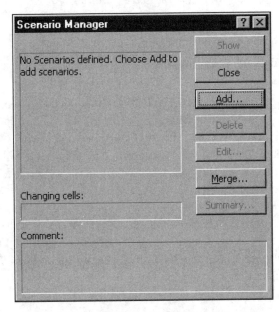

Figure 11.22 The Scenario Manager dialog box.

2. You don't have any scenarios defined yet, so click the **Add** button to create a scenario. The Add Scenario dialog box appears, as shown in Figure 11.23.

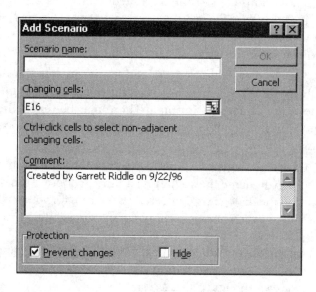

Figure 11.23 *The Add Scenario dialog box.*

3. In the Scenario name text box, type **Best Guess**.

4. Press **Tab** twice to highlight the entire comment that says Created by [Your Name] on MM/DD/YY and type **This is what I expect sales to be**.

5. Drag the dialog box down by its title bar so cells B5, C5, and D5 are visible, then click in the **Changing cells** text box. Highlight the information currently displayed in the Changing cells text box and press the **Delete** key. This is where you can define which cells will have different values for the scenario.

N O T E   The cells you specify as the Changing cells should not contain formulas. Instead, these should be cells containing values that formulas depend on. For example, B5 is the cell containing the January sales value, but several formulas in the worksheet depend on this value for their results. Therefore, B5 is a good choice for a Changing Cell.

6. Click on cell **B5**, then hold down the **Ctrl** key while you click on **C5** and then **D5**.

7. After checking to make sure your Add Scenario dialog box looks like the one shown in Figure 11.24, click **OK**.

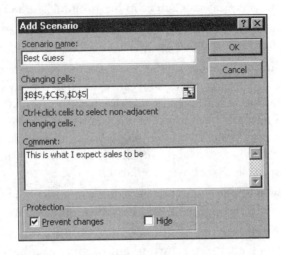

Figure 11.24 *The completed Add Scenario dialog box.*

The Scenario Values dialog box appears, as shown in Figure 11.25.

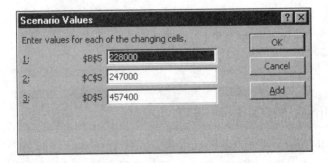

Figure 11.25 *The Scenario Values dialog box.*

8. Click the **Add** button to display the Add Scenario dialog box and try another scenario.

9. In the Scenario name text box, type **Wishful Thinking**, and edit the Comment box so the comment is **Not a chance**, then click **OK**.

10. Edit the values in the Scenario Values dialog box so the values are **328000** for $B$5, **347000** for $C$5, and **410000** for $D$4, then click **Add** again so you can add one more scenario.

11. In the Scenario name text box, type **The Sky is Falling!** and edit the Comment box so it says **You're in big trouble**. Then click **OK**.

12. Edit the values in the Scenario Values dialog box so the values are **128000** for $B$5, **147000** for $C$5, and **210000** for $D$5.

    The Scenario Manager dialog box appears once again, this time with the three scenarios listed. You can now click on any of the scenario names in the Scenarios list. Click the **Show** button and the worksheet changes to show the values for that scenario. You can switch among the scenarios while still in the dialog box and view the changes on the worksheet. When you close the dialog box, the worksheet displays the values from the last chosen scenario.

    As you switch between the three scenarios, notice that the numbers in cells E5, B14 through E14, and B16 through E16 change.

13. When you're finished experimenting with the scenarios, switch to the Best Guess scenario to return to our original numbers and then click **Close** to clear the Scenario Manager dialog box.

14. Save your work.

NOTE

Your scenarios are saved with the workbook so they're available whenever you use this worksheet in the workbook.

OUTLINING WORKSHEETS

As your skills improve and your applications for Excel expand, there will be times when you'll need to manage worksheets, and probably workbooks, containing massive data. Managing and tracking large worksheets can be very difficult and confusing. Excel has a feature called *outlining* that consolidates portions of your worksheet's data, and thereby makes large worksheets more manageable. Let's go over what outlining is and then give you some hands-on experience creating outlines.

Excel 97 is designed on the premise that most people use their worksheets to calculate totals. After all, that's a worksheet's chief application. You calculate totals in columns and in rows to come up with subtotals. Then you calculate your subtotals to come up with grand totals. Next you calculate these grand totals to come up with grand-grand totals. Before long, your worksheet contains a massive grand total in the last row of your worksheet, while the data for this grand total starts in cell A1. Managing such a worksheet, or a similar scenario, can be a nightmare.

Outlining is a feature in Excel that allows you to consolidate all your subtotals, totals, grand totals, grand-grand totals, and so on. Outlining will display only the totals you choose, without displaying the accompanying data used to make up these totals. Having the ability to display only totals and not the data that makes up the totals is why this feature is called outlining.

Before you try your hand at outlining, lets talk a little about levels of data. Most worksheets employ a natural hierarchy as it relates to levels of data. The lowest level of data is a simple value in a cell. These values are not formulas—they're simply values. The next level of data are formulas that calculate this lowest level of data. Then you move to the next level of data which are more formulas that calculate the previous formulas and so on.

The outlining feature's main task is to view selected levels of data without having to view all the data. Let's go through an illustration to help you understand outlining better.

1.   Create a new worksheet by right-clicking any of the existing sheet tabs and choosing **Insert**, **Worksheet** from the shortcut menu.

2.   In Figure 11.26 you'll see a worksheet with several levels of data. Re-create this worksheet by entering the data into your worksheet as shown.

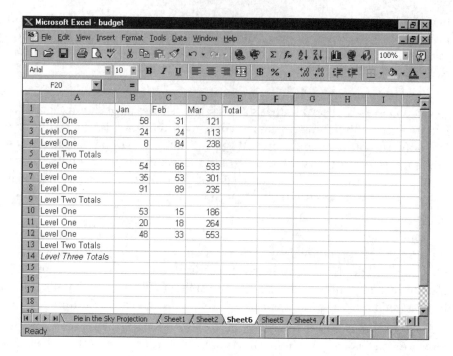

Figure 11.26 *Data for worksheet with levels of data.*

3. Using the **AutoSum** button on the Standard toolbar, let Excel calculate the sums of the Level Two Totals for Jan, Feb, and Mar. Highlight cells B5, C5, and D5, then click the **AutoSum** button. Repeat this process for the totals in rows 9, 13, and 14.

4. Highlight cells E2 through E14 and click on the **AutoSum** button to calculate the row totals. Your worksheet should now look like Figure 11.27.

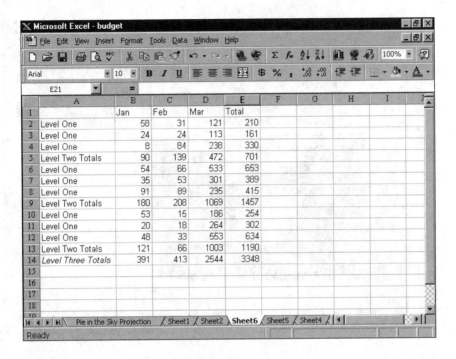

Figure 11.27 *A worksheet with many levels of data.*

5. Highlight cells A2 through E14. These are the data and formulas we want to outline.

6. From the Data menu, choose **Group and Outline**, **AutoOutline**. Your screen should look like Figure 11.28.

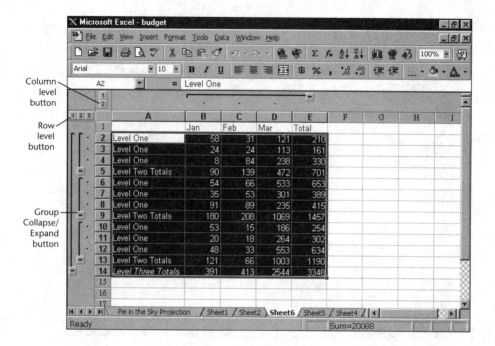

Figure 11.28 Outlined data.

You just had Excel automatically outline your worksheet. You'll notice it has placed outlining symbols on the top and right side of the worksheet. The symbols allow you to determine what level of data you want to see and what level of data you don't want to see.

Let's look a little closer at the outlining symbols and tools. You can see that the basic outlining symbol is a line with a bracket on one end and a box attached to the other end with a minus sign in the middle of it. Each cell that contains a formula (total) has an outlining symbol indicating which cells contain the data that makes up the total. For example, if you look at the Level Two Totals in cell B5, and then look over to the left to the outlining symbol, you'll notice that rows 2 through 5 are bracketed. This is because the total of rows 2 through 4 are contained in row 5—B5 to be exact. Notice that rows 6 through 9 and rows 10 through 13 are also bracketed. The totals are in row 9 and in row 13 respectively.

The box with the minus sign in it is the outlining tool called the Group Collapse/Expand button. The minus sign indicates that the group is fully expanded. To collapse a group and hide the data in the group, simply click on the **Group Collapse/Expand** button.

Follow these steps to collapse your worksheet.

1. Click the **Group Collapse/Expand** button for row 5.
2. Click the **Group Collapse/Expand** button for row 9.
3. Click the **Group Collapse/Expand** button for row 13.

Your worksheet should look like Figure 11.29.

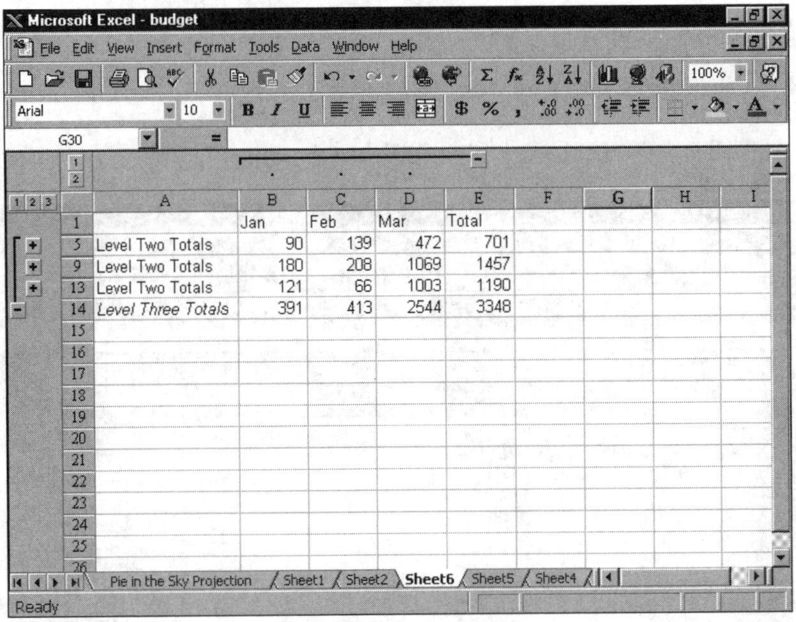

Figure 11.29 *A collapsed worksheet.*

Excel has hidden all the data in each group and displays only the group totals. The minus sign inside the box has been replaced with a plus sign to indicate that the group can be expanded to display more data.

You only had one Level Three Total. Notice it brackets the entire worksheet. Larger worksheets obviously would contain more Level Three Totals, as well as Level Four Totals, etc.

You can gain a sense of how useful consolidation can be with a large worksheet. It simplifies your data and lets you see only what you want to see. It allows you to choose the level of data that's important to you.

Another benefit in outlining is that sometimes you only want to print totals, without having to print the entire worksheet (which could expand several pages of data). Moreover, you'll want those totals on only one page. Outlining allows you to suppress the data you don't need and print only the totals that are relevant for you.

Now, note the outlining symbol above the worksheet. Since your example used only one column total, there's only one outlining tool. If you had used more column totals, then you would have had more outlining symbols for the columns.

❖ Click the **Group Collapse/Expand** button on the top of the worksheet.

Your worksheet should look like Figure 11.30.

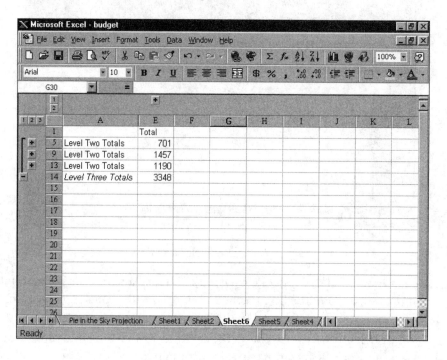

Figure 11.30 *Collapsed columns.*

Notice that all the data columns for the group were collapsed (Jan, Feb, Mar) and only the total column remained.

One final explanation before we get off this topic. Have you wondered what the two vertical buttons numbered one, two, and three are for? These buttons are called the Row Level button and the Column Level button. You can click the **Row Level** button to display the corresponding level of data you want to see. You can also click the **Column Level** button to display the level of data you want to view in your columns.

Suppose you want to see all levels of data in the sample worksheet. Do the following.

1. Click box **2** on the Column Level button.

2. Click box **3** on the Row Level button.

These steps told Excel to display the columns by 2 data levels, which is the maximum in your example, and display the rows by 3 data levels, which is again the maximum in the example.

Add more data to your worksheet, especially column totals, and practice using Excel's outlining feature. When you're finished, don't forget to save your work.

A FINAL THOUGHT

In this chapter you learned to use just a few of Excel's tools for proofing and analyzing your worksheet data. You now know how to ensure that your data is free of spelling errors and how to view the data in a variety of ways using the PivotTable and Scenario Manager. In the next chapter you'll learn about one of the biggest time savers in Excel—Macros.

CHAPTER 12

Automating Your Work with Macros

UNDERSTANDING MACROS

Without a program, your computer is nothing more than a big, expensive paperweight. A program is a set of instructions, in a language your computer can understand, which allows your computer to perform useful (or so one would hope) tasks. Excel is a big computer program that tells your computer what to do. A *macro* is nothing more than a little program (in this case, inside Excel) that tells Excel what to do.

Don't let the word *program* scare you. You can use Excel macros to cut time-consuming, repetitive tasks down to size without knowing the first thing about

309

programming. Excel lets you record any series of Excel actions for later use, just as you would record a series of sounds on a tape recorder for future playback.

Suppose you routinely format groups of selected cells in some particular way—perhaps centering their contents, surrounding them with a border, and adjusting the column width to accommodate the longest entry. To do this manually, you have to perform three separate tasks requiring numerous mouse actions or keystrokes. However, if you record these tasks as a macro, you can perform them all at once with a couple of mouse clicks or keystrokes to run (play) the macro.

Another common use for a macro is to automate the typing of frequently entered text, such as your name, address, or company name. Recording frequently entered text as macros saves time and eliminates typos—assuming you type things correctly while recording the macro.

This cell formatting example is a very simple illustration of what you can do with macros. Literally any series of tasks can be consolidated into a single macro—no series of tasks is too simple or too complex.

Consider the toolbar buttons, which are actually shortcuts for performing tasks. Some buttons, such as the Open button, don't save you much time. Instead of clicking on the **Open** button, you could simply choose **File**, **Open...**. It may hardly seem worth the effort to use a button to save one keystroke or mouse click. However, because opening files is something that is repeated many times during a typical Excel session, the button can accumulate a savings in time that is worthwhile.

Let's discuss the issue of programming. You don't need to know anything about programming to make use of macros. However, if you take the time to learn a little about Excel's programming language, you can extend your macros' potential flexibility and complexity enormously.

Even if you don't do any programming and just use Excel's macro recorder, you are actually programming. Huh? Let us explain. When you turn on the macro recorder and perform the tasks you want included in the macro, Excel creates a computer program for you and runs the program when you run the macro.

NOTE

The programming language Excel uses to create your macros is called *VBA* (Visual Basic for Applications). This language is an extension of the BASIC programming language that comes with many computers. In fact, you may already have some familiarity with BASIC. If you already know a little about any version of BASIC, you won't have any trouble adapting to VBA. If you have no clue about the ins and outs of programming but have some healthy curiosity, you can quickly learn some simple VBA programming from the documentation included with Excel.

PLANNING A MACRO

There are a couple of things to take into account before you start recording a macro. The first is planning.

When you record a macro, everything you do (including mistakes) is recorded in the macro and turned into program code. For example, if you start recording a macro while in one worksheet and then realize that you want to use the macro on another worksheet, you switch to the other worksheet and start performing the tasks you want to be part of the macro. The problem is, whenever you run the macro, the first thing it will do is switch to a different worksheet, which probably isn't what you want to do at that point. Recording a macro with a lot of mistakes can also slow down the execution of the macro.

If you want the macro to manipulate some selected cells, you need to perform the macro recording tasks on a single active cell in the worksheet. Select that cell before starting the recording process. This way, when you run the macro, it performs on the current selection.

You also need to consider whether the macro uses absolute or relative referencing. The concept is the same as the absolute versus relative referencing discussion in the copying formulas section of Chapter 5. If your active cell is A1 when you start recording the macro using absolute referencing, and you click on cell D6, the first thing the macro does when played is move to cell D6. If you were using relative referencing—which is the default—the macro would move three columns to the right and five rows down, which is D6's relative position from A1. As a general rule, relative referencing allows your macros to operate correctly in a variety of situations.

STORING MACROS

Macros are stored on *module sheets.* Module sheets are very much like worksheets, but their only purpose is to maintain macros and their instructions. Module sheets can be stored as one of the sheets in the workbook you're working in or the Personal Macro Workbook. You instruct Excel where to store your macros.

When macros are stored in the workbook you're working with, they are called *local macros.* When you select the **Store macro in this workbook** option (we'll show you where to select this option later), Excel stores your macro in a hidden workbook. When you open any workbook, the Personal Macro Workbook also opens, albeit as a hidden file. The macros are called global or personal macros because they can be executed from any workbook.

If you need to view the Personal Macro Workbook, possibly for editing macros in it, you can reveal the file by using the **Unhide...** command from the Window menu. Don't forget to hide the Personal Macro Workbook when you're finished with any edits. The Personal Macro Workbook is created by Excel when you store your first global macro. If the Unhide... command doesn't appear when you go to view the Personal Macro Workbook, it simply means that no macros have been created and stored there yet. This will become clear as you progress through this chapter.

In planning your macros, you should decide if the macro will be used with several workbooks or just one. For example, if you planned a macro that creates PivotTables exclusively from the data in your SALES file, then you should store your macro in the SALES file by choosing the **Store macro in This Workbook** option. However, if you planned a macro that generates your company name, centers it, bolds it, and italicizes it, this macro can be used in more than one workbook, and you should store this macro as a global macro by choosing the **Store macro in Personal Macro Workbook** option. You'll see where this option appears as you work through the example in this chapter.

You can also store macros in a new workbook, but in order to use the macros, you would always have to open the new workbook where the macros are stored. It's better to store them locally in the workbook you will use them in, or globally.

RECORDING A MACRO

Let's start recording the cell formatting macro now.

1. Start Excel and open the **BUDGET** workbook if it isn't already on your screen. Create a new worksheet by right-clicking on any of the existing sheet tabs and choosing **Insert...**, **Worksheet**. It isn't necessary to record the macro on an unused sheet, but doing so ensures that you won't mess up any existing worksheet data while recording your macro.

2. Click on cell **B2** to make it the active cell and then choose **Tools**, **Macro...**, **Record New Macro...** to display the Record Macro dialog box, as shown in Figure 12.1.

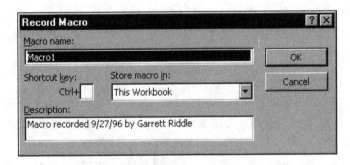

Figure 12.1 *The Record Macro dialog box.*

For this macro, any active cell will work. Using a cell that is at least one row down and one column over allows you to see all sides of the border the macro adds. You could allow Excel to name the macro for you (in this case Macro1) but that's not very descriptive, so let's give it a new name.

3. With the Macro name text box highlighted, type **CellFmt** and press the **Tab** key to highlight the contents of the Description box.

4. In the Description box, type **Formats selection center aligned, places border and AutoFits column width**. This macro works on any group of selected cells, so you'll want to make sure it's available whenever you need it.

5. Click on the **Arrow** next to the Store macro in drop-down list to display all the storage options, as shown in Figure 12.2.

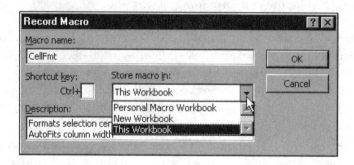

Figure 12.2 *The drop-down list of Store macro in options.*

6. Click on **Personal Macro Workbook** in the drop-down list to ensure that the macro is available on any worksheet you may open now or in the future.

7. Click on the **OK** button to begin the macro recording session. You can tell you are recording a macro because the status bar displays the message `Recording`. There is also a small toolbar floating on the screen with Stop Recording and Relative Reference buttons, as displayed in Figure 12.3.

   Before performing the macro tasks, you need to make sure you're using Relative References so the macro works on any group of selected cells and not just on B2.

8. Click on the **Relative Reference** button on the Stop Rec toolbar. Now you can proceed to format the active cell for center alignment, place a single-line border around it, and AutoFit the selection.

9. Display the shortcut menu for the active cell by right-clicking on it. Choose **Format Cells...**, click on the **Alignment** tab, and choose **Center** in the Horizontal area of the dialog box. Don't click OK yet.

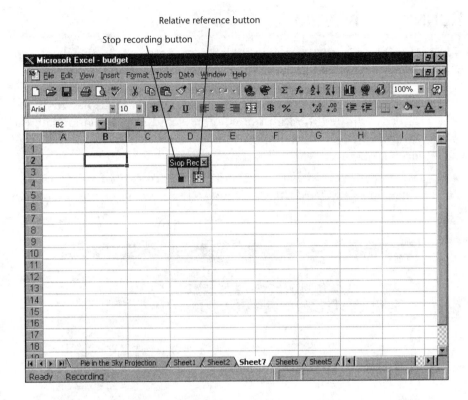

Figure 12.3 *The Stop Rec toolbar and the status bar displaying* `Recording`.

10.   Click on the **Border** tab, then select **Outline** in the Presets section of the dialog box, and click **OK**.

11.   Choose **Format**, **Column**, **AutoFit Selection**.

12.   Click on the **Stop Recording** button in the floating Stop Rec toolbar, and then click on another cell so you can see the border around the cell. Since the cell is empty, you can't tell if the type in the cell is centered or the width is adjusted to accommodate it. You'll see the complete results of the macro when you run it on a real selection.

RUNNING A MACRO

Now that you've recorded a macro, let's select some cells in the sheet containing your database and try it out.

1. Click on the **Sheet2** tab (the database sheet) to display it. If you already adjusted the width of column A and B to accommodate the largest entries, reduce their widths now so at least some of the text in each is obscured.

2. Select cells A2 through A12 and choose **Tools**, **Macro**, **Macros....** Click on **PERSONAL.XLS!CellFmt** so that it is highlighted, as shown in Figure 12.4.

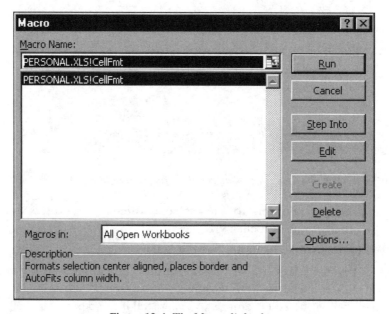

Figure 12.4 *The Macro dialog box.*

Your Macro dialog box may contain the names of other macros if there are any others stored in the PERSONAL.XLS dialog box or on any other open workbook.

N O T E

3. Click the **Run** button to execute the macro.

The list of items in column A is now center-aligned, with a border around it and with the column width adjusted to fit the largest entry.

That's all there is to running a macro from the Macro dialog box. Now let's take a look at ways to make it even easier to run a macro.

UNHIDING THE PERSONAL MACRO WORKBOOK

Let's change the options for the CellFmt macro in the PERSONAL.XLS workbook. The PERSONAL.XLS workbook is hidden, so before you can make any changes to the CellFmt macro, you have to unhide the PERSONAL.XLS workbook.

1. Choose **Window**, **Unhide...** to display the Unhide dialog box, as displayed in Figure 12.5.

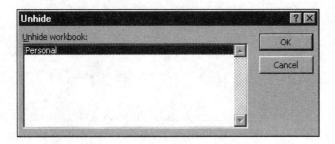

Figure 12.5 The Unhide dialog box.

If there are any other open but hidden workbooks, these are listed along with Personal.

2. Click on **Personal**, if it isn't already highlighted, and click the **OK** button. The Personal workbook with one tab, Sheet 1, is displayed as shown in Figure 12.6.

3. Choose **Tools**, **Macro**, **Macros...** to bring up the Macro dialog box.

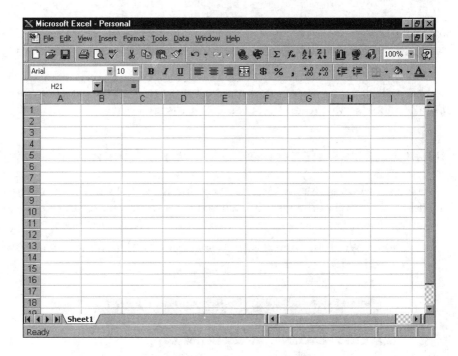

Figure 12.6 *The Personal workbook.*

4. Select **CellFmt**, if it isn't already highlighted, and click on the **Edit** button. The Microsoft Visual Basic screen will appear, as shown in Figure 12.7.

   With the macro displayed, you could edit it to correct mistakes or add functionality. Even if you do not know the first thing about programming, you may find it interesting to look over the macro. You'll be surprised at how easily you'll understand what's going on.

WARNING

Unless you know what you're doing and have a reasonable understanding of Visual Basic, you should not edit the macro in any way. Even making some seemingly innocuous changes could leave the macro completely useless.

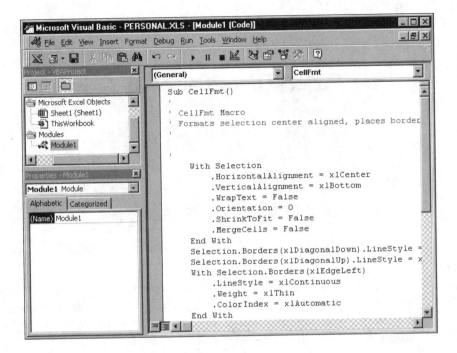

Figure 12.7 The Microsoft Visual Basic screen.

5. Exit out of the Visual Basic Editor by clicking on the **Close** button. You will return to the PERSONAL.XLS workbook.

ASSIGNING MACROS TO MENUS AND SHORTCUT KEYS

Now that the workbook containing your macro is unhidden, you can switch back to the Budget workbook and change the macro options. The Record Macro dialog box has a Shortcut key area. This area allows you to create a keystroke that will initiate the playing of the macro you have designated.

1. Choose **Window**, click on **BUDGET**, and move to a blank worksheet.

2. Now that you're back in familiar territory, choose **Tools**, **Macro**, **Macros...** and click on **PERSONAL.XLS!CellFmt**.

3. Click the **Options...** button to display the Macro Options dialog box as shown in Figure 12.8.

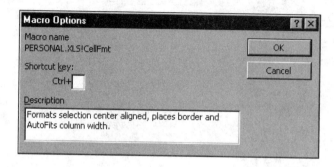

Figure 12.8 *The Macro Options dialog box.*

You can enter any of the 26 letters of the alphabet (uppercase or lowercase) in the shortcut key dialog box. You have more than 52 possible shortcut key combinations, but be very careful. Excel lets you assign letters that have already been designated as a shortcut key for other functions. For example, if you choose **Ctrl-f** as the shortcut key combination for a macro, then **Ctrl-f** is no longer the shortcut for Find. We know that the letter *e* hasn't been taken, so let's use that for this example.

4. Type **e** in the shortcut dialog box and click on the **OK** button.

5. Exit the Macro dialog box by clicking the **Close** button.

That's all it takes to create a shortcut key. Now let's add your macro to a menu.

1. Choose **Tools**, **Customize...** to bring up the Customize dialog box shown in Figure 12.9.

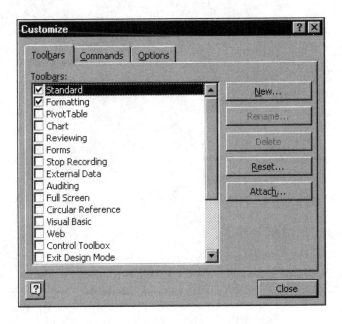

Figure 12.9 *The Customize dialog box.*

2. Click on the **Commands** tab. Scroll down the Categories list and select **Macros**.

3. Press and hold your left mouse button on the **Custom Menu Item** option in the Commands list. While still holding your left mouse button down, move your pointer up to the Tools menu as shown in Figure 12.10.

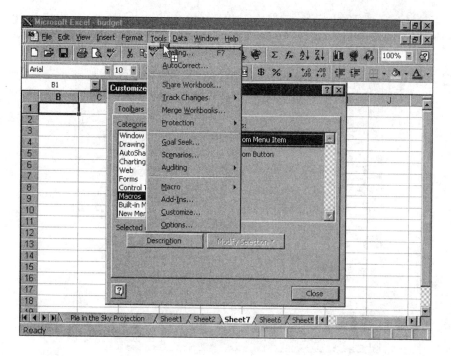

Figure 12.10 *Assigning a macro to a menu.*

The Tools drop-down menu will appear, and if you move your mouse pointer down the list you'll notice a horizontal line that follows it. This line serves as an insertion point indicator.

4.   Drag the mouse pointer below the Macros option and release the left mouse button. The words `Custom Menu Item` appear with a border surrounding them.

5.   Right-click on **Custom Menu Item** to call up the shortcut menu.

6. Click on **Name:** and delete the text in the adjoining dialog box. Type **Center/Border/AutoFit** and press **Enter**. Your menu should look like Figure 12.11.

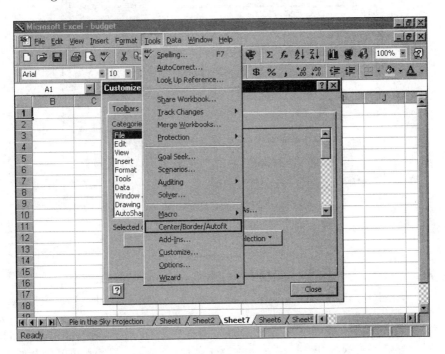

Figure 12.11 Adding a macro to the Tools menu.

7. Right-click on **Center/Border/AutoFit** to recall the shortcut menu.

8. Select **Assign Macro...**, and the Assign Macro dialog box will appear as shown in Figure 12.12.

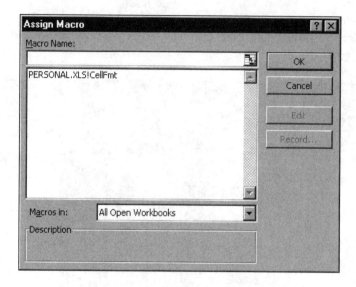

Figure 12.12 *The Assign Macro dialog box.*

9.   Click on **PERSONAL.XLS!CellFmt**, and click the **OK** button.

10.   Click on the **Close** button to exit the Customize dialog box. The text you typed—**Center/Border/AutoFit**—is the text that appears in the Tools menu. The menu width will adjust to accommodate as much text that will fit on one line across the screen. However, it's best to keep the menu text reasonably short so the menu doesn't obscure too much of the screen.

The whole point of using macros is to save time. That being the case, choosing **Tools**, **Macro**, **Macros...**, selecting a macro name, and then clicking the **Run** button is far too tedious a process for executing a simple macro. You now have two ways to run the macro: from the Tools menu and the shortcut key. Let's use them both.

1.   Select cells B2 through B11 (the category column) and choose **Tools** to display the Tools menu, as shown in Figure 12.13.

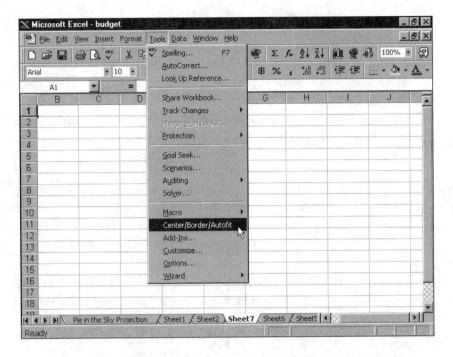

Figure 12.13 The revised Tools menu.

2. Click on **Center/Border/AutoFit**. There now, wasn't that easier? To use the shortcut key on a column that needs reformatting, you can close the Budget workbook without saving it, and then open it again.

3. Close the Budget workbook by choosing **File**, **Close** and click on **No** when asked if you want to save the changes. Then reopen the Budget workbook and go to Sheet2.

4. Once again, select cells B2 through B11 and press the shortcut key combination, **Ctrl-e**.

ASSIGNING MACROS TO TOOLBAR BUTTONS

This is getting just a bit too easy, don't you think? Well, we're still not finished making life easier with macros. You can also assign a macro to a button on a toolbar.

1. Close the BUDGET workbook again without saving, and reopen it as before.

2. Choose **Tools, Customize...** to display the Customize dialog box.

3. Click on the **Commands** tab if it isn't already chosen, and select **Macros** from the Categories options.

4. Click and hold your left mouse button on the **Custom Button** option in the Commands list. While still holding your left mouse button down, move your pointer up to the Formatting toolbar.

 NOTE You can create some space on a toolbar for new macro buttons, or just to remove some clutter, by dragging the button you want to remove down onto the worksheet. You have enough room to add another button to the Formatting toolbar, so you don't need to worry about it now.

5. Drag the button between the Italic and Underline buttons. Release the mouse button to accept the button position, as shown in Figure 12.14.

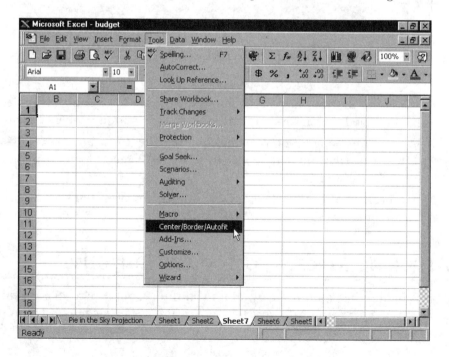

Figure 12.14 *The new button on the Formatting toolbar.*

6. Right-click on the selected button to display the shortcut menu.

7. Click on **Name:** and delete the text in the adjoining dialog box. Type **Center/Border/AutoFit**.

8. Select **Assign Macro…**, and the Assign Macro dialog box will appear.

9. Click on **PERSONAL.XLS!CellFmt**, and click the **OK** button.

10. Click on the **Close** button to exit the Customize dialog box.

11. Select B2 through B11 again and then click on your new smiley-face macro button.

Restoring the default toolbar setting is just as easy.

1. Choose **Tools, Customize** to bring up the Customize dialog box.

2. Click on the **Toolbars** tab of the Customize dialog box, and select **Formatting** from the Toolbars list.

3. Click the **Reset…** button. A dialog box will appear asking you if you're sure you want to make these changes. Click **OK**.

ASSIGNING MACROS TO BUTTONS ON THE WORKSHEET

If you thought assigning macros to a toolbar was neat, wait until you assign a macro to a button on the worksheet. You may have occasions where you'd like a *floating* button. Floating macro buttons are good when you want the button to stay in a particular area of the worksheet, namely close to the chart or data that the macro is designed to manipulate. Try the following exercise and see what you think.

1. Close the Budget workbook again without saving the changes, and reopen it as before.

2. Place the mouse pointer over any button on the toolbar that is displayed, right-click the mouse button to display the shortcut menu, and choose **Forms** to display the Forms toolbar, as shown in Figure 12.15.

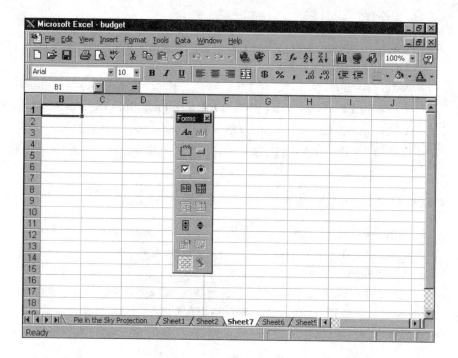

Figure 12.15 *The Forms toolbar.*

3. Click on the **Button** button (the second button down in the right column).

4. Place your mouse pointer somewhere outside cells B2 through B11. Click and drag the mouse to the approximate size you want the button, but don't obscure cells B2 through B11. (Don't make your button too small or you won't be able to read the temporary name that Excel gives it.)

5. When you release the left-mouse button the Assign Macro dialog box will appear. Again, you can assign any available macro in the Assign Macro dialog box.

6. Select **PERSONAL.XLS!CellFmt** and then click **OK**. Your floating button is probably named Control 1 and is currently selected. When the button is selected you can change the size, name or font of the button. Let's change the name before you use the button.

7. Click inside the button and delete the previous name. Type **Cell Format**, and click anywhere on the worksheet.

8. Select cells B2 through B11 and click on your new floating Worksheet Button to execute the macro. Notice when you place the mouse

pointer on top of the floating button the thick cross pointer changes to a pointing finger. When the mouse pointer is a pointing finger, you can click on the floating button to activate the macro.

9. Scroll down the worksheet and watch your floating macro button scroll with the worksheet. Scroll back up to have it reappear on the screen.

NOTE   To select a floating button that's attached to a worksheet in order to cut, paste, copy, etc., you must first right-click on the button to bring up the shortcut menu. An easier way is to hold the **Ctrl** key down before clicking on the floating button.

ASSIGNING MACROS TO DRAWING OBJECTS

Now the fun really begins. You can assign macros to any worksheet or drawing object. You can even import graphical objects from other programs into Excel and turn them into macro buttons. Using objects as macro buttons, your designs and choices are virtually limitless. We'll use a simple oval shape in our demonstration, but you can use your creativity in the future.

1. Close the Budget workbook again without saving and reopen it, as before.

2. Click the **Drawing** button on the Standard toolbar. The Drawing toolbar will appear.

3. Click on the **Oval** button (the fourth button to the right of AutoShapes).

4. Place your mouse pointer near cells B2 through B11. Click and drag the mouse to the appropriate size you want the button, but don't obscure cells B2 through B11.

5. Right-click on the new object to reveal the shortcut menu. Select **Assign Macro...**. Again, you can assign any available macro in the Assign Macro dialog box.

6. Select **PERSONAL.XLS!CellFmt** and then click **OK.**

7. Select cells B2 through B11 and click on your new floating oval object to execute the macro.

That's all there is to making macros easier to execute. You shouldn't have any more excuses for not using them, even though they involve that nasty programming stuff.

1. Choose **Window**, click on **PERSONAL.XLS**, and then choose **Window**, **Hide**.

2. Save your work and exit Excel if you're not proceeding to the next chapter. If you wish to exit, Excel will ask if you wish to save the changes made to PERSONAL.XLS (the Personal Macro Workbook). Click on the **Yes** button to save your work.

A FINAL THOUGHT

This chapter covered the basics of planning, recording and executing macros. We strongly encourage you to invest more time and energy exploring the vast power of macros and macro programming. It is time well spent.

The next chapter looks at the process of linking worksheets.

CHAPTER 13

Linking Worksheets

UNDERSTANDING LINKING CONCEPTS

You may or may not have been working in only one workbook throughout the exercises we've covered so far. You have probably, however, been working in more than one worksheet throughout these exercises. The worksheets you've been creating have no special relationship to each other, except that some contain information about a single company.

There are many situations that call for tying data from two or more workbooks together. This process of tying data together is called *linking*. You can also link data between worksheets in the same workbook.

There's nothing magical or mysterious about linking. When you link data from one worksheet to another, you are simply using the referencing concepts that have been discussed since we started creating formulas. However, when you create links to other worksheets—whether they are in the same or a different workbook—the reference includes the workbook name (if it's a different workbook), the sheet name, and then the cell address or range.

Linking is commonly used for several different purposes. You can use linking to break a large, complex worksheet into smaller, more manageable chunks. You might want to keep some confidential data in a separate worksheet to keep prying eyes away, or you may want to segregate your worksheet by company, department, or activity.

A very good reason for linking to worksheets in different workbooks is to summarize data from several company divisions. Suppose your company has offices in three cities and each creates a worksheet detailing weekly sales activity. By linking, the manager at each location could send a disk containing the workbook to company headquarters, where the new numbers could be brought into the summary, or master worksheet.

N O T E   Of course, you don't have to place confidential information in a separate sheet. You can hide any portion of a worksheet that you do not want in plain sight. However, it can be less cumbersome to place the data in another worksheet so it's available to you by switching to that sheet, rather than having to unhide and rehide it every time you want to see it.

When you create links, you are dealing with at least two worksheets: a source worksheet and a dependent worksheet. The *source worksheet* contains the data that you want to bring into the dependent worksheet. After a link is created, the linked data in the *dependent worksheet* is automatically updated when the linked data in the source worksheet is updated.

Linking worksheets is different from a simple copy-and-paste operation. If you copy a value from one worksheet and then paste it into another, you are simply copying the value and not establishing a link. If the value in the source worksheet (the one you copied from) changes, the value in the dependent worksheet does not change.

If you try to use copy and paste to copy a formula from one worksheet to another, it does not work at all. The requisite workbook and worksheet portions of the reference are not copied; you end up with an invalid formula.

CREATING LINKS

If the worksheets you want to link are already created, you can simply open them and create the link references from the source worksheet(s) to the dependent worksheet. In our case the worksheets and workbooks we want to link are not created. So you need to create them before we can discuss linking them. The following section will guide you through creating multiple workbooks.

Creating Multiple Workbooks

Before we can demonstrate how to link workbooks and worksheets, you must first create multiple workbooks to use in our linking examples. You'll create three simple worksheets in separate workbooks to track sales data for Spokane Locks and Bagels' three locations. These are the source worksheets. You'll then create a dependent worksheet to let you summarize the data from the source worksheet.

1. Start Excel. If the Budget workbook or any other workbooks containing data are on your screen, close them and click on the Standard toolbar's **New** button to open a fresh workbook.

2. Type **SALES** in cell A1.

3. In cell A3 type **Total Sales**, press **Enter** to confirm the entry, and then double-click on the column heading border of column A to adjust the width to accommodate the entries. Your screen should now look like Figure 13.1.

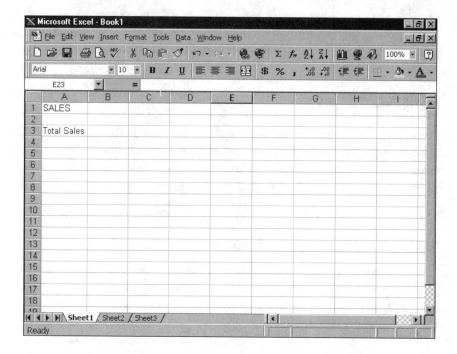

Figure 13.1 *The first sales sheet.*

Let's copy the worksheet to two other sheets in two new workbooks. This worksheet is simple enough that you can enter the data manually into the other worksheets. But copying the worksheet can be a real time saver when you want to create multiple worksheets with an identical structure.

4. Choose **Edit**, **Move or Copy Sheet…** to display the Move or Copy dialog box shown in Figure 13.2.

5. Click on the **Arrow** next to the text box under To book to display the list of books you can move or copy the worksheet to.

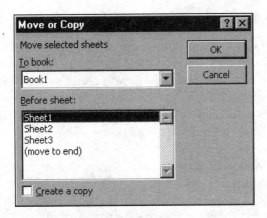

Figure 13.2 *The Move or Copy dialog box.*

6. Select **(new book)**. Then click the **Create a copy** check box and click **OK** to make the copy. Let's create a third source workbook by copying your current worksheet, but this time you'll use the shortcut menu to perform the copy.

7. Place the mouse pointer on the active sheet tab at the bottom of the worksheet and press the right mouse button to bring up the shortcut menu.

8. Select **Move or Copy...** to display the Move or Copy dialog box, as shown in Figure 13.2.

9. Click on the **Arrow** next to the text box under To book to display the list of books you can move or copy the worksheet to.

10. Select **(new book)**. Then click the **Create a copy** check box and click **OK** to make the copy.

11. Click on the Standard toolbar's **New** button to create a new empty workbook so you can enter the structure for the summary sheet.

12. In cell A1, type **MASTER SALES SHEET**.

13. In cell A3 type **Downtown**; in A4 type **Valley**; and in A5 type **Northside**.

Adding Data to the Workbooks

Now that you've created multiple workbooks, let's create the data for each worksheet. Once you have entered the data, you can begin linking the source worksheet to the dependent worksheet. You could switch to each of them one at a time, but it's often easier to be able to see a portion of all the worksheets at once. To do this you can use Windows 95's ability to organize the four workbook windows into four equal-sized tiles on the screen.

1. Choose **Window, Arrange...** to display the Arrange Windows dialog box, as shown in Figure 13.3.

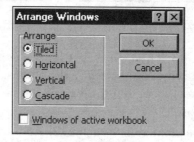

Figure 13.3 *The Arrange Windows dialog box.*

2. The **Tiled** option is the default, so just click the **OK** button to tile the four windows, as shown in Figure 13.4.

   You can easily tell which window is active, because it is the one with the highlighted title bar and scroll bars. You can change active windows by choosing **Window** and then the name of the window you want. The easiest way to change active windows is to simply click on it. Let's add location and sales information in cells B1 and B3 of each of the source windows.

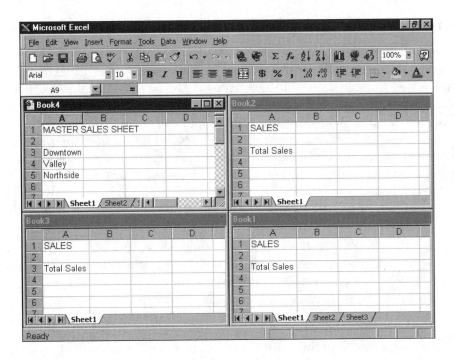

Figure 13.4 *The tiled windows.*

3. Click anywhere in the window in the upper-right portion of the screen. In Figure 13.4 this window is Book2.

4. In cell B1 type **DOWNTOWN**. In B3 type **$31,000** and then click anywhere in the window below (Book1) to make it the active window.

5. In cell B1 type **VALLEY**. In B3 type **$27,500** and then click in the window on the lower left (Book3) to make it the active window.

6. In cell B1 type **NORTHSIDE**. In B3 type **$58,000** and then click in the Master Sales window in the upper-left corner.

Creating Linking Formulas

Now you're ready to link your workbooks. In order to link workbooks together, you must create linking formulas. As with any other Excel formula, the linking formula starts with an equal sign. Also, as with any other Excel formula, once the equal sign is entered, Excel allows you to click on cells and cell ranges to include their addresses in the formula. In creating linking formulas, you can also click on cells from a different workbook and have their address entered into your formula. We have tiled the three source workbooks and the one dependent workbook (Master Sales) to illustrate this.

1. Click in cell **B3** of the Master Sales window, which is where the Downtown sales figure will be. Type =.

2. Click twice on cell **B3** in the Downtown sheet (Book 2 in the figure). The formula in the formula bar is `=[Book2]Sheet1!$B$3`. Press the **Enter** key. Now you can add the other links.

3. With cell B4 in the Master Sales sheet selected, type =.

4. Click twice on cell **B3** of the Valley window and press **Enter**.

5. With cell B5 in the Master Sales sheet selected, type =. Click twice on cell **B3** of the Northside window, and press **Enter**. The sales numbers for each location are now linked to the master sheet, as shown in Figure 13.5.

   If any of the sales numbers in the source sheets change, the numbers in the dependent Master Sales sheet also change. Let's try changing one of the numbers to see if it works.

6. Change the sales number in the Downtown sheet to **$41,000** and observe the corresponding change in the Master Sales window.

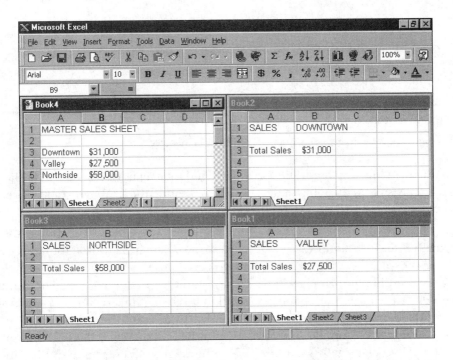

Figure 13.5 The tiled windows with sales numbers.

Not only can you create links between different workbooks, but you can also create links within the same workbook between separate worksheets or pages. To link within a workbook, you start with an equal sign as in the above example. Then click on the desired page tab within the workbook to activate the page. Finally, click on the desired cell to create a link between the sheets. The actual linking formula references the worksheet name and the cell address as shown in Table 13.1. Table 13.1 also provides examples of how referencing formulas look in different examples within Excel.

Table 13.1 *Linking using correct referencing*

Type of Reference	Example of How Referencing Should Appear
Normal reference	=C6
Worksheet reference in the same workbook	=Sheet1!C6
Worksheet reference	=[Workbook1]Sheet1!C6

In the earlier linking illustration, you arranged four separate workbooks so that each was visible at the same time. This made creating the linking formula easier because you just had to click on the appropriate workbook and cell address.

If you want to create a link within the same worksheet, you should use Excel's Split command to view your active worksheet in two or four panes. Once the worksheet is split, say in half, you could use one half to select the cell where the linking formula will be housed and type the equal sign. Then you could use the other half to select the cell that is being linked and click on it to have it entered into your linking formula. To activate the split command, choose **Window**, **Split**. Placing the cursor in the first row cells, the first column cells, or in a cell totally surrounded by other cells, will determine if the window will split into two or four panes. The cursor position will also decide if the window splits vertically or horizontally. You can play with the splitting command to get a sense of it.

If you want to create a link within a workbook, you should use Excel's New Window command to view multiple pages of the same workbook. When you have two or more copies of your workbook, then you can view different pages simultaneously. To create a new window of your current workbook, simply select **New Window** from the Window menu. The title bar will show the original workbook name followed by a colon and the number of the new window. For example, the second window of your SALES workbook would be named SALES:2. The original workbook will be temporarily renamed SALES:1. Then use the **Arrange...** command from the Window menu to view both SALES:1 and SALES:2.

Maintaining Links

You'll often find yourself making changes to linked documents without having the master worksheet open at the same time. As a result, every time you open a dependent worksheet Excel will offer to examine the source worksheets and update the appropriate fields.

Let's save and close the workbooks now.

1. Close the Downtown workbook, saving it with the name **Downtown**. Close the Northside workbook and save it with the name **Northside**. Use the name **Valley** to save the Valley workbook and, finally, save the Master Sales workbook with the name **Master**. Now let's open the Master workbook to see how Excel handles a dependent document.

2. Open the Master workbook. Excel prompts you with a message dialog box asking if you want to update the linked data contained in the Master workbook, as shown in Figure 13.6.

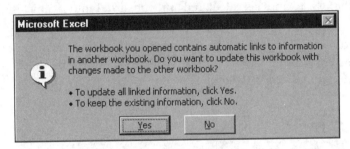

Figure 13.6 The Excel message dialog box to update links.

3. Click the **Yes** button to update the links and open the workbook.

So why wouldn't Excel just assume that you want all links maintained at all times and stop asking you that annoying question when you open a worksheet that contains links? Well, you might want to make changes to one of the individual worksheets without affecting the Master worksheet yet. You can make these changes without having the Master worksheet open. The Master worksheet will not automatically show the updated figures until you give Excel permission to update the links. This could come in handy.

Converting Formulas to Values

You may have occasion where you want linking to be discontinued—or you might want to turn a formula into its value and remove the underlying references. With Excel you can convert and replace any formulas to their values, including linking formulas. Once converted, the formulas remain regular values. Let's conduct an exercise in turning off linking.

To turn off linking by converting linking formulas to their values, follow these steps.

1. Making sure that the Master workbook is still up on your screen, open the Downtown workbook.

2. Make cell B3 of the Master workbook the active cell. Notice the linking formula displayed in the formula bar.

3. Click in the formula bar and select the entire formula by highlighting it.

4. Press **Ctrl-=**. Then press **Enter**.

The highlighted formula is calculated and converted into a value. Make B3 the active cell. Notice the value has replaced the linking formula in the formula bar.

Just to make sure the linking has been deactivated, make Downtown the active workbook and click in cell B3. Type **$85,000**. Notice the Master workbook's value remains at **$41,000**.

LINKING BY PICTURES

Sometimes linking via a linking formula may not be the best approach to join data together. Excel provides another option for linking data from one worksheet or application to another. We'll call this method *linking by pictures*.

Linking by pictures involves highlighting a range of data you want to take a picture of. Once the picture is taken from the source worksheet, it can be placed in the dependent worksheet. Any changes made to the data from the supporting worksheet will automatically change in the dependent worksheet.

There are two major differences between linking by pictures and linking through external references. The first difference is that the picture is an object, meaning that it can be resized, moved, copied and overlapped. The second difference is that the picture does not reference any particular cell(s), but refers to an *area* of the source or supporting worksheet. Therefore, any object that appears in the specified area becomes part of the picture, including all formatting.

You may be wondering what the advantages are to linking by pictures. One advantage has already been alluded to. With picture linking, you can include the formatting as well as the data. When the format changes in the source worksheet, then the picture automatically changes. This is not possible with linking formulas.

A second advantage has also been alluded to. That is, any object that resides in the area of the original or source worksheet will be pictured in the dependent worksheet. Remember, linking by pictures is not concerned with particular cell addresses, but with a particular area you designate. All objects in this area appear in the dependent worksheet. This feature is helpful for creating forms.

Another advantage is that since pictures are objects, you can manipulate them in a variety of ways. You can resize them, move them, group them, etc. You'll be surprised at some of the looks you can generate by reshaping objects.

Finally, a tremendous advantage of linking via pictures is that once the data is linked into the dependent worksheet, you cannot alter the data from the dependent worksheet. Of course the data can be altered from the source worksheet, but the resulting copy is not changeable. The advantage is that you can create documents (like forms) for areas where you don't want the data altered.

Let's try a very simple illustration to demonstrate linking data by pictures. You should start fresh by closing any workbooks you currently have open. Follow the steps as we demonstrate various features of linking data by pictures.

1. Close any existing workbooks that are open and create two new workbooks by clicking on the Standard toolbar's **New** button.

2. Choose **Window**, **Arrange...** to display the Arrange Windows dialog box.

3. The Tiled option is the default, so just click the **OK** button to tile the two windows.

4. Save the workbook on the left as **Picture1** and the workbook on the right as **Picture2**.

5. Enter the text as shown in Figure 13.7.

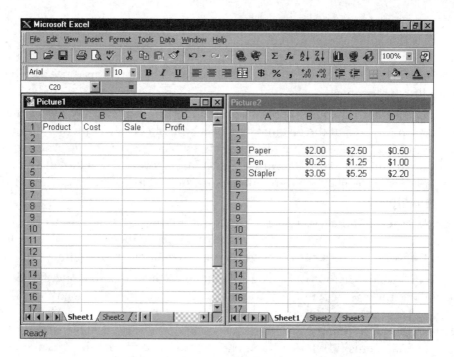

Figure 13.7 *Tiled workbooks with data.*

6. Highlight and copy the data in Picture 2 (Cells A3 through D5) using the **Edit**, **Copy** command.

7. Click on the Picture 1 workbook in cell **A3**.

8. Click the **Edit** menu while holding down the **Shift** key, then select **Paste Picture Link** (don't confuse the Paste Picture command with Paste Picture Link).

You have just successfully linked data using pictures. Your screen should now look like Figure 13.8.

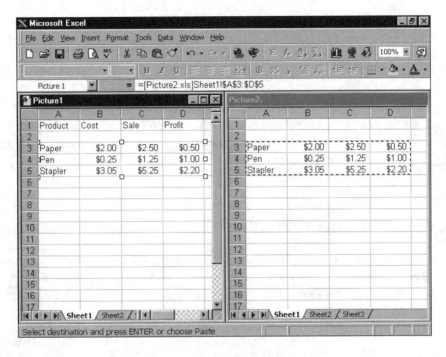

Figure 13.8 *Two workbooks linked via pictures.*

Let's make sure the data is linked properly. Click on cell **C1** in the Picture2 workbook. Type $10.75 to replace the $2.50 value. Make **C3** the active cell and type $8.75 to replace the $0.50 value. Note that both changes also occurred in the Picture1 workbook.

Make Picture1 the active workbook and click on the picture you just pasted. Notice that there are size boxes around the picture. Click and hold the picture as you move your mouse down, and place the top of the box near cell A12. Release the mouse button. Notice that the entire picture moves. Also notice that you are not actually moving data into cells. Pictures are independent of the cells.

Since your picture is like any other graphic object, you can use the drawing tool bar to alter its look. Click on the Standard toolbar's **Drawing** button. While your picture is selected, click on the **Shadow** button and select a shadow style. Click away from the picture, anywhere in the workbook, so you can see the effects of the shadow on the picture.

For more information on how to link between Excel and other applications, please see Chapter 16. For more information on manipulating objects and pictures in Excel, refer to Chapter 9.

NOTE

CONSOLIDATING WORKSHEETS

We have discussed consolidating data by creating links and through external referencing of several workbooks and worksheets. *Consolidation* is simply the process of combining data from several sources into a summarized form. Let's look at some other ways Excel consolidates data from many worksheets into a summary worksheet.

Consolidating Manually

One of the simplest ways to consolidate data from several worksheets is to create a summary sheet where you paste the data from the individual worksheets onto the summary sheet. This is a fairly straightforward method, as long as you don't have too many individual worksheets to copy from. When pasting, however, you must remember to use the **Paste Special...** command.

The following are steps used to consolidate worksheets using the **Copy** and **Paste Special...** commands.

1. Activate one of the worksheets that contain the data you want to include in the consolidated or summary sheet. Highlight the range of cells to be copied.
2. Choose **Edit, Copy**.
3. Activate the cell in the upper-left range where the data will be copied in the summary worksheet.
4. Choose **Edit, Paste Special...**. Click on the **Add** option in the Operation section of the Paste Special dialog box, as shown in Figure 13.9.

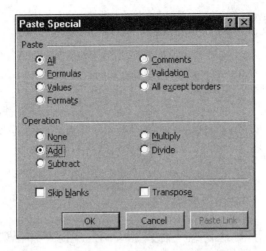

Figure 13.9 *The Paste Special dialog box.*

5. Continue to activate each worksheet you want to copy data from and consolidate on the summary sheet. Paste and add the copied data directly on top of the existing data in the summary sheet.

As you continue copying your data on top of the existing data in the summary sheet, Excel continues to add the new data with the existing summary sheet data. This is one of the simplest ways to consolidate data. The only drawback to this method is that the summary sheet you create is not linked to the individual sheets. Consequently, if the data in the original sheets changes, the summary sheet is outdated. The only way to update your summary sheet is to repeat the consolidation process.

Automatic Consolidation

Excel has a built-in feature for consolidating several worksheets into one summary worksheet. With this consolidation feature, Excel will even create links to the summary worksheet automatically. All you have to do is instruct Excel which worksheets and ranges to include by clicking on them or typing their names in the Consolidate dialog box.

Let's go through the steps used to consolidate worksheets using the Consolidate dialog box.

1. Close any of the workbooks you currently have open, and create two new worksheets by clicking on the Standard toolbar's **New** button.

2. Tile the two workbooks horizontally by choosing **Window**, **Arrange...** and then select the **Horizontal** option from the Arrange Window dialog box. Click **OK**.

3. Use the top workbook, Sheet1, for the Summary worksheet you're creating. Click in cell **A1** to activate the Summary worksheet and mark the starting position of the consolidated data.

4. Click on the lower workbook (Sheet2), and type the numbers **222** in cells A1 through D4. Figure 13.10 shows how your worksheet should look at this point.

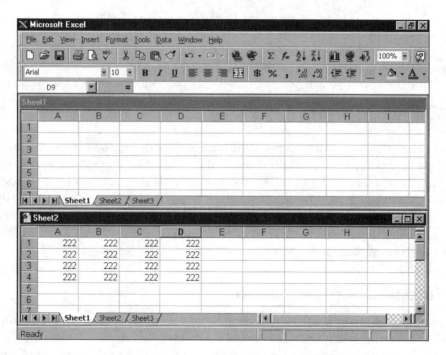

Figure 13.10 *Entering data for automatic consolidation.*

5. Click on the **Sheet2** tab of the lower workbook. Enter the numbers **333** in cells A1 through D4.

6. Click on the **Sheet3** tab of the lower workbook. Enter the numbers **444** in cells A1 through D4.

7. Activate the top workbook and move to cell A1.

8. Choose **Data**, **Consolidate...** to bring up the Consolidate dialog box, as shown in Figure 13.10. If the Consolidate dialog box obstructs your view, just drag it out of the way.

9. Highlight the range A1 through D4 in the lower worksheet. This is the data you want to consolidate. As you highlight the range, the range reference is entered in the Reference box of the Consolidate dialog box.

10. Click the **Add** button. The selected range is added to the All References box.

11. Activate **Sheet2** and **Sheet3**, clicking the **Add** button between each one.

12. Since you want a sum of the data, you don't need to change the Function in the drop-down list in the upper-left hand corner of the Consolidate dialog box. You should note, however, that you can select a different function if desired.

13. Since you want the summary sheet linked to the individual worksheets, click on the **Create Links to Source Data** check box. The dialog box should now look like the one pictured in Figure 13.11.

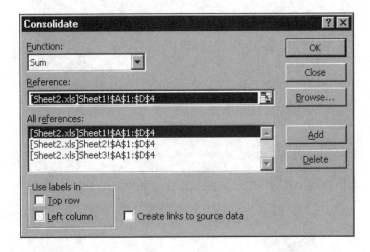

Figure 13.11 *The completed Consolidate dialog box.*

14. Click on the **OK** button to consolidate the data you selected.

Notice that the cells of the summary sheet contain the value 999. This is because you consolidated Sheet1, Sheet2, and Sheet3. In other words, for each cell in the range of A1 through D4, Excel added 222+333+444. To make sure the worksheets are linked, you can change any number in the lower worksheet and observe the changes above.

A FINAL THOUGHT

In this chapter, you learned to take advantage of Excel's powerful features for working with multiple workbooks. In the next chapter, you'll learn about some of the ways you can customize Excel's working environment to suit your needs.

CHAPTER 14

Customizing Excel

This chapter covers a variety of ways to customize your working environment in Excel. It also contains a potpourri of Excel information that didn't fit logically in any of the other chapters.

Some of the sections in this chapter, such as "Using AutoSave," will allow you to work in Excel with greater confidence knowing your data is automatically protected, even if you forget to save your document. Other sections show you how to specify options such as how Excel calculates formulas, whether you are prompted for summary information when saving workbooks, and how many sheets are in a workbook by default.

You'll also learn to alter your perspective of the worksheet by changing view options.

Setting Excel's Options

Excel's Options dialog box provides tremendous flexibility and allows you to change most of the ways you interact with the program. We'll examine some of the more interesting options in the dialog box without changing them. However, we will offer some recommendations for these options.

Start Excel, if it isn't already running. Make sure there is a worksheet on your screen. Since we aren't stepping through the procedures discussed in this chapter, it doesn't matter what worksheet is on the screen. Let's take a look at some of Excel's flexible options by starting with the General worksheet tab.

General Tab

To display the General tab of the Options dialog box choose **Tools**, **Options...**, and then click on the **General** tab, as shown in Figure 14.1.

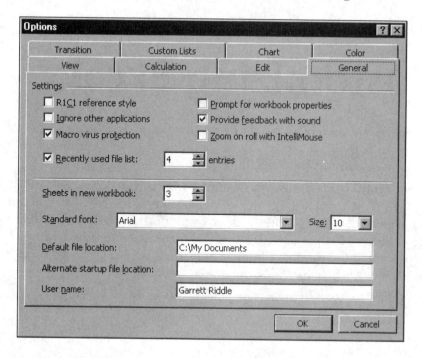

Figure 14.1 *The General tab of the Options dialog box.*

- ❖ **A1 or R1C1 reference style**. You have a choice between using the A1 or R1C1 Reference Style on the General tab. The reference style determines how you refer to cells in the worksheet. You want to leave this as the default, A1, unless you are more comfortable with an old spreadsheet program from Microsoft called Multiplan. Even if you are more familiar with Multiplan, you're still better off sticking with the default since that's the way all modern spreadsheet programs refer to cells.

- ❖ **Macro virus protection**. To help prevent the possibility of contaminating your system, Excel will warn you before opening a workbook that contains a macro. This option won't determine whether macros in a workbook actually contain a virus, but it is a good reminder to be careful when using someone else's workbook.

- ❖ **Prompt for workbook properties**. By selecting this option, Excel will ask you for title, subject, author, and comment information for each new workbook you save. If you have trouble keeping track of your files, this is a helpful feature.

- ❖ **Recently used file list**. This option allows you to adjust the number of recently used files displayed at the bottom of the File menu. You can display anywhere from zero to nine files.

- ❖ **Sheets in new workbook**. This option on the General tab defaults to 3 sheets. You can always add or delete worksheets from a workbook, so the value in this option doesn't matter too much. However, if you consistently use more or less worksheets in a workbook, you may want to increase or decrease the value to save you the trouble of doing it later.

- ❖ **Standard font** and **Size**. These options on the General tab allow you to specify which of the available fonts and sizes you want to use for future worksheets. Changing the defaults does not change the fonts or sizes on existing worksheets. You might consider changing the font or size if you find the default difficult to read on your screen. Keep in mind that if you change to a larger size, you won't be able to see as much data on your worksheet at one time.

- ❖ **Default file location**. This option on the General tab allows you to specify which directory you want to use for your Excel files. The directory appears when you choose **File, Open…**. We recommend specifying a directory for the Default file location so your files are always where you expect them to be. To enter a Default file location, click in the text box and type the complete path where your files are stored.

For example, if your files are stored on drive C in a directory called MYFILES, which is one level below the Excel directory, you would enter **C:\EXCEL\MYFILES** in the text box.

❖ **Alternate startup file location**. Did you know that any Excel file placed in the XLSTART directory will automatically open when you start up Excel? This shortcut feature is very useful if you often find yourself working on the same documents, or if you want to autostart a file that resides on a shared network drive. If, however, you want to open files from a directory other than XLSTART when you start Excel, you should type the full pathname of the directory location in the Alternate startup file location box.

❖ **User name**. This option on the General tab displays the name that was entered when Excel was first installed on your computer. If you aren't the person who installed the software, you can simply delete the name in the text box and enter yours. They can always change it back when they return from vacation.

Edit Tab

To display the Edit tab on the Options dialog box, choose **Tools**, **Options…**, and then click on the **Edit** tab, as shown in Figure 14.2.

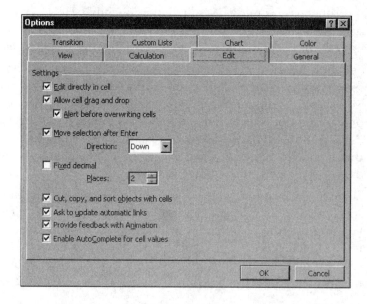

Figure 14.2 The Edit tab of the Options dialog box.

❖ **Edit directly in cell**. This option allows you to edit your data directly in the cell, as opposed to having to click on the formula bar and editing your data there. Editing your data directly in the cell is usually the fastest way to make changes to your worksheet. We can't see why anyone wouldn't want to keep this feature active.

❖ **Allow cell drag and drop**. This option on the Edit tab really makes using your mouse with Excel worthwhile. When the Allow cell drag and drop option is selected, the mouse pointer changes from a plus sign to an arrow when it is placed near the border of cells. This allows you to use your mouse for things like copying, pasting, moving, and selecting cells. Otherwise, these tasks would have to be done from the keyboard.

❖ **Alert before overwriting cells**. This option is probably a good one to leave on. When selected, Excel will inform you if you are copying or moving data to an area that already contains data. This option prevents data from being accidentally overwritten.

❖ **Move selection after Enter**. This (default) option on the Edit tab causes the active cell to move one row down after you accept an entry by pressing **Enter**. If you want to be able to press **Enter** without moving to another cell, click in the check box to remove the check.

❖ **Fixed decimal**. This option is useful if you almost always enter numbers with a certain number of decimal places. It can save you time if you don't have to enter the decimal point. If you specify a certain number of decimal places (2 is the default) and click in the **Fixed decimal** check box, Excel enters a decimal point for you. You can always override this option by manually entering a decimal point.

❖ **Cut, Copy, and Sort objects with cells**. This option on the Edit tab is for advanced users. Basically, Excel allows objects (usually graphics like circles, squares, triangles, etc.) and text to be "attached" to one particular cell. You may have a column of objects attached to separate adjacent cells. The **Cut, Copy, and Sort objects with cells** option allows for deleting, copying, and sorting to be performed on cells that have objects and text attached to them.

❖ **Ask to update automatic link**. This option activates a dialog box when you open a document that is linked with other documents. With the Ask to update automatic link activated, Excel updates the data contained in the dependent document. (See Chapter 13 for more information on linking.)

Calculation Tab

To display the Calculation tab on the Options dialog box, choose **Tools**, **Options...**, and then click on the **Calculation** tab, as shown in Figure 14.3.

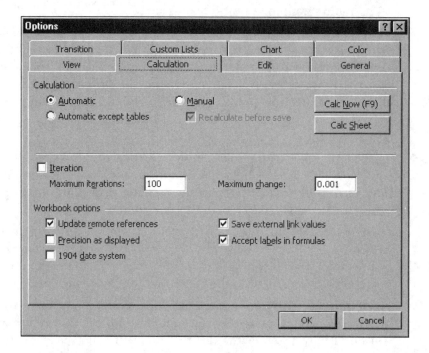

Figure 14.3 *The Calculation tab from the Options dialog box.*

❖ **Calculation**. The options in the Calculation area on the Calculation tab let you choose whether Excel calculates automatically (the default) or manually. You can also choose to have Excel calculate automatically except for tables (such as PivotTables).

As you have worked through the steps in this book, you probably noticed that when you changed numbers that formulas referred to, the recalculations occurred almost instantly. This is because the examples in the book are very simple and very small. However, if you are working with larger, more complex worksheets containing many formulas and functions requiring recalculation when numbers are changed, there can be quite a long delay while Excel performs the calculations.

The actual length of time required for calculations depends on the size and complexity of the worksheet, as well as the speed of your computer. If your computer is fast enough, even very large worksheets may recalculate fast enough to satisfy you. However, when you find that the delays become burdensome as you are entering or editing worksheet data, consider switching to manual recalculation by clicking on the **Manual** option button.

Be sure to keep the **Recalculate before save** box checked so the numbers are brought up-to-date when you save the workbook. However, even if you've selected **Manual** calculation, Excel normally recalculates when you're saving anyway. Deselecting the Recalculate before save option will prevent Excel from updating or recalculating the worksheet.

❖ **Iteration**. The **Iteration** option on the Calculation tab deals with circular references of the type where a formula in the first cell references a formula in a second cell, and the formula in the second cell references the formula in the first cell. This causes a circular reference error message. However, by selecting the Iteration option, Excel will calculate the formulas based on 100 iterations (you can increase or decrease this number) or until the values change to be less than 0.001 (the default which can also be changed), whichever comes first.

❖ **Calc Now (F9)**. The Calc Now (F9) option is used to calculate all open workbooks. You can also calculate all open workbooks by pressing **F9** on your keyboard.

❖ **Calc Sheet**. The Calc Sheet option on the Calculation tab is used to calculate the worksheet only. The shortcut key is **Shift-F9**.

❖ **Update remote references**. The Update remote references option refers to linking workbooks with other applications. When you open a workbook that is linked by remote reference to a document or application other than Excel, you have the option to relink and update the references (calculate the formulas) to the documents that are no longer linked. (See Chapter 13 for more on linking).

❖ **Precision as displayed**. The Precision as displayed option on the Calculation tab is used to determine how certain rounded values are displayed. For example, look what rounding does if you were to add 5.006+5.006=10.012. When formatted as currency (rounded) you would get $5.01+$5.01=$10.01. Although the rounded result is correct, it may not be acceptable for presentation purposes. By selecting the **Precision as displayed** option, the values are converted to $5.01+$5.01=$10.02.

When using the **Precision as displayed** option, be very careful because the underlying values are permanently changed to the displayed values. You will not be able to change them back to their original values. For example, 5.006 would be permanently changed to 5.01.

❖ **1904 date system**. This option on the Calculation tab allows you to change the base date of January 1, 1990 (the first date that coincides with the serial value of 1), which is used by Microsoft Excel for Windows 95, to the base date of January 2, 1904, which is used by Microsoft Excel for Macintosh. See Chapter 3 on Entering Dates and Times for more about dates and serial values.

❖ **Save external link values**. The Save external link values option of the Calculation tab stores both link information and actual linked data in the same worksheet. As a result, a worksheet that has massive links to external documents can take a long time to open and take up a lot of disk space. By deselecting **Save external link values**, you can reduce the space needed for your worksheet and help the worksheet to open faster.

View Tab

To display the View tab on the Options dialog box, choose **Tools**, **Options...**, and then click on the **View** tab, as shown in Figure 14.4.

The View tab of the dialog box is a bit different than the other tabs of the Options dialog box we have looked at so far. Any changes to the settings in the other tabs of the dialog box become the new default settings for new workbooks. This is also true of the changes made in the Show area of the View tab in the Options dialog box. However, changes made in areas outside of the Show area of the View tab only affect the current worksheet.

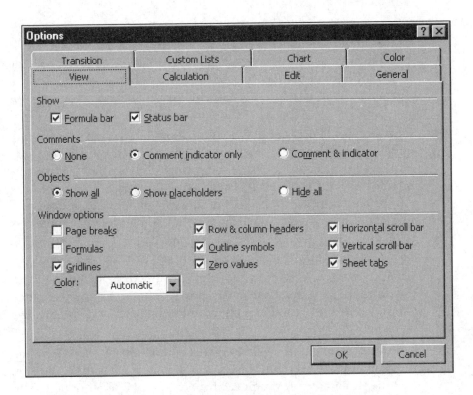

Figure 14.4 The View tab of the Options dialog box.

This dialog box lets you turn on or off various screen elements that can make it easier to navigate in Excel, but can also add clutter to your screen. A good rule of thumb is to remove any elements that you don't use. Let's explain each of the options on the View tab.

❖ **Formula bar** and **Status bar**. These options in the Show area on the View tab is to suppress the Formula bar and Status bar from displaying. Although you have the option to remove these tools, it becomes very difficult and awkward to navigate in your worksheet without them.

❖ **Comments**. The Comments area of the View tab gives you three choices about how to handle any comments attached to your worksheet. You can decide between displaying an indicator (a red triangle in the upper-right-hand corner of the cell where a note is attached), the comment and an indicator, or nothing at all. (See Chapter 6 for more about how to add, delete and enter notes.)

❖ **Show all**. This option in the Objects area of the View tab allows you to see all the objects in your worksheet. The objects in question here are graphic elements, such as charts and pictures. Showing all of them (the default) presents you with the most accurate representation of what your printed page will look like. Not surprisingly, it can slow down your navigation through the worksheet, especially on a slower computer.

❖ **Show placeholders**. This option in the Objects area of the View tab is used when you don't necessarily need to see your objects on the screen but need to know where they are on your worksheet. This option replaces your objects with gray rectangles as a placeholder. Showing only the placeholder can speed things up and does not affect the printing.

❖ **Hide all**. This option in the Objects area of the View tab allows for when you don't want to see your objects or a placeholder for them. You can make both completely disappear by using the **Hide all** option. This option also prevents the objects from printing. Don't worry, you can have your objects back by selecting either **Show all** or **Show placeholders**.

SHORTCUT

You can toggle between displaying objects, displaying placeholders, and hiding objects by using the shortcut key, **Ctrl-6**.

❖ **Page breaks**. This option in the Windows options area on the View tab allows you to choose whether Excel displays horizontal and vertical lines where your printed pages end. This can be a very useful option for determining where portions of your worksheets fall on the printed pages as you enter and edit data, without having to use **Print Preview**.

❖ **Formulas**. This option can be especially useful for finding and displaying all the formulas on a worksheet without selecting one cell at a time. It's easy to forget where you placed your formulas, particularly in larger worksheets, and this can shed some light on the situation. Figure 14.5 shows a portion of the Budget worksheet with the formulas displayed.

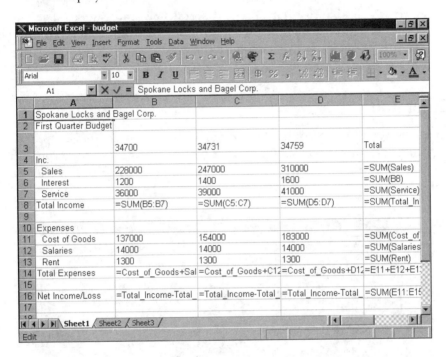

Figure 14.5 Part of the budget worksheet with formulas displayed.

❖ **Gridlines**. This option in the Windows options area of the View tab allows you to remove all gridlines in the selected worksheet and view the worksheet on a clean, white screen. This can be useful when you don't want the individual cells to clutter your view.

❖ **Color**. With this option you can change the color of the gridlines in your workbook by selecting a color from the Color drop-down list box.

❖ **Row & column headers**. This option in the Window options area of the View tab will suppress the letter headings across the columns and the number headings down the rows.

❖ **Outline symbols**. This option allows for the selection and deselection of outlining symbols. (A discussion on outlining and outlining symbols can be found in Chapter 10).

❖ **Zero values**. This option in the Window options area of the View tab sup-presses (does not display) any cell that has a zero value in it. If a formula returns a zero value to a cell, the zero in that cell is also suppressed.

❖ **Horizontal scroll bar**, **Vertical scroll bar**, and **Sheet tabs**. These options remove both scroll bars and sheet tabs from view. This would only seem to be worthwhile if you were attempting to get a good screen presentation of your worksheet.

Color Tab

To display the Color tab of the Options dialog box, choose **Tools**, **Options...**, and then click the **Color** tab. On Excel's default Color tab palette you'll find a selection of 56 colors, and even these can be modified. Figure 14.6 shows the Color tab.

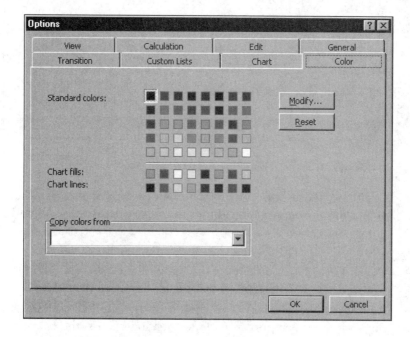

Figure 14.6 *The Color tab of the Options dialog box.*

❖ **Standard colors**. The Standard colors portion of the Color tab con-sists of every solid color that makes up a palette.

❖ **Chart fills**. The Chart fills portion of the Color tab depicts the default colors used for the filling sections on charts. It also depicts the default order in which the colors are used.

❖ **Chart lines**. The Chart lines portion of the Color tab represents the default colors used for chart lines. It also depicts the default order in which the colors are used.

❖ **Modify…**. The **Modify…** button on the Color tab allows you to change the colors on your existing palette. Once the **Modify** button is clicked, a Colors dialog box appears. By clicking on the **Custom** tab of the Colors dialog box you can select a color and adjust the hue, saturation, and luminosity.

❖ **Reset**. The **Reset** button on the Color tab will return the Color tab to its default status.

❖ **Copy colors from**. The Copy colors from dialog box on the Color tab allows you to copy a custom palette from one workbook to another in order to achieve a consistent look. Once both workbooks are open and the destination workbook is active, clicking on the **Copy colors from** arrow and selecting the source workbook from the drop-down list will copy the custom palette to the source workbook.

TRANSITION TAB

To display the Transition tab of the Options dialog box, choose **Tools, Options…**, and then click the **Transition** tab, as shown in Figure 14.7. The Transition tab was developed to help people who use other spreadsheet applications, such as Lotus 1-2-3, make an easy transition to Excel.

❖ **Save Excel files as**. This option allows you to change the default settings you save your Excel files in.

❖ **Microsoft Excel menu or Help key**. The Microsoft Excel menu or Help key options in the Settings portion of the Transition tab allow you to change the keyboard character that activates the menu bar. The default character is the slash key. If you want the key to activate the Help for Lotus 1-2-3 Users dialog box instead of Microsoft Excel Menus, select **Lotus 1-2-3 Help**.

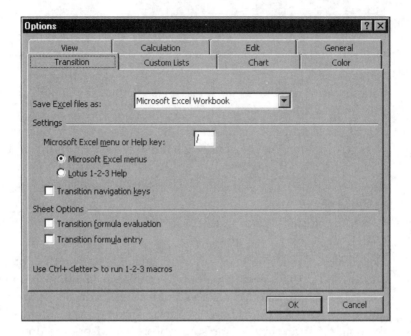

Figure 14.7 *The Transition tab of the Options dialog box.*

SHORTCUT

A shortcut for accessing the menu bar is to press the **Alt** key along with the letter on the menu bar that is underlined. This will activate the menu and display the commands. You can then simply type the underlined letter of the command to activate it.

❖ **Transition navigation keys**. Selecting this option alters how the keyboard shortcuts and function keys will perform.

❖ **Transition formula evaluation**. This option in the Sheet Options portion of the Transition tab manages the way calculations are performed on a Lotus 1-2-3 worksheet that is opened in Excel.

❖ **Transition formula entry**. This option allows Lotus 1-2-3 functions to be entered using Lotus 1-2-3 syntax. Excel then automatically converts the Lotus 1-2-3 function into an Excel function.

Custom Lists Tab

To display the Custom Lists tab of the Options dialog box, choose **Tools**, **Options...**, and then click the **Custom Lists** tab, as shown in Figure 14.8. The Custom Lists tab allows you to create and maintain lists that are used in Excel's automatic series feature. As discussed in Chapter 3, Excel will automatically create a series of values when you enter the first value and then use the fill handle to extend the first entry into other cells. Let's create and use a custom list to illustrate this feature.

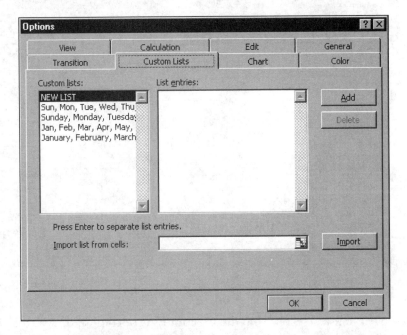

Figure 14.8 The Custom Lists tab of the Options dialog box.

1. Choose **Tools**, **Options...** and click the **Custom Lists** tab. If it isn't already selected, click on the **NEW LIST** option.

2. Click in the **List entries** text box.

3. Type **Ten, Jack, Queen, King, Ace.**

4. Click the **Add** button, then click **OK**.

5. Move to cell A3 of the workbook you have open, and type **Ten**.

6. Drag the fill handle on the lower-right edge of the cell through cell K3. Your custom list will appear as shown in Figure 14.9.

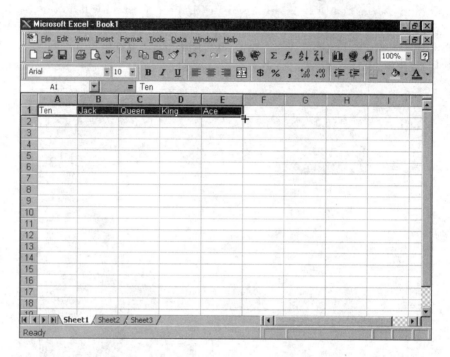

Figure 14.9 Adding a custom list.

To remove the list, select it from the Custom Lists portion of the Custom Lists tab in the Options dialog box. Click on the **Delete** button, and when Excel warns you that the list will be permanently deleted, click **OK**.

❖ **Custom lists.** The Custom lists box on the Custom Lists tab stores the names of custom lists that are created. The names of the lists are actually the first few names on the list. Excel has created four default lists (they are day and month lists), and you can create more by choosing **NEW LIST**.

SHORTCUT

Once you've created a new list, you can use it in your Excel worksheet by typing in the first item on the list and then dragging the fill handle of the cell to display the remaining list entries.

❖ **Import list from cells**. This option on the Custom Lists tab allows you to import lists developed in worksheets as a custom list that can be reproduced for future use. You can produce a custom list by highlighting the range you want to import from your worksheet and clicking the **Import** button.

CHART TAB

To display the Chart tab of the Options dialog box, choose **Tools**, **Options...**, and then click on the **Chart** tab, as shown in Figure 14.10. The Chart tab allows you to control how worksheets are plotted and charted. To see these options, you must have a chart selected prior to choosing the **Options...** command from the Tools menu. For more information about creating and selecting charts, see Chapter 8.

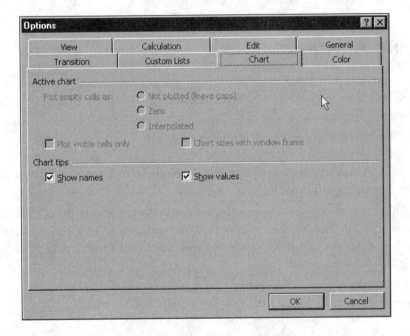

Figure 14.10 *The Chart tab of the Options dialog box.*

The Active chart area on the Chart tab tells Excel how to handle empty cells that are included in a range charts are created from. By default, Excel ignores empty cells.

❖ **Not plotted (leave gaps)**. This option in the Empty cells plotted as section of the Chart tab is the same as Excel's default option, which is to ignore empty cells.

❖ **Zero**. This option of the Empty cells plotted as section treats empty cells as if they contained a value of zero.

❖ **Interpolated**. The interpolated option of the Empty cells plotted as section of the Chart tab instructs Excel to interpolate values (average adjoining values in the data range for any blanks) for the cells and then plot them.

❖ **Plot visible cells only**. This option of the Active Chart area on the Chart tab instructs Excel to include cells in hidden rows and columns as part of the data series, or not to include them.

❖ **Chart size with window frame**. This option in the Active chart section of the Chart tab instructs Excel if the chart size should be adjusted when the document window size is adjusted.

USING AUTOSAVE

Office 97 includes a host of extra programs designed to enhance your work with Excel. You already used one of these, the Scenario Manager, earlier in the book.

The add-in we're going to discuss here is AutoSave. There is no more important procedure in Excel, or any other computer program for that matter, than saving your work. It doesn't matter what skills you master or what sort of elaborate worksheets you create if you lose them to a power failure or some other computer mishap.

Of course you can save your work manually, but anything that can be done to automate the process and relieve you of that burden is welcome. AutoSave does just that. With AutoSave you can instruct Excel to save your work automatically at specified intervals.

Let's take a look at AutoSave now. You can skip the first two steps if AutoSave is already one of the choices on your Tools menu.

1. Choose **Tools, Add-Ins...** to display the Add-Ins dialog box, as shown in Figure 14.11.

   The dialog box displays the add-in programs on your computer's hard disk. The ones with checks in their check boxes are currently available to Excel.

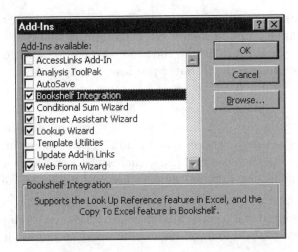

Figure 14.11 The Add-Ins dialog box.

2. Click the **AutoSave...** check box (if it is unchecked) and then click OK to make AutoSave available.

N O T E Browse through the other add-ins to familiarize yourself with their functions. In addition to these, several companies offer other add-in programs for performing various specialized tasks. You'll see advertisements and reviews for these in some of the popular computer magazines. You may also receive offers for some of these through the mail after you send in your registration form.

3. Choose **Tools**, **AutoSave** to display the AutoSave dialog box, as shown in Figure 14.12.

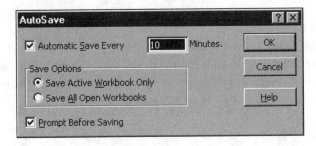

Figure 14.12 The AutoSave dialog box.

By default, the check box in the upper-left portion of the AutoSave dialog box is checked and the default save interval is ten minutes. The rule of thumb for how often you should AutoSave is the same as for how often you should save manually. Save often enough that if you lose your work just before the next save, you won't be too upset. For most folks, that's somewhere between 10 and 20 minutes.

The Save Options area of the dialog box lets you choose whether AutoSave saves only your active workbook (the default), or all open workbooks. Since saving all open workbooks could cause each save to take a few extra precious seconds, it's usually best to have AutoSave just save the active workbook.

The final check box lets Excel prompt you before proceeding with a save. We strongly recommend that you use this option. In this way, if you have made some changes to the worksheet that you do no want saved, you can cancel the save.

If you choose to be prompted before the save, Excel displays the AutoSave confirmation dialog box, as shown in Figure 14.13, after the specified number of minutes.

Figure 14.13 *The AutoSave confirmation dialog box.*

If you want to proceed with the save, click the **Save** button. If you don't want to save, click **Cancel**. The **Skip** button also works, but its primary purpose is to allow you to skip saving certain workbooks and save others when you've chosen to have AutoSave save all open workbooks.

Just because your work is being saved to your computer's hard disk every so often, don't feel too secure about the safety of your data. If you have important data stored on your computer, you must also back it up on floppy disks, tape (if you have a tape backup system), etc. This is critical, because things can go wrong that are more serious than a power failure.

If your computer breaks down, is stolen, or burned in a fire, you can at least restore your important data to another computer from your backups.

CHANGING VIEWS

There are a couple of options for changing the view of your worksheet that are not part of the Options dialog box. The first of these is called **Custom Views…**.

As you work with larger worksheets, you may find yourself jumping back and forth between the far reaches of the worksheet to view and edit different portions. You can use the Go To method we discussed earlier, but even that method can become confusing. An easier way to move around the worksheet is to assign names to the various views you want to move to in **Custom Views…**.

To add a named view, move to the portion of the worksheet you want to be able to return to and then use **Custom Views…** to assign it a name. Let's take a look at **Custom Views…**.

1. Choose **View**, **Custom Views…** to display the Custom Views dialog box, as shown in Figure 14.14.

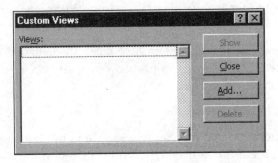

Figure 14.14 *The Custom Views dialog box.*

2. Click on the **Add…** button to display the Add View dialog box, as shown in Figure 14.15.

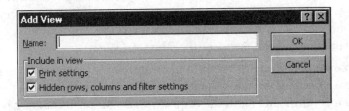

Figure 14.15 *The Add View dialog box.*

3. Enter a name for the view and click **OK**. You usually want to keep the print settings and hidden rows and columns with your views, so keep these check boxes checked.

Figure 14.16 displays an example of the Custom Views dialog box with several views to choose from.

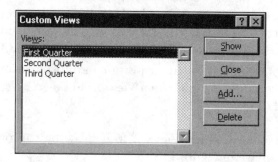

Figure 14.16 *The Custom Views dialog box with several named views.*

The views you name in Custom Views only relate to the active worksheet. You can use Custom Views to switch between workbooks, or even among worksheets in the active workbook.

N O T E

After you have added views, you can move to them by choosing **View, Custom Views...**, highlighting the desired view, and clicking on the **Show** button.

Zooming the Workbook

Let's take a look at one other useful feature for changing the view of your worksheet. Until now, you've been looking at your worksheets at the default zoom (100%). If you want to step back from your worksheet to get a bigger picture, you can zoom out to a smaller percentage. You can also zoom in to see more detail in a smaller portion of the worksheet.

The **Zoom...** command on the View menu is used to either magnify your worksheet or demagnify it, whichever you choose. Sometimes you may want to see your entire worksheet and the only way to accomplish that task is to shrink it so that it all fits into the window. At other times you may want to magnify a certain area of the worksheet to have a better view of that section.

Selecting the **Zoom...** command from the View menu displays the Zoom dialog box as it appears in Figure 14.17.

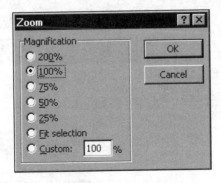

Figure 14.17 *The Zoom dialog box.*

The Zoom dialog box consists of one enlargement option (**200%**), three reduction options (**75%**, **50%**, and **25%**), a **Fit Selection** option (this will determine the best fit to view the highlighted portion of your worksheet so that it fills the window), and a **Custom** option (which allows you to choose a percentage between 10% and 400% for enlargement or reduction).

The zoom percentage you choose only affects the appearance of your screen. It has no effect on what is printed.

N O T E

Also, zoom percentages are saved as part of your named views in **Custom Views...**.

The following steps will guide you through magnifying or demagnifying your worksheets.

1. Choose **View, Zoom...** to display the Zoom dialog box.
2. Choose the **200%** enlargement option, one of the three reduction sizes (**75%**, **50%**, or **25%**), the **Fit Selection** option, or enter a custom size in the custom window.
3. Select **OK**.

The larger the number, the less worksheet area you are able to see. Figure 14.18 displays a portion of the Budget worksheet zoomed to 200%.

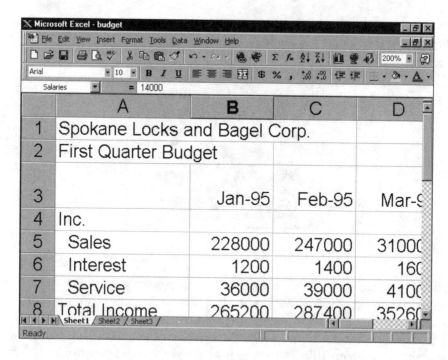

Figure 14.18 *An example of a 200% zoom.*

You can also use the Zoom Control box on the Standard toolbar to quickly select your desired magnification. By selecting the pull-down menu you can select one enlargement option, three reduction options, or one selection option that will fill the screen by giving you the best fit for any selected cell(s).

A FINAL THOUGHT

In this chapter you learned to customize Excel in a variety of ways. Of course, there are no limits to the ways you can work with Excel, and you should now have a good start on that journey of exploration. In the next chapter you will explore Excel's toolbars and ways to customize them to your liking.

CHAPTER 15

Switching and Customizing Toolbars

As you have seen throughout this book, toolbars are often the fastest and easiest way to initiate Excel tasks. With a click of the mouse, you're off and running with an operation that might otherwise take several mouse clicks or keystrokes.

You can make toolbars even more useful by customizing them to include just the buttons you use most often for a particular type of operation, or by creating custom buttons.

DISPLAYING AND POSITIONING TOOLBARS

Excel automatically displays the Standard and Formatting toolbars and positions them at the top of the screen. You have also seen Excel display other toolbars such as the Chart toolbar when editing charts, and you have displayed the Drawing toolbar by clicking on the Standard toolbar's **Drawing** button.

Let's see how you can choose other toolbars and position them wherever you want them on the screen.

1. Start Excel, if it isn't already running, and make sure there is a worksheet on your screen. You don't need to have any particular workbook open since you are displaying and moving toolbars without actually using the buttons.

    The shortcut menu is the fastest way to choose which toolbars are displayed on your screen. There is also a Toolbars dialog box which makes additional toolbars available, as well as a few extra options. Start with the shortcut menu.

2. Right-click on any of the toolbar buttons on the Standard or Formatting toolbar to display the toolbar shortcut menu, as shown in Figure 15.1.

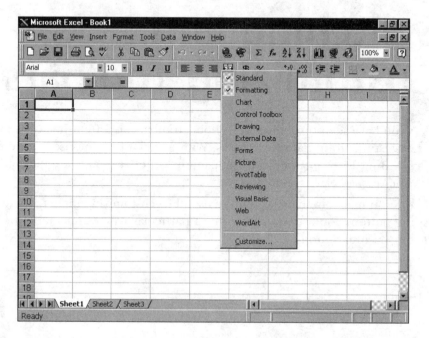

Figure 15.1 The toolbar shortcut menu.

The toolbars that are currently displayed have a check mark in front of their names on the shortcut menu. You can remove a toolbar from the screen by clicking on its name. Clicking on a toolbar name without a check mark will cause it to be displayed. Let's display the PivotTable toolbar now.

3. Click on **PivotTable** to display the PivotTable toolbar, as shown in Figure 15.2.

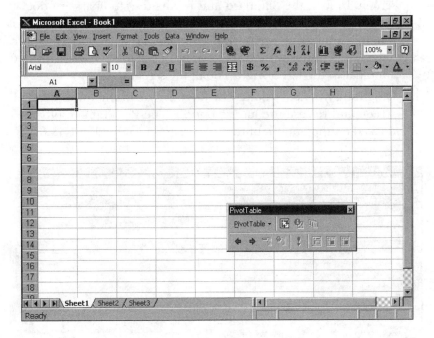

Figure 15.2 *The PivotTable toolbar.*

N O T E

All the available toolbars and their respective functions are listed in Appendix C. You can mix and match buttons to create your own custom toolbars, or create your own custom buttons. As with other toolbars, you can see what the function of each of these buttons is by simply moving the mouse over a button and reading the ToolTip.

Toolbars can be moved by moving the mouse pointer to one of the areas between a toolbar border and the buttons and then dragging. However, if the toolbar is floating, it's easier to move it the same way you move other windows—dragging it by the title bar. You can remove a toolbar by clicking on its name in the shortcut menu or by simply clicking on a floating toolbar's close box.

Often, having a toolbar floating on the screen obscures important information or is distracting, even if you move it out of the way. One solution to this problem is to dock it in one of the docking positions. There are four docking locations: the top, bottom, and sides of the screen. In fact, the Standard and Formatting toolbars are docked at the top of the screen now. You can dock a toolbar by moving it to any one of the docking areas, though it should be noted that you can't always use buttons with drop-down lists or tear-off palettes if you dock a toolbar to the left or right side of the screen.

4.   Drag the PivotTable toolbar by the title bar to the lower edge of the screen and release the mouse button. The PivotTable toolbar is now docked on the bottom of the screen, as shown in Figure 15.3.

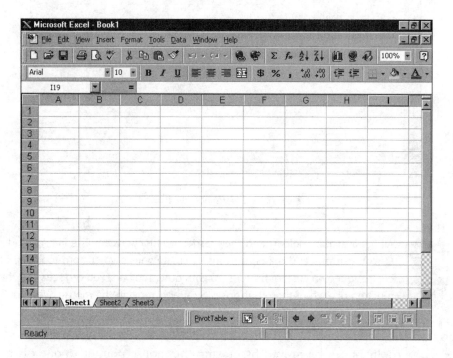

Figure 15.3 *The PivotTable toolbar docked on the bottom of the screen.*

The horizontal position depends on where the outline was when you released the mouse button. You can move the toolbar right or left by positioning the mouse over any space between the buttons and the edges of the toolbar.

NOTE For a toolbar with very few buttons such as this one, it's a good idea to position it at the far left or right of the docking area so there will be room for another toolbar, should you decide to add one.

The Standard and Formatting toolbars, which are docked, can also be moved. Let's undock the formatting toolbar and position it as a floating toolbar near the top of the worksheet.

1. Position your mouse pointer over the two small lines at the far left side of the Standard toolbar, as shown in Figure 15.4. These lines make up the *move handle.*

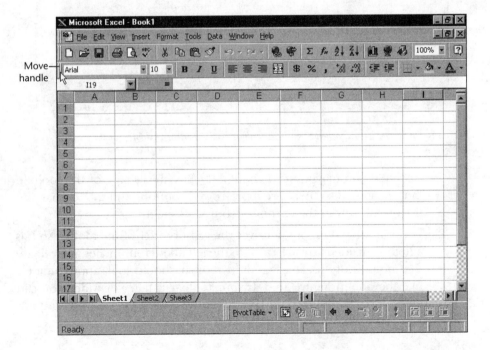

Figure 15.4 The Standard toolbar's move handle.

2. Press and hold your left mouse button on the move handle, and drag the Standard toolbar down so the top edge of its outline is just below the column headings. Now release the mouse button. The Standard toolbar should be positioned approximately like the one in Figure 15.5.

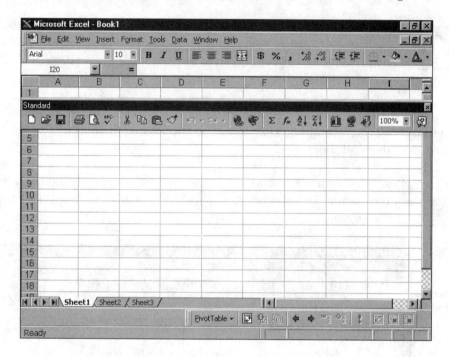

Figure 15.5 *The undocked Standard toolbar positioned near the top of the worksheet.*

At times, you may want to change the size and shape of the toolbar. Let's change it so there are more rows of buttons and the toolbar can fit comfortably in the corner of your worksheet.

3. Position the mouse pointer over the right border of the toolbar so it is a double-headed arrow. Drag it to the left about four inches and release the mouse button. The Standard toolbar should look approximately like the one in Figure 15.6. If your toolbar is taller or wider, you can grab one of the borders and resize it until it's just the way you want it.

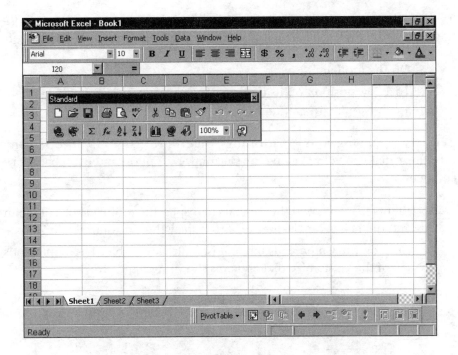

Figure 15.6 *The Resized Standard toolbar.*

Before moving on, let's redock the Standard toolbar so it will be in its normal position the next time you use Excel.

4. Drag the Standard toolbar up to the top of the screen and release the mouse button to redock it above the Formatting toolbar.

CREATING CUSTOM TOOLBARS

Now that you know how to display and position the toolbars supplied by Excel, let's look at how to customize toolbars. There are several ways to modify toolbars to suit the way you work. You can alter existing toolbars by adding, removing, or changing the position of buttons. You can also start from scratch with a new toolbar equipped with your choice of buttons.

With the Customize dialog box on the screen, you can remove or reposition any button on a toolbar that is currently displayed by simply dragging it:

❖ Off the toolbar

❖ To a new position on its toolbar

❖ To any other visible toolbar

Let's try removing and positioning some buttons. You can open the Customize dialog box by clicking the **Customize...** option in the toolbar shortcut menu.

1. Right-click on any of the toolbars to display the toolbar shortcut menu and then click on **Customize...** to display the Customize dialog box.

2. Click on the **Commands** tab, if it isn't already visible. The Commands tab of the Customize dialog box is shown in Figure 15.7.

Figure 15.7 The Commands tab of the Customize dialog box.

The Commands tab of the Customize dialog box contains all the existing commands you can use to add to a toolbar or menu. The commands are separated into logical categories to make it easy to find the command you want.

Before you add any buttons, let's make some room on the Formatting toolbar so you won't obscure any buttons when you add a new one to it.

Let's say you decide that you don't need the Bold, Italic, and Underline buttons because you have already memorized the keyboard shortcuts (**Ctrl-B** for bold, **Ctrl-I** for italic, and **Ctrl-U** for underline). Let's remove these buttons from the Formatting toolbar now.

3. Drag the **Bold** button from the Formatting toolbar onto the worksheet and then release the mouse button. Repeat the process for the **Italic** and **Underline** buttons so the toolbar looks like the one in Figure 15.8.

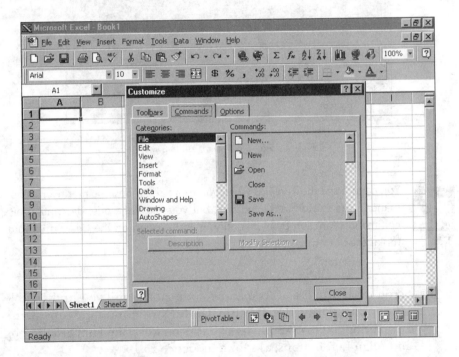

Figure 15.8 *The Formatting toolbar without the Bold, Italic, and Underline buttons.*

Let's add buttons for Double Underline, Strikethrough and Vertical Text. All these commands fall within the Format category but you could, of course, add buttons from different categories.

4. Click **Format** in the Categories list to display the Format commands, as shown in Figure 15.9.

Figure 15.9 *The Format commands.*

N O T E You cannot see the ToolTips when you move the mouse pointer over a command in the Customize dialog box, but you can see a brief description of a command's function by highlighting it and clicking on the **Description** button at the bottom of the dialog box.

5. Scroll down the list of formatting commands until you find Double Underline. Drag the **Double Underline** command up to the Formatting toolbar, so the insert line is between the Font Size list box and Align Left buttons, as shown in Figure 15.10.

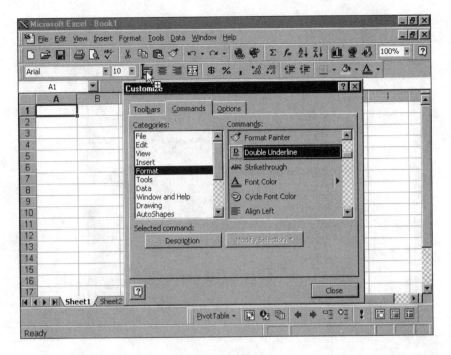

Figure 15.10 *Positioning the Double Underline button on the Formatting toolbar.*

6. Release the mouse button to accept the placement of the Double Underline button. If the button ended up to the left or right of its intended position, you can simply drag it left or right to reposition it where you want it.

7. Drag the **Strikethrough** command to the position just to the right of the Double Underline button and release the mouse button.

8. Drag the **Rotate Text Down** button to the position just to the right of the Strikethrough button and release the mouse button. The Formatting toolbar should now look similar to the one in Figure 15.11.

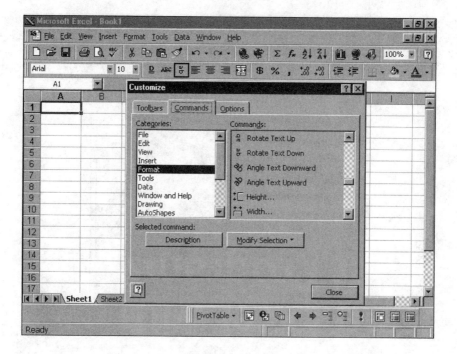

Figure 15.11 *The Formatting toolbar with its three new buttons.*

Now let's create a custom toolbar with just the buttons we want.

9. Click on the **Toolbars** tab of the Customize dialog box to display the Toolbars options, as shown in Figure 15.12.

You can use the check boxes in the Toolbars list to choose which toolbars to display. Notice that if you use the scroll bar to scroll down the list of toolbars there are more toolbars to choose from in the dialog box than are available from the shortcut menu.

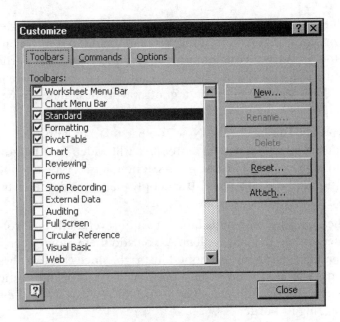

Figure 15.12 The Toolbars tab of the Customize dialog box.

10.   Click the **New** button to display the New Toolbar dialog box, as shown in Figure 15.13.

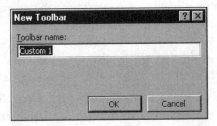

Figure 15.13 The New Toolbar dialog box.

When you create a new toolbar, choose a name that denotes the group or category of buttons you plan to add to it. If you are creating a toolbar with a conglomeration of buttons with no particular relation, except for the fact that you want them on a toolbar, a name such as "My Toolbar" might be a good way to designate your toolbar. In fact, that's exactly what you can do right now.

11. Type **My Toolbar** in the New Toolbar text box and click **OK**. A new blank toolbar appears. The toolbar will widen and lengthen as you add buttons to it. The way you see it now, it isn't wide enough to fit the entire title, "My Toolbar." If you only plan to add one or two buttons to a toolbar, use a very short name.

12. Click on the **Commands** tab. Let's add several buttons from assorted categories to the new toolbar. As you add them, don't worry too much about getting them positioned just right since you can always reposition them. Also, you should position the buttons in a single row. If some of them end up stacked vertically, you can resize the toolbar by dragging its border.

13. Click on the **File** category, drag the **Open** button onto the new toolbar, and release the mouse button.

Just because a button is already in use on one toolbar doesn't mean you wouldn't want it on another. You may want to equip My Toolbar with the buttons you use most often so you won't need to display any other toolbars.

N O T E

14. Click on **Up** in the Categories list, drag the **Up** command to the right of the Open button on the new toolbar and release the mouse button.

15. Click on the **Charting** category, drag the **Chart Type...** command to the right of the Arrow Style button, and release the mouse button. The new toolbar should now look like the one in Figure 15.14.

The new toolbar will be listed on the toolbar shortcut menu and on the Toolbars tab of the Customize dialog box, so you can display and remove this toolbar from your screen like any other toolbar. Let's leave the Customize dialog box on the screen since you will be using it in the next section.

Figure 15.14 My Toolbar with the three buttons added.

DESIGNING CUSTOM TOOLBAR BUTTONS

If putting together your own collection of buttons doesn't provide you with enough options, you can also change the image of any of the buttons on any toolbar. The simplest approach, if you can find an existing image you like, is to copy the image to the button you want to change.

If you need an even more custom image than that, you can edit a button's image or design your own using the Button Editor or just about any other paint-type graphics program.

WARNING

We're not very creative when it comes to graphic design. On second thought, "not very creative" is an overstatement. Drawing stick figures is about as far as we got in art class. So don't expect any great-looking (or even good-looking) button images from these examples.

The first thing to do is replace the image of one of the buttons on My Toolbar with one from the Change Button Image menu. Let's replace the image on the Open button with an image from the Change Button Image menu. The Change Button Images are normally used to attach macros, as you learned in Chapter 12, "Automating Your Work with Macros." However, you can copy any image you want. Since these do not already have functions assigned to them, they are a natural choice.

1. With the Custom dialog box still up on your screen, right-click on My Toolbar's **Open** button. The Custom shortcut menu appears.

2. Move your mouse pointer down to **Change Button Image**, as shown in Figure 15.15.

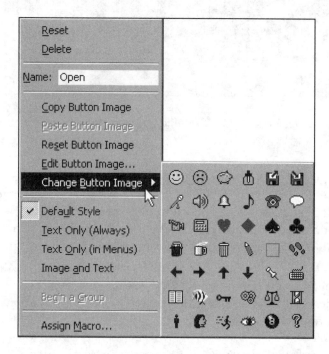

Figure 15.15 *The Change Button Image options.*

3. Click on the **heart** image just to the left of the calculator in the third row down. The Open button on My Toolbar should now look like the one shown in Figure 15.16.

Figure 15.16 *Now My Toolbar has a heart.*

Let's edit the heart button to customize it even further.

4.   Right-click on the **Heart** button to display the shortcut menu.

5.   Click on **Edit Button Image...** to display the Button Editor dialog box, as shown in Figure 15.17. Each small box in the Picture portion of the dialog box represents one dot or pixel of the image. You can click on a color in the Colors portion of the dialog box and then apply that color to any dot in the picture by simply clicking on it. If you want to apply the color to a series of dots, you can drag the mouse over the dots to paint the color.

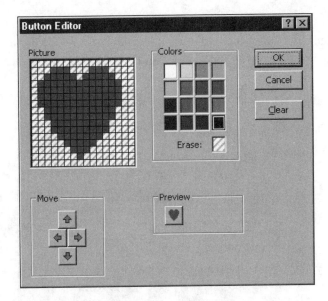

Figure 15.17 *The Button Editor dialog box.*

Clicking on the **Erase** box allows you to erase any of the dots that are filled with color by dragging or clicking on them.

You can use the arrow buttons in the Move portion of the dialog box to move the entire image up, down, left, or right, if the image doesn't already extend to the edges of the Picture box.

The **Clear** button lets you remove the entire image so you can start fresh and create your image.

Let's add a black horizontal line on the top and bottom rows and erase a few dots in the middle of the heart to create an open heart.

6. Click on the black box in the Colors portion of the dialog box and drag across the top and bottom rows of the Picture portion of dialog box. If you make a mistake, you can remove black "dots" by clicking on them again.

N O T E

The Preview portion of the Image Editor dialog box shows, in actual size, what your button will look like as you edit it.

7. Click the **Erase** box, and erase a few dots in the middle of the heart so the picture portion looks like Figure 15.18.

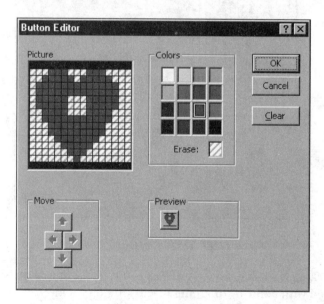

Figure 15.18 *Using the erase feature to modify an image.*

8. Click **OK** to close the Button Editor dialog box and accept the modifications.

The Button Editor doesn't offer a wide variety of graphics tools to create complex images. If you want more design flexibility, consider using a more sophisticated paint-type program to create an image. You can then copy your design to the clipboard and paste the image onto the button of your choice using the technique just described.

Before you finish this chapter, let's get the screen back to normal. Remove the PivotTable toolbar, delete the "My Toolbar" toolbar, and reset the Formatting toolbar back to its original configuration.

1. Click on the check mark next to the **PivotTable** option in the Toolbars list on the Toolbars tab of the Customize dialog box.

2. Click on the **Formatting** option so it is highlighted, and then click the **Reset…** button.

3. Excel will ask you if you're sure you want to reset the changes you made to the Formatting toolbar. Click **OK** to confirm the reset.

4. Scroll down the toolbars list until you can see My Toolbar.

5. Click on **My Toolbar** in the toolbars list to remove the check mark, and if you want to delete the toolbar, click the **Delete** button.

6. Excel will ask you if you're sure you want to delete the "My Toolbar" toolbar. Click **OK** to confirm the deletion.

7. Click on the **Close** button to remove the Customize dialog box. Your screen should be back to the way it looked before you started this chapter.

A Final Thought

In this chapter, you learned to display, position, and customize your toolbars to make them work as efficiently as possible for you. Don't forget to refer to Appendix C for a complete listing of Excel's toolbars and their button functions.

The next chapter covers how to use Excel with other programs.

CHAPTER 16

Using Excel with Other Programs

No program is an island. Gee, that sounds familiar. But seriously, few computer users rely solely on one program. If you are using Excel—and it's probably safe to assume you are since you're reading this book—you have other programs at your disposal.

If you have Microsoft Office 97, which includes the Word for Windows word processing program and the PowerPoint presentation program, you have the ability to create compound documents using parts of two or more of the programs. Even if all you have are Windows 95 and Excel, you have the mini-applications that come with Windows, such as NotePad and WordPad.

WHY USE OTHER PROGRAMS WITH EXCEL?

For as long as people have been creating paper documents, they've been adding bits and pieces of various types of information together—cutting out a picture from one place and pasting it into another, cutting out a chart here and pasting it into a report there. In computer jargon, documents that include pieces from several applications are called *compound documents.*

The technology to create computerized compound documents has been like the Holy Grail—very elusive. Finding such a technology would mean far greater computer productivity. The possibilities seemed endless, but the search for a means to accomplish it seemed never-ending.

In several places throughout this book, we have mentioned the value of using other, more specialized programs for accomplishing certain tasks. For example, you can create and edit toolbar buttons with the Button Editor. However, using a more flexible program, such as Paint, allows you greater freedom of expression and control.

Certainly Excel isn't the best tool for every job. It's an incredible spreadsheet program that specializes in creating and formatting number-oriented documents. But when it comes to creating text-oriented documents, you'll want to use a word processing program with all the tools for formatting words, such as Word for Windows.

"Use the best tool for the job" may sound like common sense. And it is. Of course you would use a word processing program if you were writing a report for your company proposing to hire new employees for your department. You want to format the report so it is as attractive—and persuasive—as possible.

But words alone probably won't make this proposal fly. The words will likely need to be backed up by some numbers demonstrating the various costs and benefits these proposed new employees will bring. The best tool for that job is a spreadsheet program such as Excel.

You can create and print the report with your word processing program. Then you can create and print a worksheet (and perhaps a chart for emphasis) from Excel and insert the worksheet and chart pages into the report. But imagine how much more convincing and professional-looking the report would be if the worksheet and chart were integrated into the body of the report.

Right there, smack dab in the middle of a beautifully formatted word-processed page, you place your worksheet and your chart, as if you had used scissors and paste but without the muss and fuss. And the worksheet and chart can be linked to the report document so when the data is changed in the workbook, the changes are instantly reflected.

AN OFFICE OVERVIEW

Microsoft Office 97 is a combination or suite of programs including Excel, Word, PowerPoint, and Access. Other, smaller programs may also be present in your version of Office, such as Binder and Outlook.

Word is a word processing program. Word processing is the single activity performed by more computer users than any other. From simple memos to complex reports or even books, word processing programs provide the tools for entering, formatting, editing text, and printing documents.

PowerPoint is a presentation graphics program that provides all the tools necessary to create dazzling presentations using overhead transparencies, 35mm slides, your computer screen, or an LCD projector.

Access is a relational database program used for creating, editing, viewing, querying, and reporting all sorts of information.

There are some tremendous advantages to using Office 97 instead of a mish-mosh of programs from other companies. First of all, the Office programs are arguably the best programs available in their respective categories.

Another advantage to using Office 97 is uniformity. As you work with the Office programs, you'll find that several major consistencies jump out at you. The menus for the programs are all very similar. Of course the options within the menus are appropriate for the particular program you're working with. Microsoft also ensures that dialog boxes, toolbars, shortcut menus, and program help all operate comparably. There's even a consistent shortcut for switching among the Office programs.

This consistency makes learning the second and third programs much easier than the first. After you've learned any one of the programs, you'll often find yourself correctly guessing about how to perform a task in one of the other programs. After a short while it will all start to feel natural and automatic.

Notice the similarity among the screen elements in the screens from Word and PowerPoint as shown in Figures 16.1 and 16.2.

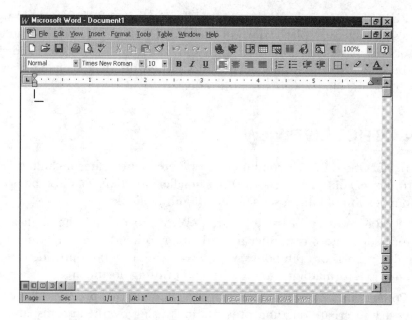

Figure 16.1 A sample screen from Word.

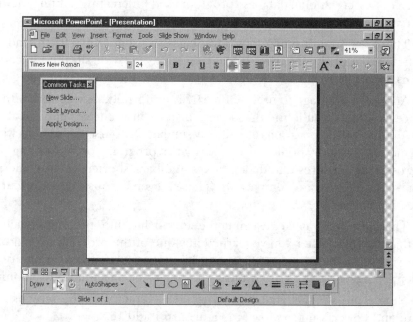

Figure 16.2 The main PowerPoint screen.

The Microsoft Office Shortcut Bar

When Microsoft Office is installed in a normal manner, the Microsoft Office Shortcut Bar appears automatically when you start Windows 95.

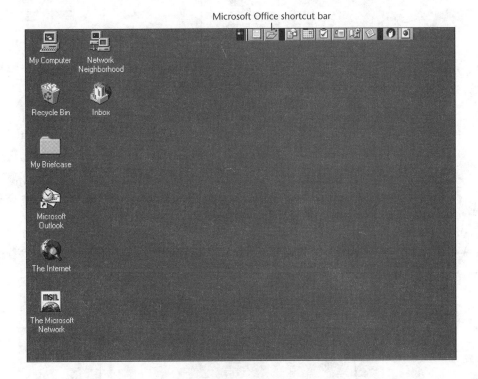

Figure 16.3 *The Microsoft Office Shortcut Bar.*

You may remember that we turned off the Microsoft Office Shortcut Bar early on in the book. To bring back the Shortcut Bar, you'll need to go into the Microsoft Office Folder and open it (The default location for this is C:\ProgramFiles\MicrosoftOffice). If you have Microsoft Office installed in a different location, you'll have to act accordingly.

1. Go to the desktop and double-click on the **My Computer** icon.

2. Double-click on the **Program Files** folder to open it.

3. Double-click on the **Microsoft Office** folder to open it.

4. Locate the shortcut to the **Microsoft Office Shortcut Bar**, as shown in Figure 16.4, and double-click on it.

Microsoft
Office Shortcut
Bar

Figure 16.4 The shortcut to the Microsoft Office Shortcut Bar.

5. You will be asked if you would like to configure the Office Shortcut Bar to start automatically whenever Windows is started. Click on the **Yes** button.

The Office Shortcut Bar should now be visible in the top-right corner of your screen, as shown in Figure 16.3. As a default, the Office Shortcut Bar doesn't contain any of the Office programs. Instead it contains shortcuts to a number of functions, such as creating or opening a new document. To add program icons to the Office Shortcut Bar, you'll need to go to the Customize dialog box.

1. Right-click on the **Office 97** symbol on the far-left corner of the Office Shortcut Bar to display the control menu shown in Figure 16.5.

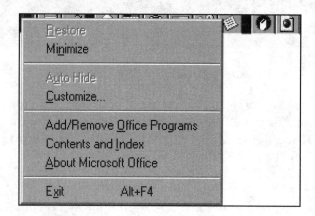

Figure 16.5 The Office 97 Shortcut Bar control menu.

2. Select **Customize...** and click on the **Buttons** tab to display the options.

3. Scroll down the **Show these Files as Buttons** list. You can click in the check box next to any of the applications you want to add to the Shortcut Bar. For this example, click in the check boxes next to **Microsoft Excel** and **Microsoft Word**.

4. Click **OK**.

To start or switch to any of your Office programs using the Shortcut Bar, just click the button for that program. If the program isn't already running, it may take a while to start. If the program is already running, clicking on its Shortcut Bar button switches you to that program almost instantly.

Remember, if you don't know which Microsoft Office Shortcut Bar button belongs to which program, position the mouse pointer over the button to see a ToolTip that tells you the name of the designated program.

NOTE

The Microsoft Office Shortcut Bar is so convenient, we recommend that you always keep it running, except when you are giving on-screen PowerPoint slide show presentations where the toolbar could be distracting.

The Right Tool for the Job

Deciding which of the Office programs to use for a particular task or project is the first—and often the most difficult—challenge. There is some overlap in capabilities, so many projects could be completed using any of the programs. Choosing the best one for the job, however, makes the job go more smoothly and gives you greater flexibility to do it the way you want to.

Picking the correct program might seem to be a matter of common sense—working with words, use Word; manipulating numbers, use Excel; creating a presentation or chart, use PowerPoint; manipulating data, use Access. Well, it's not quite that easy, because there's a shared set of capabilities among the members of the Office ensemble.

Word, for example, has a table feature for manipulating rows and columns, and can even perform calculations like Excel. Excel, in addition to extensive number handling capabilities, can also create dazzling charts. Access might appear to be the best choice for data management, but Word and Excel also have the ability to create databases and to sort and select portions of the database that meet certain criteria. PowerPoint also lets you work with text and create charts.

The path to the best choice becomes even murkier when you take into account the ability to link portions of any of these programs to any other. So how do you decide?

As a general rule, Word is the best choice for primarily text-oriented documents. When you need to work extensively with numbers and calculations, Excel is usually the preferred tool. Excel also makes the most sense for charts, especially those that reflect data in an Excel spreadsheet. PowerPoint is usually the tool to turn to for presentations that pull together elements from the other two programs. Access is the best choice for complex data management.

Ultimately, the best advice we can give you is to learn the capabilities, strengths, and weaknesses of all the Office 97 programs. It also helps if you know what elements you want to include in your document. If you know what the programs can do, and what you want to accomplish, choosing the right one can be as easy as picking the correct socks to go with your shoes.

The following are some more concrete examples of tasks and which program is best suited to each job.

Word makes putting together almost any written document a breeze. From business and personal letters to book-length manuscripts, simple memos to annual reports, Word has the tools to make your documents appear just the way you want.

For number-oriented documents, from household budget worksheets to forecasts for multinational corporations, from a cash flow analysis for a sandwich shop to a portfolio analysis of a multimillion dollar pension fund, Excel provides tools for deftly manipulating numbers to answer the questions you have and finding the best solutions when you are wondering *what if*....

Excel is also the first place to turn when you want to transform the numbers from your Excel worksheet into charts. A column chart showing the relationship between income and expenses is a sure way to clarify the numbers. A pie chart comparing the contribution each division is making to the company makes a stronger statement than numbers alone. A line chart showing the ups and downs of the various investments in a pension fund can help make you better choices than just staring at a bunch of numbers.

The complex database management tasks Access performs include accounting systems where the various pieces of the system are tied together. For example, you could have accounts receivable or accounts payable entries automatically posted to the general ledger.

The text-oriented documents created in Word, the number-oriented worksheet documents created in Excel, and the forms or other portions of data created in Access, can all be used as parts of a presentation. The point of most documents created in Word, Excel, and Access is to persuade and enlighten, so it makes sense that by simply putting them together you can create a persuasive presentation. True enough. But if you want to use the right tool for the job (that is the section heading after all), PowerPoint is the likely choice.

Let's say you are making a presentation to the board of directors to convince them to recommend the acquisition of another company. You might use Word to create an analysis of the proposed acquisition, but you could also use salient portions of the analysis in conjunction with Excel charts to create slides for the presentation. Within PowerPoint itself, you might add slides with bulleted lists of important points, as well as speaker's notes to use during the presentation.

PowerPoint lets you add music, digitized speech, and even video clips to create a multimedia presentation with the kind of production values you would expect to find in a Pepsi commercial. If you can't convince the board with all those tools at your disposal, maybe it's time to move on to the next project.

The next two sections describe some of the nifty new features in the latest versions of Word and PowerPoint. We won't give Access any further discussion here since it isn't used nearly as often as the other two programs.

A Quick Look at Word for Windows

When it comes to word processing programs, there are none with more capabilities—combined with incredible ease of use—than Word for Windows 97. Of course, this new version includes all the features you expect in a world class word processing program. However, some of its new features truly set this program apart from the competition. Figure 16.6 shows a text document in Word for Windows.

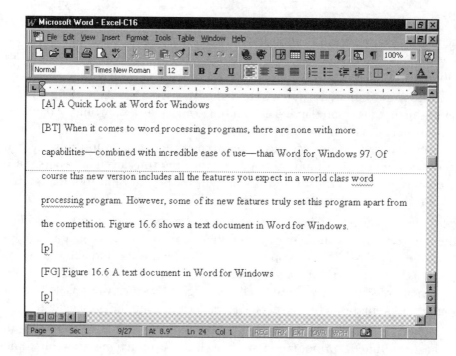

Figure 16.6 A text document in Word for Windows.

Almost Unlimited Undo

If you are as prone to mistakes as most of us are, this feature alone is worth the price of admission. Word 97 keeps track of every change you make to your document, and you can undo any individual change or sequence of changes. You can also redo any series of changes you undid.

AutoCorrect

This feature actually corrects your mistakes automatically as you type them. No human intervention is required, which suits most people just fine. Suppose you have a nasty habit of typing **teh** instead of *the*, or **recieve** instead of *receive*. AutoCorrect automatically corrects these and many other common mistakes as soon as you press the **Spacebar**.

AutoCorrect can also ensure that the first letter of each sentence and the names or days, such as Monday, Tuesday, etc., are in uppercase. You can also add your own common mistakes to the list of items so they will be automatically corrected.

AutoSummarize

You can automatically summarize the key points of a document with the AutoSummarize feature. AutoSummarize can be adjusted to varying levels of detail and will create a brief summary of your documents. You can choose between creating a new summary document, or highlighting the key points within an original document. Whatever your intentions may be, AutoSummarize will provide you with a fast and easy way to peruse documents.

AutoFormat

Wouldn't it be great if you had your own personal designer to format your documents professionally? Word does! AutoFormat can analyze your document and apply the formatting it thinks is best suited to the content. Of course, AutoFormat doesn't always make a good guess, so you have the opportunity to choose from several format templates, or reject the changes altogether.

Wizards

Word's Wizards present you with a series of dialog boxes to help you create a variety of documents. You can create the structure for several types of letters, memos, newsletters, fax covers, web pages, and tables by simply answering questions in the Wizards dialog boxes. With Wizards, you can create sophisticated documents, even if you don't know how to use most of the features involved in their creation.

A Quick Look at PowerPoint

If you make presentations, whether to small or large groups, you may wonder how you ever got along without PowerPoint. This program provides all the tools you'll need to create multimedia presentations, overhead transparencies, and 35mm slides.

Your presentations can incorporate text, charts, graphics, and even sound and video (if your computer has the ability to handle these extras). You can also print copies of your presentation to hand out to the audience, or create speaker's notes to help the presenter remember what to say.

Of course, you can also easily incorporate documents and pieces of documents created in other Office programs into PowerPoint presentations. Figure 16.7 shows a PowerPoint screen with a slide from a presentation.

Figure 16.7 A PowerPoint presentation slide.

One of PowerPoint's best features is the way it can lead you by the hand through the entire process of creating a presentation. All you need to worry about is what you want to present—PowerPoint will do the rest.

Even if you've never used previous versions of PowerPoint and have no idea where to begin creating presentations, there's no need to panic. PowerPoint makes creating presentations easy, even for novice users.

The AutoContent Wizard

Word and Excel have Wizards, but PowerPoint's AutoContent Wizard is special. This Wizard provides a brief interview and then creates an entire presentation for you—almost. Just add your own specific text, add any graphic objects and your presentation is complete.

The Clip Gallery

The Clip Gallery provides a new, easier way to add an expanded collection (more than 1,000 pieces) of special graphics, movies and sounds to your presentations. You can choose from groups of thumbnail sketches, or let PowerPoint do the work with the Auto Clip Art feature.

Record Narration

If you hate public speaking, or if you just want to duplicate a presentation, you'll love the Record Narration feature. All you need is a sound card and microphone to create voice-narrated slide shows.

Animation

You can animate virtually every element of a slide, whether it be text, elements of a graph, or movies. Text and objects will move in and out of a slide according to the style you select. You can adjust the timing and motion according to your preferences.

Freehand Drawing

As you give electronic presentations you can use the freehand drawing tool to add temporary annotations to your slides.

Some PowerPoint Terminology

❖ **Slides** are the heart of every presentation you create in PowerPoint and can be presented electronically on screen, or as overheads and 35mm slides. Slides can contain text, graphics, charts, and even sound and video.

❖ **Outlines** contain the text of your slide presentation. You can enter text for your slides directly on the slides or in an outline.

❖ **Speaker's notes** provide the presenter with a page that corresponds to each slide and contains a small image of the slide with any additional notes.

❖ **Audience handouts** are printed copies of your presentation that can be created with the Handout Master. You can have two, three, or six slides per handout page, and you can add additional elements, such as other text or graphics. For example, you may want each page of the handout to include your company logo.

❖ **Placeholders** let you quickly add the type of element you're likely to want in a particular area of a slide. When you pick a layout for your presentation, placeholders for such elements as text, graphics, and charts are included. Just click or double-click in the placeholder (depending on the type of placeholder) to add or edit the element.

❖ **Objects** are the individual elements that make up presentations. Text elements—such as titles or bulleted lists, graphics and charts—are individual objects and can be moved, sized, rotated, and even overlapped by other objects in a presentation.

WHAT IS OLE AND WHY SHOULD I CARE?

There are three ways to insert information from another Windows 95 program into a document:

❖ Paste from the Clipboard

❖ Embed an object

❖ Link an object

When you select information in a document and then choose **Edit**, **Cut**, or **Copy** (or use a keyboard shortcut or toolbar button to cut or copy), the information is stored on the Clipboard. The Clipboard is a temporary holding area that stores information until you cut or copy something else. The Clipboard only holds the last thing you cut or copied and replaces it with the next thing you cut or copy.

You can retrieve the Clipboard's contents by positioning your insertion point where you want the information to go—whether in a different location in the same document, a different document in the same program, or even a document in a different program—and then choosing **Edit**, **Paste**.

Cutting or copying and then pasting information is simple and straightforward, but has some limitations. Typically, the information you paste is treated as ordinary text or graphics that either can't be edited at all, or must be edited using the available tools of the program in which you pasted it.

In Chapter 13, "Linking Worksheets," you learned how to use a simple form of linking to tie several source worksheets to a dependent worksheet. This is a valuable form of linking, but it's only the beginning.

Dynamic Data Exchange—Baby Steps

With the advent of Windows version 3.0, a technology called DDE (Dynamic Data Exchange) was introduced, enabling users to create truly compound documents. Not only could these compound documents include information from multiple applications, but the data could be updated as the source data changed. DDE was a step in the right direction, but hardly a panacea.

Creating compound documents with DDE could be intimidating, often requiring writing a bit of programming code, and often was dangerous. It was common for DDE documents to cause applications, and Windows itself, to crash. With DDE, you learned to save your work often or suffer the consequences.

OLE 1.0—The Holy Grail? Not Quite

The first implementation of OLE 1.0 after the release of Windows version 3.1 removed many of the obstacles to creating compound documents. Using OLE, embedded data was easier to edit and linked data was less likely to cause system crashes. Also, for the first time, you could create useful compound documents without a degree in Rocket Science.

OLE isn't really a separate technology from DDE, just an evolutionary progression. In fact, OLE is based on the underlying DDE technology. It just added a friendlier interface and additional features.

As wonderful as OLE 1.0 was, it still suffered from some of the same instability problems as DDE. It was more stable, but not stable enough. Links to source data were still easily broken. While it made embedding data easy, editing embedded data still had to be done in the source application, away from the document where the object was embedded.

OLE 2.0—The Genuine Article

OLE 2.0, the latest version of OLE, which is supported by all the main Office applications and many other Windows 95 applications, has everything computer users have been searching for—almost. Links created using OLE 2.0 are much more stable. You do not have nearly as many lost links or system crashes as you once had to put up with.

Perhaps best of all is the way you can edit embedded objects. Embedded objects can now be edited in place, a process sometimes called *visual editing*. With in-place editing, you edit the object right in the document where it's embedded. This way, you can see your edits in context, which greatly enhances efficiency.

When you edit an embedded object, the menus and toolbars of the application the object was *created* in usually replace the menus and toolbars of the application the object is embedded in. You're able to edit the embedded object without ever leaving the document. You'll see how in-place editing works in conjunction with Paint later in this chapter.

WARNING

Documents using OLE require more of your computer's resources than simple documents created in one application. If you have a slower computer with relatively little memory, you may be better off avoiding OLE. Trying to create compound documents with your weakling computer may take more time and patience than it's worth.

On second thought, the benefits of OLE are so compelling you might want to upgrade or replace your computer so you have enough muscle to make working with OLE bearable.

Linking or Embedding? That's the Question

When creating a compound document, the first decision you have to make is whether to link the data to or embed the data in the document. Let's take a look at the differences.

Linking places a representation of the data from one document into another. The primary advantage is the data in the representation is updated when the data in the source document is updated.

Linking would be the right choice if you were putting a portion of an Excel worksheet, such as a budget, into a Word document where you wanted to be sure the Word document always reflected the latest budget numbers.

One disadvantage of linking is that the data isn't quite as easy to edit. You don't have the advantage of in-place editing. When you double-click on the linked data, the source document appears in its original application. It's not a big problem, just a little less convenient.

Another disadvantage to consider is that the document containing the source data must be available in order to edit the linked data. If you delete the source document, you are not able to edit the linked data.

Choose embedding if you don't need the data updated from a source document. A graphic image, such as clip art or a Paint image, doesn't usually have to be updated and is a perfect candidate for embedding.

Embedding makes editing easier by allowing in-place editing. The menus and toolbars are replaced with the menus and toolbars of the application the embedded document was created in. In the example of an Excel worksheet in a Word document, the Word menus and toolbars would be replaced with the Excel menus and toolbars. This allows you to edit the worksheet data in the context of a Word document with Excel's tools.

The primary disadvantage of embedding is that it makes the document larger by roughly the size of the source document. For example, if you embed a 15,000 byte Excel worksheet into a 15,000 byte Word document, the result is a Word document of about 30,000 bytes. Linking, on the other hand, adds very little to the size of the document.

OLE Samples

Describing how OLE works isn't nearly as effective as actually seeing a couple examples of OLE in action. First, we'll show you an example of an Excel worksheet in a Word for Windows document. Then, you'll see a Paint image linked to an Excel worksheet.

 Paint is one of the accessory programs included in the Windows 95 package. It can be used to create, edit, and view pictures.

N O T E

A sample Word for Windows document with a portion of the Spokane Locks and Bagel budget worksheet is displayed in Figure 16.8.

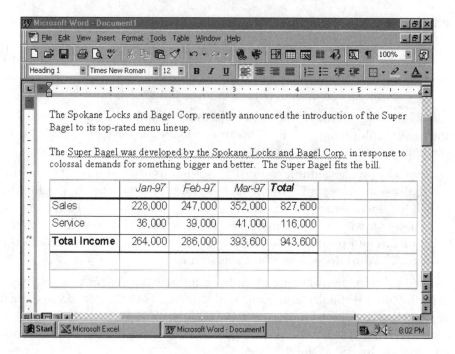

Figure 16.8 An Excel worksheet in a Word document.

The worksheet looks like it's just part of the Word document. But double-click anywhere on it and—zap! As you can see in Figure 16.9, the Excel menus, toolbars and formula bar are available and you can edit the worksheet as though you were in Excel.

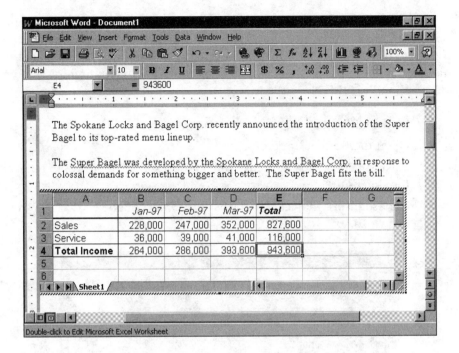

Figure 16.9 *The embedded worksheet, ready to be edited.*

Using OLE

Here are some steps for creating OLE objects on your own. We'll embed a Paint image into an Excel worksheet. If you don't have Paint, you may be able to follow along using another program. Although embedding objects from the supplemented programs included in Office 97 works exactly the same way in all the Office 97 programs, this isn't necessarily the case when using other Windows programs.

Some other programs may not support the latest version of OLE, and some programs may not support OLE at all. If the program in which you want to embed an object doesn't operate in exactly the same way as described in this chapter, don't panic. Refer to that program's documentation to see how, and if, it handles OLE objects.

1. Start Excel if it isn't already running.

2. Open the Budget workbook.

3. Make sure cell A1 is the active cell, and press the **Delete** key to remove the sheet's title.

4. Choose **Insert**, **Object...** to display the Object dialog box, as shown in Figure 16.10.

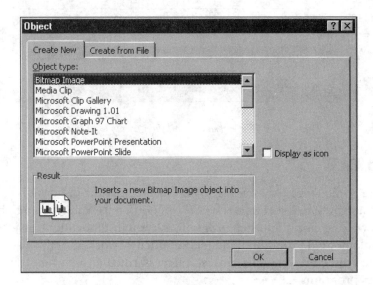

Figure 16.10 *The Create New tab of the Object dialog box.*

5. Click on the **Create New** tab if it isn't already selected. The names in your Object Type list may differ from the figure, depending on the programs installed on your computer.

You'll also notice a check box in the middle-right portion of the dialog box next to **Display as Icon**. This option lets you display a small icon to represent the type of embedded object.

6. Scroll down the list to **Paintbrush Picture** and click on it. The Result portion of the dialog box tells you what would happen if you selected this object type.

 If Paintbrush doesn't appear in your list, you may need to run the Windows 95 setup program to install the paint application. For further help, see the setup instructions that came with Windows 95.

NOTE

7. Click the **OK** button.

The title bar still says Microsoft Excel, but Excel's menus and toolbars have been replaced by the Paint menus and toolbar. The Bitmap Image box also appears on the screen, as shown in Figure 16.11.

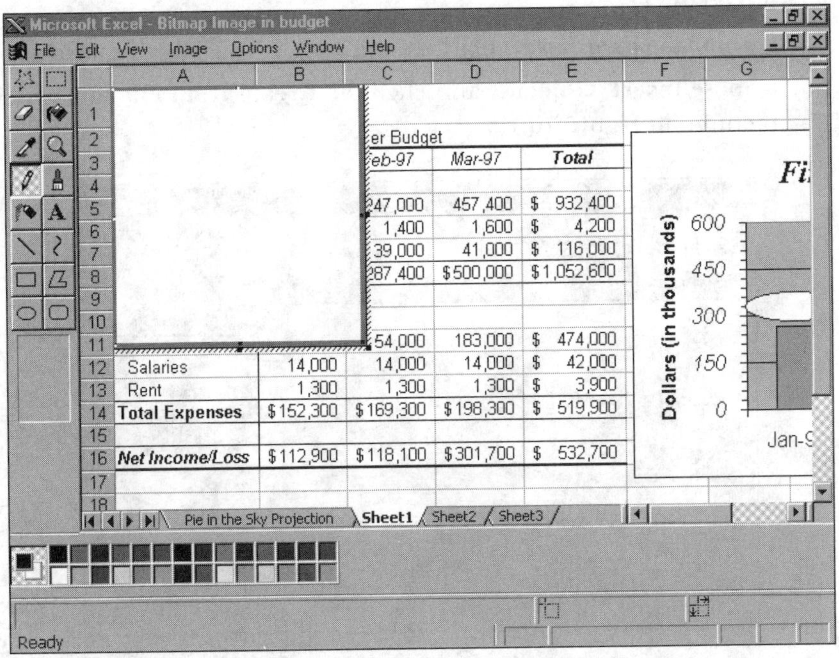

Figure 16.11 *The Paint menus, toolbar, and Bitmap Image box in Excel.*

There are a number of formatting features that you can explore in Paint. For the purposes of this exercise, feel free to add any text or graphics you want.

(You can use the ToolTips to figure out what various buttons will do.) When you're finished, you can click anywhere outside the text entry box on the Budget worksheet to exit Paint and return to Excel. If you want to edit the Paint image again, double-click on the image to bring back the text entry box, menus, and toolbars.

Linking an Excel Worksheet into a Word Document

When linking one document into another, you have the choice between linking the entire document or just a portion of it. Since there are fewer steps to linking an entire document, that's what we'll do.

To link an Excel worksheet with a Word document:

1. Start Word and open the document you want the Excel worksheet linked to.

2. Position the insertion point where you want the worksheet data to appear.

3. Choose **Insert**, **Object...** and click the **Create from File** tab, which is pictured in Figure 16.12.

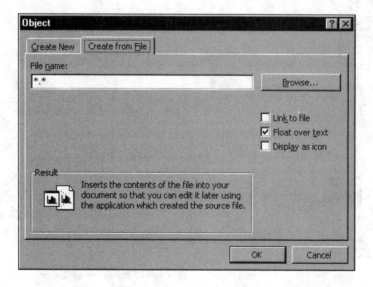

Figure 16.12 The Create from File tab of the Object dialog box.

4. Click the **Link to File** check box in the lower-right portion of the dialog box. This check box tells Word to create a link to the file rather than embed it.

5. Click **Browse** to locate the file you want to link into the Word document. After you've located the drive and directory where the Excel worksheet is stored, click on the worksheet's name and then click **OK**.

    After a few seconds (it could be longer if you have a slow computer), the worksheet appears in the Word document, as shown in Figure 16.13.

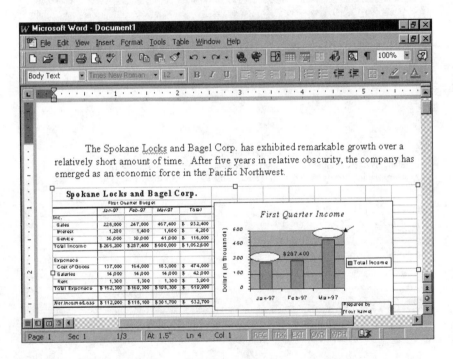

Figure 16.13 *An Excel worksheet linked to a Word document.*

The worksheet is now an object in the Word document that can be moved and sized. To edit the worksheet data, just double-click on the object. The worksheet will appear in a separate Excel window. Any changes you make in the worksheet will be reflected in the Word document (don't forget to save any changes you make to the data from Excel).

As you can see, the problem with linking an entire worksheet is that it can take over the whole document, leaving little room for the surrounding text. For this reason, you may choose to insert selected cells. One other option is to insert the worksheet as an icon.

To insert a worksheet as an icon, click on the **Display as Icon** option in the Create from File tab of the Object dialog box. After the file is linked it will appear as an icon, as shown in Figure 16.14.

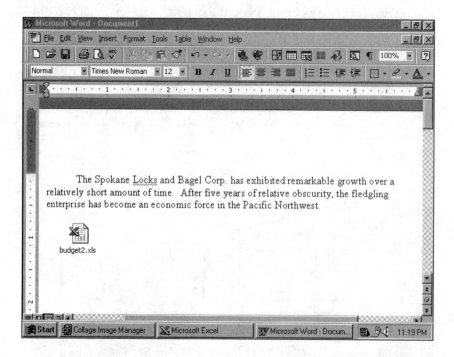

Figure 16.14 *A linked worksheet displayed as an icon.*

The icon lets the reader know that there is additional information available. To view the worksheet, all you have to do is double-click on the icon.

The **Display as Icon** option is only a good idea if the people reading your document have Excel on their computer. Also, if you print a document with a linked file that's displayed as an icon, the icon prints out just as it appears on the screen.

Organizing Projects with Binders

Office 97 users have another option available for merging documents from different sources—the Office binder. A binder allows you to tie together a group of Office 97 documents by utilizing Windows' drag-and-drop feature. All you have to do is create a binder and then drag in files from My Computer or the desktop area. You can then work with individual documents, or apply formatting features like page numbers or headers/footers to the entire collection.

To create a binder, minimize all other applications you may be working with and go to the desktop.

1. To start Binder click on the **Start** button, move to the Programs Option and click on the **Microsoft Binder** icon.

   If Binder doesn't appear as an option, you may need to run the Office 97 setup program to install the application. For further help, see the setup instructions that came with Office 97.

   Your screen should look like Figure 16.15.

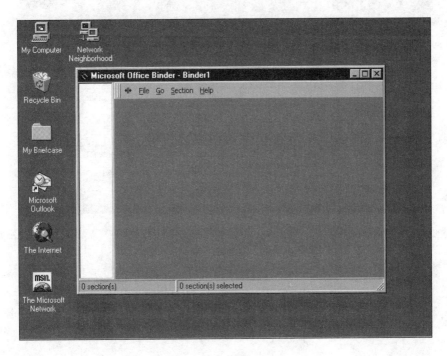

Figure 16.15 The Office Binder.

When you're working with a binder, the pane on the left side of the window will show each of the documents that make up the binder. The pane on the right side will contain the specific document you're working on.

2. Double-click on the **My Computer** icon, and select a file you would like to add to the binder.

3. Press and hold your left mouse button down, and drag the selected file to the pane on the left side of the window. Release the mouse button to copy the document to the binder. Your screen should now look like Figure 16.16.

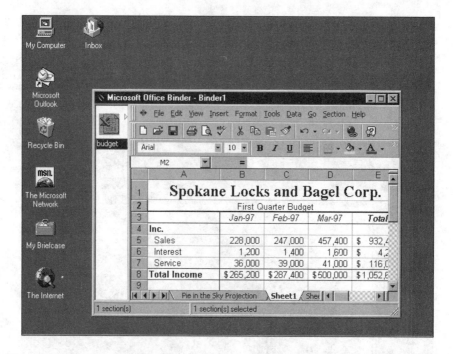

Figure 16.16 Adding a document to a binder.

You can now edit the document by clicking on the right pane.

4. Select another document you'd like to include in the binder and drag it into the left pane. You can switch between documents by clicking on the corresponding icon in the left pane.

The binder can now essentially be treated like any other document in Office 97. To save, preview, print or modify a binder, just select the appropriate command from the File menu.

A FINAL THOUGHT

In this chapter, you learned some of the basic concepts behind using Excel with other programs and using OLE to share data between applications. This just scratches the surface of Excel's ability to work with other Windows programs. Combining Excel with other programs adds up to more than the sum of the programs and greatly enhances your ability to create complex documents.

In the next chapter, you'll journey out into cyberspace and take a look at using Excel to create and read documents on the World Wide Web.

CHAPTER 17

Excel and the Internet

As you've already seen while working with Excel, computers are revolutionizing the way our world operates. Technology is advancing at an increasingly rapid rate, and no task is too great or too small for computers to handle. Sometimes the idea of keeping up with all these changes seems a little overwhelming, but the rewards usually outweigh the initial inconveniences.

In recent years, perhaps no single aspect of computing technology has generated as much change or attention as the Internet. An *internet* is a collection of computer networks that allow connected computers to communicate directly with each other. An *intranet* is a network within an organization or business. These networks are connected in a number of different ways, including optical fiber, telephone lines and satellite systems. To connect with an internet, all you basically need is a modem connection to a server and the appropriate *TCP/IP* (Transmission Control Protocol/Internet Protocol) software.

Most of the time when people refer to the Internet, they're talking about a global connection of networks. However, internets exist on a number of different levels, ranging from global to local. As a result, you can communicate with someone down the hall or halfway around the world in the same basic manner. The most common form of communication on the Internet is electronic mail (e-mail), which allows a message to be sent from one computer to one or more additional computers. Other common Internet utilities include *Gophers* and *FTP* (File Transfer Protocol) *sites*. Gophers allow users to create and access computer file directories, while FTP sites can be used to transfer files from one computer to another.

The largest system of resources available on the Internet is the *World Wide Web* (commonly referred to as the Web). The Web provides access to a virtually unlimited amount of information, ranging from news reports to video clippings and sound files. Unlike most other Internet services, the Web bases a large part of its functionality on graphics. Web users can point and click on designated text or objects in one site to move to another selected site. This way users can interact with their computer to direct their travels through cyberspace.

Because there are several different types of computers, Web pages are all written in a basic format called *Hypertext Markup Language* (HTML). Without getting too involved, HTML is essentially a programming format that uses a combination of ordinary text and common-language commands called *tags*. Computers then process these commands with the help of a *browser*, a program that deciphers HTML into text, images and sound (Figure 17.1).

The beauty of the Web is that it simplifies the relationship between users and their computers. Both experienced computer programmers and novices alike can create and use multimedia documents for the Web. It doesn't matter if you want to advertise products from your business or post pictures of a family pet—the only limits are your imagination.

What's more, you don't need any fancy programs or expensive computer equipment—a basic text editor and knowledge of HTML is all it really takes. And now, thanks to Microsoft, you don't even really need either of those. Office 97 will automatically convert text documents, charts, drawings and anything else you've created into HTML format. In addition, you can use Office 97 to create and view new HTML documents.

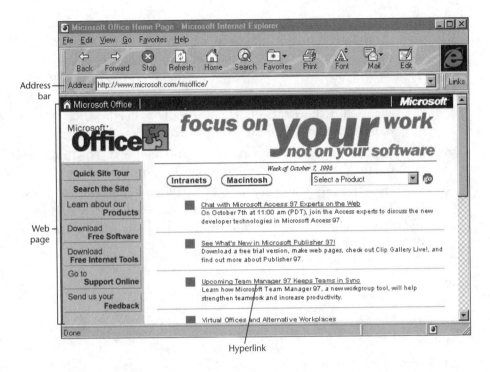

Address bar

Web page

Hyperlink

Figure 17.1 *Viewing a Web document with a browser.*

HTML—The Language of the Internet

Let's face it, the term Hypertext Markup Language immediately conjures up images of pocket protectors and slide rules. The mere mention of the word programming is enough to make people shrug their shoulders and turn off their computers. After all, computers are confusing enough when using a program that someone else wrote, let alone trying to write one of your own.

Don't be scared by all the fancy names and jargon—HTML really is easy to use. All you need to understand are a few basic concepts:

❖ The fundamental building blocks of HTML documents are *tags*. Tags are essentially commands (i.e., bold, center, or italic). They consist of a left angle bracket (<), a tag name, and a right angle bracket (>).

❖ Tags are usually paired together to turn on and off a command. The end tag looks exactly like the start tag, except a slash (/) precedes the text within the brackets. Tags usually will take the form of <COMMAND> text </COMMAND>.

❖ Every HTML document consists of head and body text. The head contains the title, and the body contains the remaining contents.

❖ Even though every Web page is unique, all pages have to follow the same basic structure. This uniformity allows browsers to read a page and understand what the author wants. The basic framework for a Web page is shown in Table 17.1.

Table 17.1 *The basic framework of a Web page*

<HTML>

<HEAD>

<TITLE> Page title </TITLE>

</HEAD>

<BODY>

Page body.

</BODY>

</HTML>

❖ Browsers won't recognize more than one consecutive space in the text of your document. As a result, if you separated two words by pressing the **Spacebar** 20 times and hitting the **Enter** key 20 more, there would only be one space between the words on your browser.

❖ HTML is not case sensitive. For example, <TITLE> is equivalent to <title>.

❖ Links to other pages are created with anchors. Placing the tags <A> and </A> around a section of text or a graphic, in addition to designating the file location, creates a link to another page.

❖   Style tags are used to format the appearance of text. There are a wide number of style tags, and not all of them are recognized the same way by different browsers. Table 17.2 contains some basic style tags.

Table 17.2 HTML style tags

OPENING TAG	FUNCTION	END TAG
<P>	Paragraph	</P>
<B>	Bold	</B>
<I>	Italic	</I>
<CENTER>	Center	</CENTER>

Now that you know some of the basics, it's time to start tying things together. If you want to, you can put together an HTML document by using Notepad or any other text editor that allows you to save in ASCII format. Because this is a book on Excel, we'll just do a quick comparison between an HTML document and a converted Office 97 document.

Table 17.3 contains the text of a sample HTML document.

Table 17.3 A sample HTML document

```
<HTML>
<HEAD>A Sample HTML Document</HEAD>
<TITLE>A Sample HTML Document</TITLE>
<P>
<BODY>
This is just a sample of what HTML coding looks like:
<P>
<B>The Bold tags make your text look like this</B>
<P>
<I>The Italic tags make your text look like this</I>
<P>
<CENTER>The Center tags make your text look like this</CENTER>
</BODY>
</HTML>
```

Well, that's about all it takes to put together an HTML document. It's not so bad, is it? If you're following along and want to complete the document, save it in ASCII format with an .htm extension at the end of the filename (i.e., sample.htm). You can open the file with a browser to view the results, as shown in Figure 17.2.

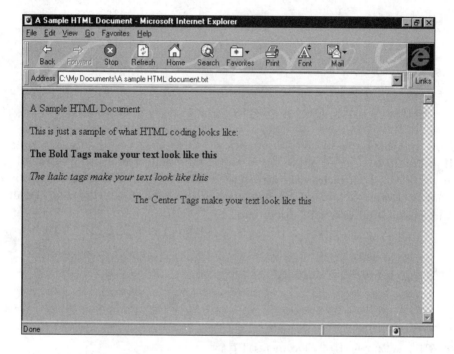

Figure 17.2 *A sample HTML document.*

 There's no room for error when putting together an HTML document. If you make typing mistake, or forget to insert a command, browsers won't be able to interpret your document correctly. The good news is that putting together a Web page is a process of trial and error, and you can just go back into the document to examine your HTML syntax.

NOTE

Now that you've seen how to do it the "hard" way, let's try duplicating the sample HTML document with Word 97.

1. Start Word if it isn't already running, and choose **File**, **New...**.

2. Type **A Sample HTML Document** and press **Enter**.

3. Type **This is just a sample of what HTML coding looks like:** and press **Enter**.

4. Click on the Formatting toolbar's **Bold** button and type **The Bold tags make your text look like this**.

5. Click on the **Bold** button again to turn it off, and press **Enter**.

6. Click on the Formatting toolbar's **Italic** button and type **The Italic tags make your text look like this**.

7. Click on the **Italic** button to turn it off, and press **Enter**.

8. Click on the Formatting toolbar's **Center** button and type **The Center tags make your text look like this**.

9. Click on the **Center** button to turn it off, and press **Enter**. Your screen should look like Figure 17.3.

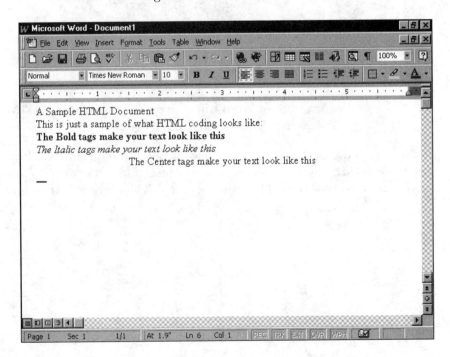

Figure 17.3 *Putting together an HTML document in Word.*

10.   Choose **File**, **Save As HTML...**. The Save As dialog box will appear.

NOTE

If the Save As HTML... command does not appear on the File menu, you need to install the Internet Assistant add-in program.

11.   Type **Sample** in the file name text box and click on **Save**. A dialog box will appear to warn you that some formatting changes may be lost, as shown in Figure 17.4.

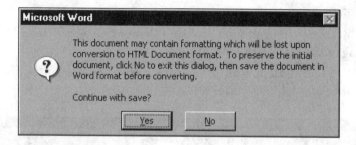

Figure 17.4 *The HTML formatting warning.*

12.   Click on the **Yes** button. Word will convert the page into an HTML document. Your screen should look like Figure 17.5.

At first glance, things probably don't look a whole lot different. However, if you choose **View**, **HTML Source** you'll see that Word has inserted its own tags into your document. To hide the HTML coding, choose **View**, **Exit HTML Source**.

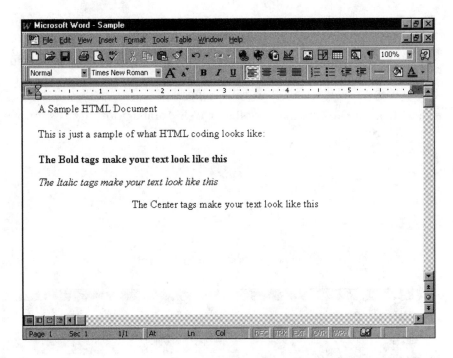

Figure 17.5 *The Word document converted into HTML.*

CREATING HYPERLINKS IN YOUR WORKSHEET

Now that we've covered some of the concepts involved with HTML programming, it's time to turn our attention back to Excel. Like the other main

Office 97 programs, Excel can be used in conjunction with a browser to view HTML documents.

If you have an Internet connection, here's all you have to do to get on-line:

1. Open Excel if it isn't already running.
2. Click on the Standard toolbar's **Web Toolbar** button, as shown in Figure 17.6.

Figure 17.6 *The Web Toolbar button.*

The Web toolbar appears, as shown in Figure 17.7.

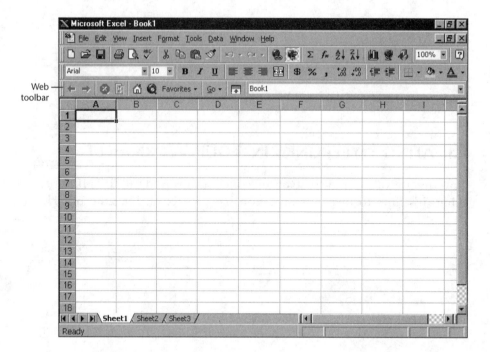

Figure 17.7 *The Web toolbar.*

3. Type the address, or URL (Universal Resource Locator), of the Internet site you want to visit in the address text box and press **Enter**. Excel will connect with your Web browser and take you to the designated site.

Having access to a server also means that you can create hyperlinks from an Excel worksheet to other sites. If you don't have an on-line connection, you can make links to your hard drive or company's network. Let's make a link to the Budget worksheet.

1. Open a new worksheet.

2. Move to cell A1.

3. Click on the Standard toolbar's **Insert Hyperlink** button, as shown in Figure 17.8.

Figure 17.8 *The Insert Hyperlink button.*

A dialog box will appear asking you if you want to save the document before adding a hyperlink. Because this is a blank document, click **No**. The Insert Hyperlink dialog box will appear, as shown in Figure 17.9.

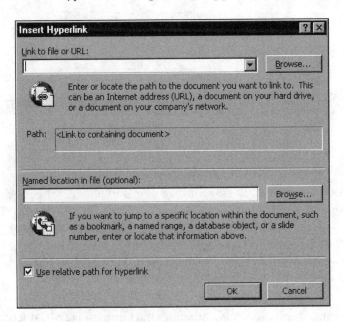

Figure 17.9 *The Insert Hyperlink dialog box.*

4. Click on the **Browse...** button in the Link to File or URL portion of the Insert Hyperlink dialog box.

5. Select the **Budget** worksheet from the Link to File dialog box and click **OK**.

6. Click **OK** in the Insert Hyperlink dialog box to accept the location. Cell A1 should now contain a colored link to the location of the Budget worksheet, as shown in Figure 17.10.

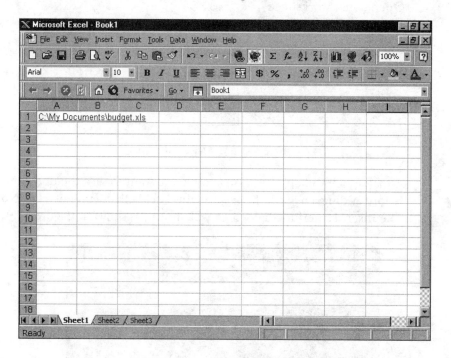

Figure 17.10 *A hyperlink to the Budget worksheet.*

Now let's check the hyperlink to make sure it works.

7. Click on cell **A1**. Excel will load the Budget worksheet, which you'll use in the following section.

ADDING WORKSHEET DATA OR CHARTS TO YOUR WEB PAGE

In the old days, implementing a table or chart into an HTML document was a programmer's worst nightmare. Thanks to Office 97's Internet Wizard, adding worksheet data or charts to a Web page is now a breeze.

Let's try saving the Budget worksheet data as an HTML file.

1. Make sure the Budget worksheet is on your screen and that you're in cell A4 of Sheet1. Choose **File**, **Save As HTML....** The Internet Assistant dialog box will appear, as shown in Figure 17.11.

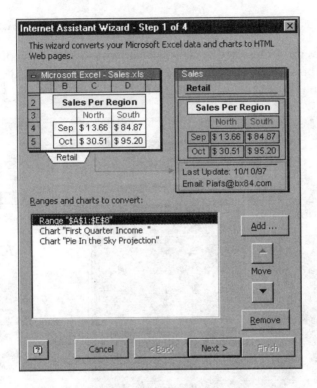

Figure 17.11 Step 1 in the Internet Assistant dialog box.

Excel automatically selects the range A1 through E8, and each of the charts in the Budget worksheet as items you might want to convert to HTML format. To convert all of these items, all you'd have to do is click on the **Next** button. To add another item to the list, you can click on the **Add...** button, and to omit something, you can click on the **Remove** button. Let's select the entire range of worksheet data in Sheet1.

2. Click on the **Add...** button to display the Internet Wizard's data conversion dialog box, as shown in Figure 17.12.

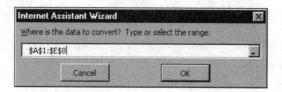

Figure 17.12 *The Internet Wizard's data conversion dialog box.*

3. Press the **Delete** key to clear the contents of the data conversion dialog box. Then click in cell **E16** and drag up to cell **A1**. Your screen should now look like Figure 17.13.

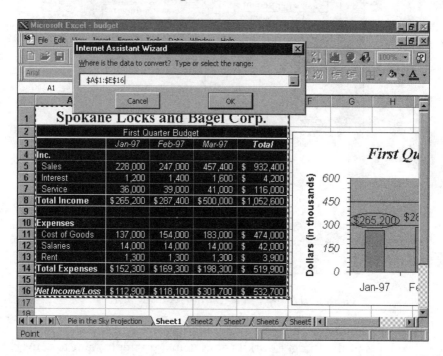

Figure 17.13 *Selecting all of the data in Sheet1.*

4. Click the **OK** button to return to Step 1 of the Internet Wizard dialog box. Select **Range"$A1:$E$8"** and click the **Remove** button to delete this selection from your document.

5. Click the **Next** button to move to Step 2 of the Internet Wizard dialog box, which is shown in Figure 7.14.

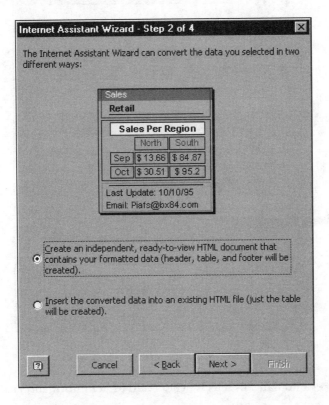

Figure 17.14 Step 2 of the Internet Wizard dialog box.

Excel offers you the option of creating a new independent HTML file for the data you selected, or inserting the data into an existing HTML document. Let's stick with creating a new HTML file.

6. Click the **Next** button to proceed to Step 3 of the Internet Wizard dialog box, which is shown in Figure 17.15.

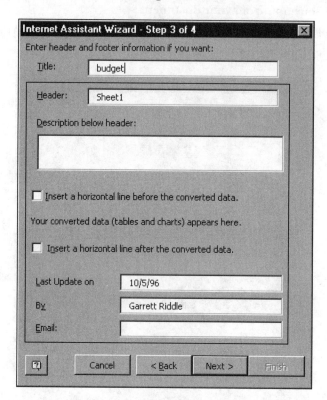

Figure 17.15 Step 3 of the Internet Wizard dialog box.

Excel automatically selects header and footer information for your chart.

7. Click on the **Next** button to accept the default suggestions and move to Step 4 of the Internet Wizard dialog box, shown in Figure 17.16.

You can change the default location of the HTML file by typing in the File path text box. Name the file **MyHTML.htm** and click on the **OK** button. Excel will convert the Selections into an HTML document and return to the Budget worksheet.

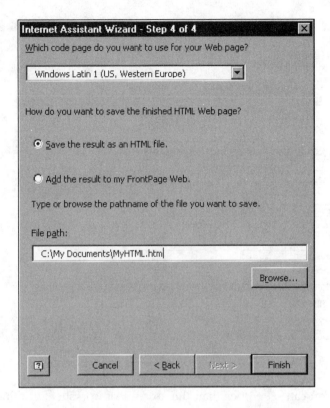

Figure 17.16 *Step 4 of the Internet Wizard dialog box.*

8.   Choose **File**, **Open. . .** .

9.   Display the drop-down list of file format options by clicking on the **Arrow** next to *Files of type*, and select **All Files**.

10. Select the MyHTML document and click on the **Open** button.

Your screen should now look like Figure 17.7.

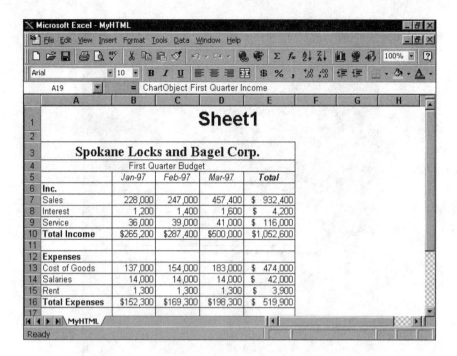

Figure 17.17 *The MyHTML document.*

As you can see, other than the absence of worksheet gridlines and formulas, the HTML document is basically the same as a normal Excel worksheet. You can still click in individual cells to edit and format the contents. You can also perform many other functions, like linking workbooks or goal seeking. Hey, this HTML stuff might not be so bad after all!

A FINAL THOUGHT

We just barely touched on a few Internet and HTML basics. If you're interested in learning more about HTML programming and the World Wide Web, there are a number of books available on the subject. You can also find some excellent resources on the Internet. The important thing to remember is that HTML doesn't have to be all that complicated.

In the next chapter, we'll wrap things up by looking at how you can customize your working environment in Windows 95.

CHAPTER 18

Customizing Windows

You learned in Chapter 2, "Getting Started—Excel and Windows Basics," to use Windows 95 productively. In this chapter, you will explore several ways to make Windows behave just the way you want.

You can use the Control Panel, a program that comes with Windows, to alter mouse operations, the desktop environment, and Windows' colors.

TAMING THE MOUSE

The Control Panel is a Windows program that provides options for customizing such aspects of Windows' environment as fonts, sound, keyboards, and printers. You can find detailed information about these options in the Windows documentation and by using Help. There are also a variety of good books that cover all these options and many more in depth.

We're just going to discuss a few of the more useful Windows customization options. One of the most useful of these involves customizing the mouse so you can work with it more easily. Let's start the Control Panel application and customize the mouse now.

1. If Excel is running, minimize the program window by clicking on the **Minimize** button in the upper-right corner of the screen (the leftmost of the three buttons in the corner of the screen). The Control Panel icon is normally found in the My Computer window. Let's open that window now.

2. Double-click on the **My Computer** icon to display the My Computer window, as shown in Figure 18.1.

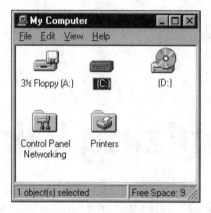

Figure 18.1 *The My Computer window.*

3. Double-click on the **Control Panel** folder to view the Control Panel icons, as shown in Figure 18.2.

    To enter one of the Control Panel's customization areas, double-click on its icon to open a dialog box. Let's go into the Mouse dialog box now.

Figure 18.2 *The Control Panel window.*

4. Double-click on the **Mouse** icon to display the Mouse dialog box, as shown in Figure 18.3.

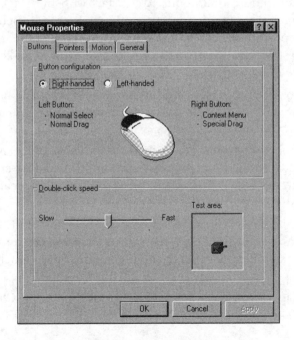

Figure 18.3 *The Mouse dialog box.*

The Mouse dialog box provides options for changing the mouse pointer speed (how fast the pointer moves across the screen as you move the mouse), changing the double-click speed (how much time you can pause between two clicks and have Windows interpret the action as a double-click instead of two single clicks), and swapping left and right mouse buttons (which may be useful for left-handed computer users). Other options are available in the various tabbed pages of the Mouse dialog box.

In the Motion tab is another feature called *Pointer Trails*, which leaves a temporary trail of mouse pointer images as you move the mouse pointer. This feature is often useful for laptop computers with LCD (Liquid Crystal Display) screens. The mouse pointer on some LCD screens has a submarine effect which can obscure the pointer as you move it from one place on the screen to another. Using the Mouse Trails feature can help you keep track of the mouse pointer in these situations. For standard desktop-type screens, this feature is usually more of an annoyance, though it can be amusing to try it out for a few minutes.

Let's try changing some of these options now to see what effect they have on mouse operations. We'll start with the tracking speed. If the tracking speed is too fast, you may have a difficult time accurately positioning the mouse pointer precisely. If the tracking speed is too slow, it will slow you down, causing you to make unnecessary mouse movements.

5. Move your mouse back and forth several inches on your desktop and observe how rapidly the on-screen pointer moves compared with how rapidly you move the mouse.

6. Click on the **Motion** tab in the Mouse dialog box. Then move the indicator in the Pointer speed portion of the dialog box all the way over to the fast (right) side of the scroll bar and repeat step 5 to see the difference.

7. Move the scroll box in the Pointer Speed portion of the dialog box all the way over to the slow (left) side of the scroll bar and, once again, repeat step 5. Notice that the mouse pointer moves much more slowly.

8. Reposition the Pointer Speed scroll box so the tracking speed is comfortable for you. Now let's take a look at the Double-Click Speed setting. The goal here is to set the double-click speed as fast as possible

but not so fast that you cannot double-click. Most people have a tough time double-clicking when it is set at the fastest speed.

Setting the double-click speed too slow can be an equally bothersome problem. For example, you might click on one screen element then move to another element and click on it, and have Windows interpret that as double-clicking on the first element. You certainly don't want the double-click speed set so slow that you have to consciously wait before clicking again to avoid having the two clicks be a double-click.

9. Click on the **Buttons** tab in the Mouse dialog box. Then point to the Test area box and double-click. If you double-clicked fast enough, the Jack-in-the-box will appear, as shown in Figure 18.4. The next double-click puts the little fellow away.

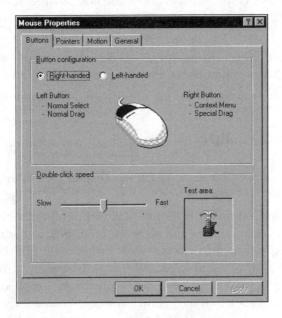

Figure 18.4 *The Mouse dialog box with the Test Area activated.*

10. If you had to try double-clicking several times before you could get the Jack-in-the-box to appear, move the Double-Click speed scroll box a little to the slow (left) side. If you had no difficulty double-clicking at the current setting, move the scroll box to the fast (right) side until you do have trouble and then back it off just enough that you can double-click comfortably.

If you want to use the Swap Left/Right Buttons, click the **Left-Handed** or **Right-Handed** options in the Buttons tab of the dialog box.

WARNING

If you swap the left and right mouse buttons, you won't notice the change until you exit the Mouse dialog box by clicking **OK**.

11.   Click **OK** to accept any changes you made and close the dialog box.

STRAIGHTENING UP THE DESKTOP

The Control Panel's Display Properties dialog box provides several options for enhancing the appearance of your Windows display, such as adding background graphic images, changing screen colors, and more.

You can also choose from several screen savers which will blank your screen and display moving images after a specified time of inactivity.

Let's take a look at these options and discuss their pros and cons.

Patterns and Wallpaper

1.   Double-click on the Control Panel's **Display** icon to display the dialog box shown in Figure 18.5.

Two Display Property options allow you to add a background to the desktop area: patterns and wallpaper. *Patterns*, as the name suggests, are designs made up of dots. These are generally not very intricate but can add a bit of visual appeal. *Wallpaper* is actually a graphic file used as background. The graphic can be one of the supplied images or you can design your own in a paint program. Wallpaper graphics can be extremely intricate. In fact, because wallpaper is displayed in a much larger size than toolbar buttons, you can use much more elaborate images for your wallpaper and still easily make out the details.

Let's start our desktop delving by choosing a pattern. To select a pattern, click on the desired pattern name in the Patterns list that appears in the Background tab of the dialog box. You may then edit the pattern if you wish.

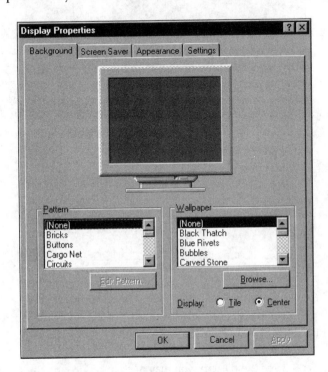

Figure 18.5 *The Display Properties dialog box.*

2. Click on the **Background** tab (if it's not already active). You can use the scroll bar to see additional pattern choices, but for now, choose one of the patterns near the top of the list.

3. Click on the **Cargo Net** pattern. You can immediately see what the effect of the pattern selection is by looking at the sample screen, as shown in Figure 18.6.

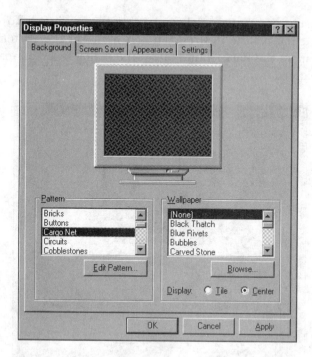

Figure 18.6 *The sample screen showing your selected pattern.*

4. With **Cargo Net** selected, click **OK** to close the Display Properties dialog box and display the pattern, as shown in Figure 18.7.

N O T E   If you can't see the pattern, you may need to reduce the size of some of your open windows. For example, if you have Excel maximized, none of your desktop will be visible, so you won't see the pattern, just as you wouldn't be able to see the top of your desk if you had papers completely covering the surface.

5. Double-click on the **Display** icon in the Control Panel window to show the Display Properties dialog box once again.

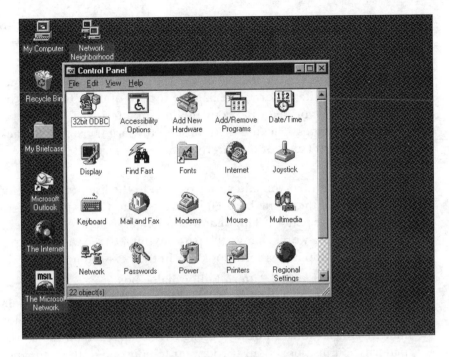

Figure 18.7 *The Cargo Net pattern covering your desktop.*

6. Click on the **Edit Pattern...** button to display the Pattern Editor dialog box, as shown in Figure 18.8.

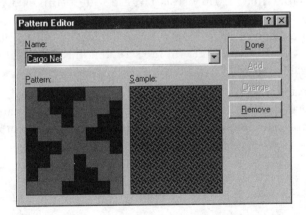

Figure 18.8 *The Pattern Editor dialog box.*

From this dialog box, you can choose different patterns to edit by using the Name drop-down list. Choosing **None** from the list lets you create your own pattern from scratch.

Each small square in the middle box of the dialog box represents one dot or pixel of the pattern. The Sample section of the left side of the dialog box lets you see what your modified pattern will look like as you make changes. Clicking the mouse in the large box adds a black dot, if there isn't already one there, and removes a black dot if there is one there.

The **Add** button lets you add a new pattern to the list after you enter a new name in the Name box. The **Change** button saves the changes you make to the pattern. The **Remove** option lets you delete a pattern from the list. We won't change the pattern, but let's see what a couple of the other supplied patterns look like in the next two figures.

7. Click **Done** to close the Pattern Editor dialog box.

8. In the list of patterns, choose **None**. Next, let's take a look at the wallpaper portion of the dialog box. The wallpaper images are color images and can add significantly greater visual appeal than the simple patterns you just looked at. If you want to edit one of the wallpaper images, you need to use another program, such as Paint.

You can use the **Center** and **Tile** options to position the image on screen. The **Center** option centers the image on your screen. If the wallpaper image you use is large enough, this is a good choice. However, if you are using a small wallpaper image, it could be hidden behind some of your open windows. The **Tile** option places as many copies as are required to fill the screen and reduces the chances that the wallpaper will be hidden.

Choosing a wallpaper image is just like choosing a pattern. Click the arrow to display the drop-down list of wallpaper images and choose the one you want. Figures 18.9 and 18.10 show two different wallpapers.

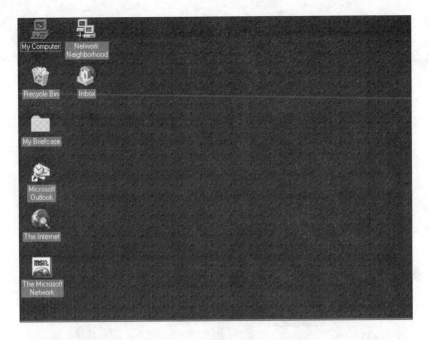

Figure 18.9 *The Blue Rivets wallpaper.*

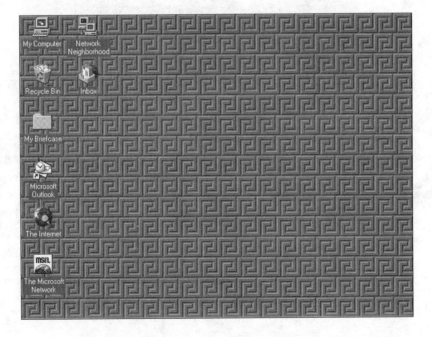

Figure 18.10 *The Carved Stone wallpaper.*

NOTE All the wallpaper names have a .bmp extension, which stands for bitmap. This is a particular type of file format that can be created by most paint-type graphics programs. If you want to create your own wallpaper file, you need to save it as a .bmp file. You also need to save it in your main Windows directory, usually C:, so that it will appear in the list of wallpaper files.

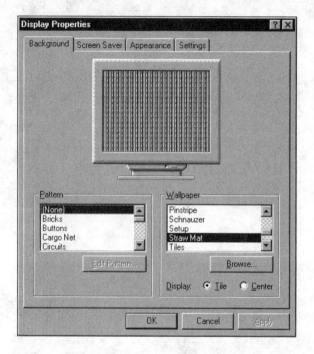

Figure 18.11 *The Straw Mat wallpaper.*

WARNING Windows 95's performance can suffer if there isn't enough memory available, and wallpaper uses memory. The more complex and larger wallpaper images use more memory than the smaller, simpler ones, but they all use memory. If you want to maximize performance and conserve as much memory as possible for your Windows programs, consider avoiding wallpaper.

9. Click **OK** to see what the wallpaper looks like on the display screen. Figure 18.12 shows the Straw Mat example.

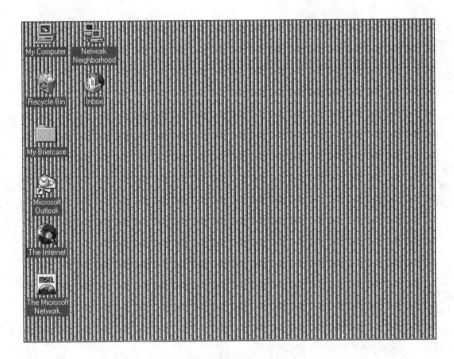

Figure 18.12 *The Straw Mat wallpaper in action.*

10.   Double-click on the **Display** icon, then choose **None** from the wallpaper drop-down list.

We'll discuss the next several features in the Display Properties dialog box without performing any actions. Leave the Display Properties dialog box open so you can refer to it as we look at the next few options.

THE SCREEN SAVER TAB

At one time, screen savers were vital for protecting your screen from phosphor burn-in, which could occur if the same image remained on screen for long periods of time. Phosphor burn-in caused the image that was burned into the screen to appear as a ghost image even when another image should have been the only one on the screen.

Newer color monitors are much less susceptible to phosphor burn-in and make screen savers unnecessary. With standard VGA monitors, an image can remain on the screen for days or weeks without causing any problems. Also, like wallpaper, screen savers can decrease performance by using some of your computer's resources to monitor periods of inactivity. For example, if you set the screen saver to activate after 10 minutes of inactivity, the computer must constantly time the length of inactivity.

Our advice is to forget about screen savers unless you have a fast enough computer that the performance decrease is unnoticeable. To choose a screen saver, select one from the list of screen saver names in the drop-down list in the screen saver portion of the Desktop dialog box, and then specify the number of delay minutes (the number of minutes of inactivity Windows will wait before starting the screen saver). You can use the **Preview** button to see what each of the screen savers look like. The **Settings** button lets you specify some options for the screen saver that you have chosen.

There is one genuine advantage to screen savers: they can help you protect confidential information by requiring a password to clear the screen saver. Normally, any keyboard or mouse inactivity clears the screen saver. However, with password protection enabled, you (or anyone else trying to use your computer) would need to enter the password you have specified. This can be a nice little security feature.

Figure 18.13 shows the Settings dialog box for the Flying Windows screen saver.

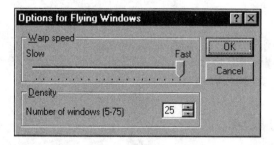

Figure 18.13 *The Flying Windows Setup dialog box.*

The setup dialog boxes for other screen savers provide different sets of options, depending on the characteristics of the particular screen saver.

Figure 18.14 shows the Change Password dialog box.

Change Password	? ☒
Change password for Windows Screen Saver	OK
	Cancel
New password:	
Confirm new password:	

Figure 18.14 The Change Password dialog box.

For security purposes, asterisks appear as you type your password. This way, if someone is looking over your shoulder, they won't see your password. Also, you are told to type the same password twice, once in the New Password text box and once in the Repeat New Password text box. This ensures that you actually typed the password you intended to type. Also, if you already had a password set, type the old password in the Old Password text box.

WARNING

If you decide to set a password, make sure it's one you can remember. Otherwise, you will not be able to get back into Windows once the screen saver is activated.

COLOR YOUR WORLD

The Appearance tab in the Display Properties dialog box lets you change the colors of various screen elements. Although the colors you choose are primarily an aesthetic decision, choosing unwise color combinations can make it hard to read portions of the screen. For example, if you choose black menu text and black menu bars, the menu text will be completely invisible.

Windows provides a variety of color combinations that make it easy to spruce up your screen.

Let's take a look at the colorful options the Display Properties dialog box displays.

1. Double-click on the **Display** icon in the Control Panel (if it's not already open) then click on the **Appearance** tab to display the screen shown in Figure 18.15.

Figure 18.15 *The Appearance options.*

The easiest way to make color changes is to choose one of the available color schemes from the Schemes drop-down list. To choose one of the color schemes, click on the arrow next to the Schemes box. Let's do that now.

2. Click on the **Arrow** next to the Schemes list box to display the list of available color schemes, as shown in Figure 18.16.

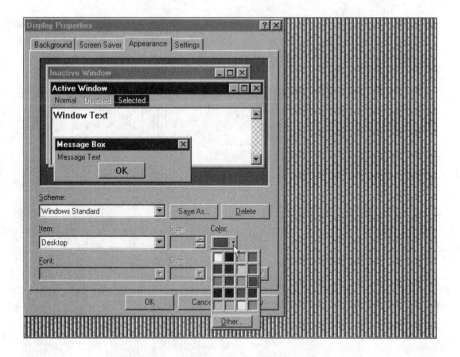

Figure 18.16 *The list of color schemes.*

We won't show you figures of different color schemes, since the figures in this book are in black and white. Try choosing several of the schemes to see their effect. When you click on a color scheme, you can see its effect by looking at the sample screen section at the top of the dialog box.

3.   Click on **Windows Standard** (or whatever scheme was already in effect) to retain that as the color scheme. You can also create custom color schemes and even custom colors by selecting colors for various screen elements from the Color Palette. Let's take a look at the Color Palette now.

4. You can change a screen element's color by choosing the element from the drop-down list of screen elements under Item, as shown in Figure 18.17. Click on that list now.

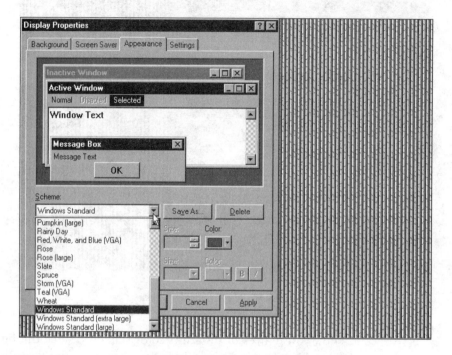

Figure 18.17 *The drop-down list of screen elements.*

SHORTCUT

Instead of choosing from the drop-down screen element list, you can simply click on the element you want to change in the sample portion of the dialog box. When you do, you'll know if you clicked on the correct element because the element's name will appear in the Screen Element box.

Having chosen the screen element you want to change, just click on the color in the color palette you want to use for that element. As you change colors for various screen elements, you can see the changes in the Sample Windows area at the top of the dialog box.

After you change all the screen elements you want to change, you can close the dialog box and the changes will remain in effect. However, if you later choose a different color scheme, your changes will be lost unless you save them with a color scheme name. To save a color scheme, click on the **Save As...** button to display the Save As dialog box, as shown in Figure 18.18.

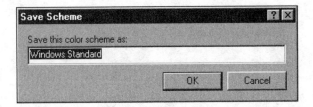

Figure 18.18 *The Save Scheme dialog box.*

You can then enter a name for your new color scheme. This name now appears on the color scheme drop-down list, so you can choose it in the future.

5. Click **OK** in the lower-left corner of the Color dialog box to close it and accept any color changes you made.

6. Close the Display Properties dialog box by choosing **OK**. Close the Control Panel window by clicking in the **Close** box in the upper-right corner.

A FINAL THOUGHT

In this chapter, you learned to customize your Windows environment in several ways. The Control Panel offers other customization options you might want to explore. Windows' Help facility includes information on the other Control Panel features, as does the Windows 95 documentation.

We hope this book has helped you gain the skill and confidence to produce usable worksheets that make your life easier and more enjoyable.

Glossary

active window	The window that is currently in use or selected.
active cell	The worksheet cell that is currently selected.
application window	The window containing the menu bar for an application.
cell formatting	Appearance changes applied to cells, such as alignment, fonts, and borders.
cell	The rectangular area on a worksheet that is the intersection of a column and a row.
comparison operators	Symbols used to compare values, such as > (greater than) and = (equal to).
comparison criteria	A set of search conditions used to find the data you're looking for in a list or database.

Control menu	The menu that contains commands for manipulating the active window. The Control menu is opened by using the Control-menu box.
Control-menu box	The icon in the upper-left corner of a window used for opening the Control menu. Double-clicking on the Control-menu box closes the window.
data series	A group of related data points that are plotted in a chart.
default	Settings that are preset. Excel comes with default settings for many options, such as column width. Most defaults can be changed.
dependent worksheet	A worksheet that uses linked data from one or more source worksheets.
document window	A window within an application window. An Excel workbook is a document window. There can be multiple document windows within an application window.
drop-down menus	A list of commands that is opened by choosing its name from the menu bar.
field names	The label in the first row of an Excel database list used to name the fields.
field	A category of information in a database list. A column in an Excel database is a field.
fill handle	The handle in the lower-right corner of the active cell or selection used for moving, copying, and filling data from the cell or selection into other cells.
header row	The first row in an Excel database containing labels for the field names.
hotkey	The keys used to initiate a command. The sequence of underlined menu letters are hotkeys.
Hypertext Markup Language (HTML)	Basic programming format that combines the use of ordinary text and common-language commands, called tags, to create pages on the World Wide Web.
icon	A pictorial representation of an object or element. Excel is started from an icon. The toolbar buttons are icons.

insertion point	The flashing vertical line indicating where text is inserted. The insertion point is sometimes called a *cursor*.
internet	A collection of computer networks that allow connected computers to communicate directly with each other.
intranet	A computer network within an organization or business.
link	A reference between two worksheets. Useful for summarizing or consolidating data from multiple worksheets or workbooks.
macro	A series of actions that has been recorded or programmed, and named, which can be executed by running (playing) the macro. An Excel macro is really a small program within Excel.
mouse	A hand-held pointing device that you move across your desktop to control the on-screen pointer. A mouse has two or three control buttons.
name list	The list of names assigned to cells or ranges of cells on the worksheet. The name list is opened from the name box on the left side of the formula bar.
Personal Macro Workbook	A workbook for storing macros that you want to have available all the time. The Personal Macro Workbook is usually hidden, but is always opened when you start Excel.
point	A size measurement, usually referring to font size. One point is approximately $1/72$ of an inch.
program	A sequence of instructions that can be run by a computer. Excel is a program.
proportional fonts	Fonts with variable-width characters. Proportional fonts usually look more professional than monospaced fonts, in which each character occupies the same width.
record	A collection of fields pertaining to one database entry.
relative reference	A cell reference that determines its position relative to the original location. Relative referencing allows formulas to work properly, even when they are copied to other areas of the worksheet.
restore button	A button in the upper-right corner of a window featuring an image of two overlapping windows. The restore button

appears when a window is mazimized, and it is used to restore the window to its previous size.

scroll bars   Devices used for navigating vertically and horizontally in a window. Vertical scroll bars are usually on the right side of the window. Horizontal scroll bars are usually on the bottom.

shortcut menu   A list of commands that is relevant to a particular area of the screen. Shortcut menus are opened by right-clicking on that area.

sort key   The field used as the basis for a database sort. Up to three sort keys can be used at one time in an Excel sort.

source worksheet   A worksheet with linked cells or ranges that provide variable information to the dependent worksheet.

ToolTip   A short description of a toolbar button that appears just below the mouse pointer when it is on a toolbar button.

TrueType fonts   A particular type of font that is scalable to practically any size on the page and the screen.

user interface   The kind of menus, dialog boxes, and other elements used to interact with the program. Windows is a graphical user interface because it incorporates many graphical elements for your interaction.

VBA   Visual Basic for Applications. This is the primary programming language used for Excel macros.

workbook   A collection of sheets (worksheets, chart sheets) that is saved with one file name. A workbook can contain up to 255 sheets.

World Wide Web   The entire collection of Web servers on the Internet.

x-axis   The horizontal plane of a chart. Sometimes called the *category axis*.

y-axis   The vertical plane of a chart. Sometimes called the *value axis*.

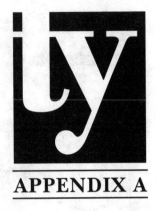

For Lotus 1-2-3 Users

There are many Lotus 1-2-3 users switching over to Excel, so Microsoft has included some tools to help former 1-2-3 users over the hump. If you are one of these, you'll be delighted at how easy it is to learn Excel. In fact, you won't even have to learn too much of Excel. You can just let Excel's help for 1-2-3 users guide you through your Excel tasks.

The first place to go to see what sort of help is available to you is the Excel Help system. Choosing **Help**, **Lotus 1-2-3 Help...** displays the Help for Lotus 1-2-3 Users dialog box, as shown in Figure A.1.

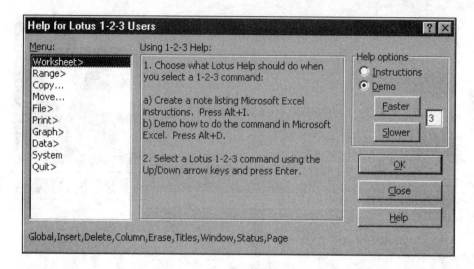

Figure A.1 *The Help for Lotus 1-2-3 Users dialog box.*

In the Help Option area of the dialog box in the upper right, you can specify whether Excel gives you instructions or demonstrates how to perform a 1-2-3 task in Excel, leading you by the hand as the task is carried out. You can also enter a number in the box just below the two option buttons to specify how quickly or slowly Excel carries out the demonstration.

In either case, you choose the command you want to learn about from the Menu list. For example, if you want to learn how to perform the /Worksheet, Insert, Column command in Excel, you would click on **Worksheet** and then **OK** (or double-click on **Worksheet**) to display the list of Worksheet commands. Next, double-click on **Insert**, and then on **Column**.

If you have chosen the **Demo** option, you are asked to confirm or change where the columns are to be inserted, as shown in Figure A.2.

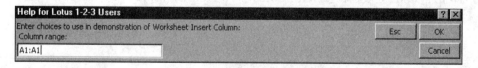

Figure A.2 *A Lotus 1-2-3 demo help dialog box.*

After entering the required information, clicking on the **OK** button causes Excel to carry out the task, using the Excel procedures.

If you have chosen the **Instructions** option, a note appears on your screen telling you how to perform the task, but letting you do it on your own. Figure A.3 displays an example of an instruction note.

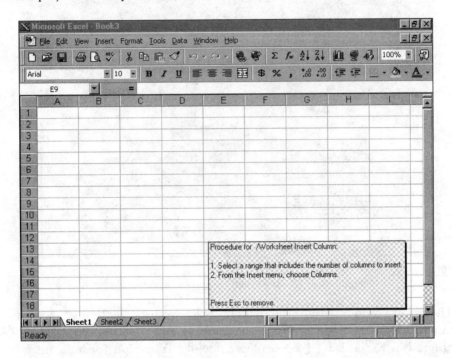

Figure A.3 *An instruction note for inserting columns.*

You can drag the note to any portion of the screen you want so it isn't in the way. When you're finished with the note, you can clear it from the screen by pressing **Esc**.

If this still isn't enough help for you, you can have Excel use your actual 1-2-3 commands to carry out tasks. You can even set up Excel to allow you to enter formulas in the 1-2-3 format and have Excel translate them for you. All these options are specified on the Transition tab of the Options dialog box (Choose **Tools**, **Options...**to display the dialog box), as shown in Figure A.4.

In the Settings portion of the dialog box, you can choose the **Lotus 1-2-3 Help** option to have Excel display the 1-2-3 help dialog box when you press the **Slash** (/) key. The **Transition Navigation keys** check box lets you use 1-2-3 keyboard navigation keys in Excel.

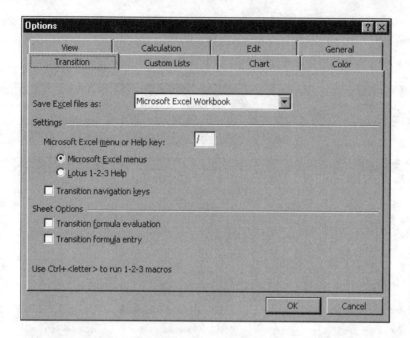

Figure A.4 The Transition tab of the Options dialog box.

The Sheet Options area of the dialog box lets you specify how you want formulas handled. Choosing **Transition formula entry** lets you enter formulas entered in Excel using 1-2-3's rules. Selecting **Transition formula entry** lets you evaluate formulas entered in Excel using 1-2-3's rules.

WARNING

While all these help facilities for former 1-2-3 users are very nice, they can impede your learning process by insulating you from the real Excel commands. If you need to use them because you have been forced to use Excel against your will and have to get a project completed before you have time to really learn Excel, fine. Otherwise, bite the bullet and stick with the normal Excel commands. You'll thank us later.

In addition to all the help facilities, you'll be pleased to know that all the 1-2-3 files you have created can be opened directly into Excel. You are prompted with a dialog box asking if you want to open the 1-2-3 version *xx* file. That's all there is to it. All the formatting and formulas you used in 1-2-3 are retained. You can even use most of the macros you created in 1-2-3 version 2.01 and some from 2.2.

Keyboard Shortcuts

Excel provides keyboard shortcuts for almost everything you can do with a mouse. We concentrated on the mouse actions to accomplish most tasks in the book. However, you save time if you use some of the keyboard shortcuts, particularly if you are a touch typist. Good typists find that removing their hands from the keyboard to use the mouse slows them down. Using keyboard shortcuts allows you to keep your hands on the keyboard.

This list of keyboard commands is not comprehensive. These are just some of our favorites. You'll find a complete guide to the keyboard commands in Excel's help facility. To view the keyboard commands in help, choose **Help**, **Contents and Index**. Select the **Contents** tab and double-click on **Reference Information**, and then on **Keyboard Shortcut References**. You are then able to choose among a variety of keyboard guides in different categories.

Table B.1 *Function Keys*

To	Press
Get help	F1
Get context-sensitive help	Shift-F1
Edit cell	F2
Close active windows	Ctrl-F4
Close application	Alt-F4
Display Go To dialog box	F5
Check Spelling	F7
Save As	F12
Save	Shift-F12
Open	Ctrl-F12

Table B.2 *Inserting, Deleting, Copying, and Moving*

To	Press
Cut selection	Ctrl-X
Copy selection	Ctrl-C
Paste selection	Ctrl-V
Clear selection contents	Delete
Undo last action	Ctrl-Z

Table B.3 *Moving and Selecting*

To	Press
Extend selection one cell	Shift-Arrow
Move up or down to edge of current data region	Ctrl-Up Arrow key or Ctrl-Down Arrow
Move left or right to edge of current data region	Ctrl-Left Arrow key or Ctrl-Right Arrow

Move to beginning of row	**Home**
Select to beginning of row	**Shift-Home**
Move to last cell in worksheet	**Ctrl-End**
Select entire worksheet	**Ctrl-A**
Move down one screen	**Page Down**
Move up one screen	**Page Up**
Move right one screen	**Alt-Page Down**
Move left one screen	**Alt-Page Up**
Move to cell A1	**Ctrl-Home**

Table B.4 *Moving within a Selection*

To	PRESS
Move down	**Enter**
Move up	**Shift-Enter**
Move left to right	**Tab**
Move right to left	**Shift-Tab**

Table B.5 *Formatting Data*

To	PRESS
Apply Currency format	**Ctrl-Shift-$**
Apply Percent format	**Ctrl-Shift-%**
Apply Date format (Day+Month+Year)	**Ctrl-Shift-#**
Apply two decimal place format with commas	**Ctrl-Shift-!**
Apply or remove bold	**Ctrl-B**
Apply or remove italic	**Ctrl-I**
Apply or remove underline	**Ctrl-U**

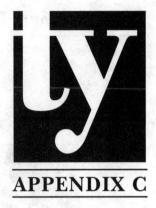

Toolbar Reference

Here are all the toolbars included with Excel. Each button is labeled with its ToolTip. Don't forget that you can create your own custom toolbars using these and many other buttons available in the Customize dialog box.

THE STANDARD TOOLBAR

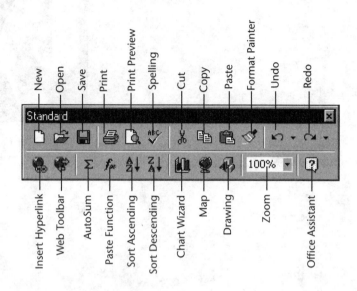

THE FORMATTING TOOLBAR

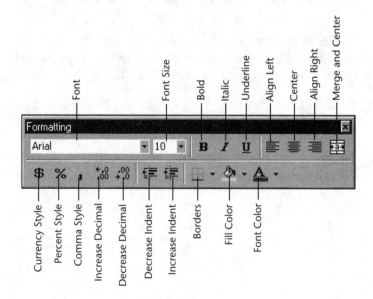

THE MICROSOFT OFFICE SHORTCUT BAR

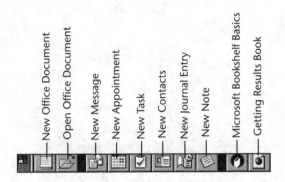

THE AUDITING TOOLBAR

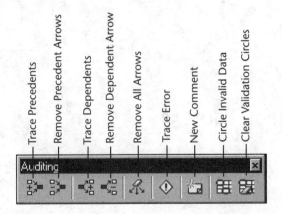

THE CHART TOOLBAR

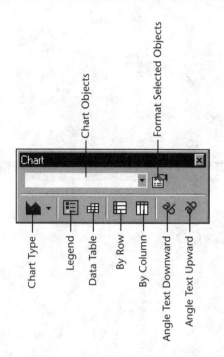

THE CONTROL TOOLBAR

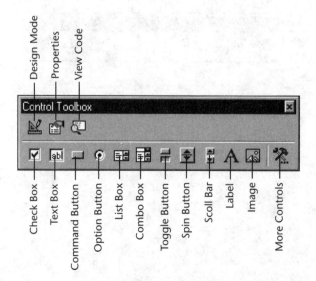

THE DRAWING TOOLBAR

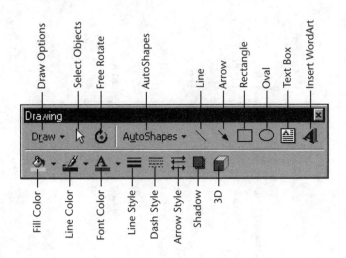

THE EXTERNAL DATA TOOLBAR

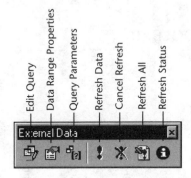

THE FORMS TOOLBAR

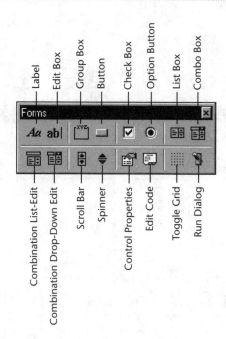

THE PICTURE TOOLBAR

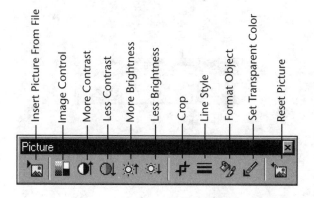

THE PIVOTTABLE TOOLBAR

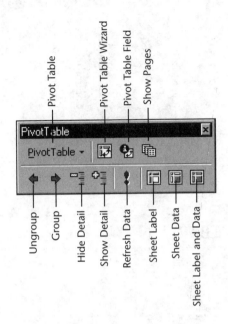

THE REVIEWING TOOLBAR

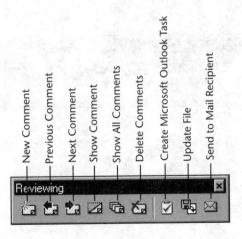

THE VISUAL BASIC TOOLBAR

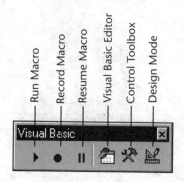

THE WEB TOOLBAR

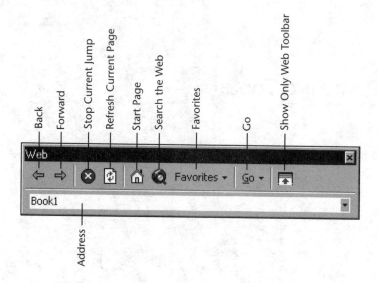

WORDART

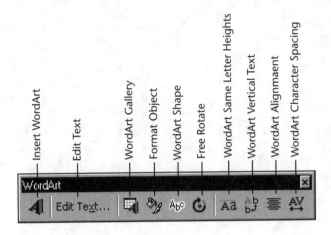

INDEX